Frommer's®

P9-CEF-295

Italian
Phrasebook &
Culture Guide

1st Edition

WILEY

Wiley Publishing, Inc.

Published by:

Wiley Publishing, Inc.

111 River St.
Hoboken, NJ 07030-5774

ISBN-13: 978-0-471-79301-4
ISBN-10: 0-471-79301-9

Series Editor: Maureen Clarke
Italian Editor: Amanda Castleman
Travel Tips and Culture Guide: Stephen Brewer
Travel Content Editor: Michael Spring
Editorial Assistant: Melinda Quintero
Photo Editor: Richard H. Fox
Cover design by Fritz Metsch

Interior Design, Content Development, Translation, Copyediting, Proofreading,
Production, and Layout by:
Publication Services, Inc., 1802 South Duncan Road, Champaign, IL 61822
Linguists: Paola Bartolotti-van Loon & Rosaria Tenace

For information on our other products and services or to obtain technical support,
please contact our Customer Care Department within the U.S. at 800/762-2974, outside the U.S. at 317/572-3993 or fax 317/572-4002.
Wiley also publishes its books in a variety of electronic formats. Some content that
appears in print may not be available in electronic formats.

Manufactured in the United States of America

5 4 3 2

Contents

An Invitation to the Reader

In researching this book, we discovered many wonderful sayings and terms useful to travelers in Italy. We're sure you'll find others. Please tell us about them, so we can share the information with your fellow travelers in upcoming editions. If you were disappointed with an aspect of this book, we'd like to know that, too. Please write to:

Frommer's Italian Phrasebook & Culture Guide, 1st Edition
Wiley Publishing, Inc.
111 River St. • Hoboken, NJ 07030-5774

An Additional Note

The packager, editors, and publisher cannot be held responsible for the experiences of readers while traveling. Your safety is important to us, however, so we encourage you to stay alert and be aware of your surroundings. Keep a close eye on cameras, purses, and wallets, all favorite targets of thieves and pickpockets.

Frommers.com

Now that you have the language for a great trip, visit our website at **www.frommers.com** for travel information on more than 3,000 destinations. With features updated regularly, we give you instant access to the most current trip-planning information available. At Frommers.com, you'll also find the best prices on airfares, accommodations, and car rentals—and you can even book travel online through our travel booking partners. At Frommers.com, you'll also find:

- Online updates to our most popular guidebooks
- Vacation sweepstakes and contest giveaways
- Newsletter highlighting the hottest travel trends
- Online travel message boards with featured travel discussions

INTRODUCTION: HOW TO USE THIS BOOK

A language so melodious it can make a chore list resemble an opera aria, Italian is spoken by more than 70 million people. And it's familiar to many chefs, artists, musicians, and others who savor Italy's rich cultural heritage.

As a Romance language, Italian is closely related to Latin, French, Portuguese, and Romanian. The modern nation of Italy is a patchwork of city-states—and its dialects still reflect these strong regional loyalties. Thus you may hear variations on the phrases found here. But rest assured: Native speakers have carefully reviewed all the material to make it universally understandable.

Our intention is not to teach you Italian: A class or audio program is best for that. Rather, we offer a travel tool that's easy to use. You don't need to memorize the contents or flip frantically to locate a topic, as with other books. Rather, Frommer's has fingertip referencing and an extensive PhraseFinder dictionary at the back, with hundreds of the most common travel phrases organized by key word.

Say a taxi driver accidentally hands you €5 instead of €10. Look up "change" in the dictionary and quickly learn how to say, "Sorry, but this isn't the right change." Then follow the cross-reference to numbers, so you can specify how much is missing.

This book may even be useful to advanced students, because it supplies speedy access to exact idioms. Elegance and *bella figura*—cutting a fine figure—are important to Italians. So is the right phrase at the right time.

As Tim Parks observed in *An Englishman in Verona*: "While Italians usually seem to like foreigners, the foreigners they like most are the ones who know the score, the ones who have caved in and agreed that the Italian way of doing things is best. . . . There is an order to follow in all things; follow it, even when it borders on the superstitious and ritualistic."

Thus, a range of travelers—from the novice to the conversationally adept—can benefit from the detailed conversation and etiquette tips here. We've also tried to make this volume useful to all English speakers, although Frommer's is based in the United States.

At each turn, we've researched the rich traditions and potential pitfalls that await visitors to Italy. Our immediate goal was to create a phrasebook that is as indispensible as your passport. Our far-ranging objective is to enrich your experience of travel. And with that, we offer this wish: *Fate il miglior viaggio possibile!*

CHAPTER ONE

SURVIVAL ITALIAN

If you tire of toting around this phrasebook, tear out or photocopy this chapter. You should be able to get around using only the terms found in the next 35 pages.

BASIC GREETINGS

For a full list of greetings, see p127.

Hello.	**Salve.**
	SAHL-veh
How are you?	**Come sta?**
	KOH-meh stah
I'm fine, thanks.	**Bene, grazie.**
	BEH-neh GRAH-tsyeh
And you?	**E lei?**
	eh lay
My name is ____.	**Mi chiamo ____.**
	mee KYAH-moh
And yours?	**E lei?**
	eh lay
It's a pleasure to meet you.	**Piacere di conoscerla.**
	pyah-CHEH-reh dee KOH-noh-shehr-lah
Please.	**Per favore.**
	pehr fah-VOH-reh
Thank you.	**Grazie.**
	GRAH-tsyeh
Yes.	**Sì.**
	SEE
No.	**No.**
	noh

OK.

OK. / Va bene.
OK / vah BEH-neh

No problem.

Nessun problema.
nehs-SOON proh-BLEH-mah

I'm sorry, I don't
understand.

Mi dispiace, non capisco.
mee dee-SPYAH-cheh nohn kah-PEE-skoh

Would you speak slower,
please?

**Può parlare più lentamente, per
favore?**
PWOH pahr-LAH-reh PYOO lehn-tah-MEHN-teh pehr fah-VOH-reh

Would you speak louder,
please?

**Può parlare più ad alta voce, per
favore?**
*PWOH pahr-LAH-reh PYOO ahd
AHL-tah VOH-cheh pehr fah-VOH-reh*

Do you speak English?

Parla inglese?
PAHR-lah een-GLEH-seh

Do you speak any other
languages?

Parla altre lingue?
PAHR-lah AHL-treh LEEN-gweh

I speak ____ better than
Italian.

Parlo ____ meglio che italiano.
PAHR-loh ____ MEH-lyoh keh ee-tah-LYAH-noh

For languages, see the English / Italian Dictionary.

Would you spell that?

Può dirmi come si scrive?
*PWOH DEER-mee KOH-meh see
SKREE-veh*

Would you please
repeat that?

Può ripetere, per favore?
PWOH ree-PEH-teh-reh pehr fah-VOH-reh

Would you point that out
in this dictionary?

**Può indicarlo su questo
dizionario?**
*PWOH een-dee-KAHR-loh soo
KWEHS-toh dee-tsyoh-NAH-ryoh*

THE KEY QUESTIONS

With the right hand gestures, you can get a lot of mileage from the following list of single-word questions and answers.

Who?	**Chi?**
	kee
What?	**Cosa?**
	KOH-sah
When?	**Quando?**
	KWAHN-doh
Where?	**Dove?**
	DOH-veh
Why?	**Perché?**
	pehr-KEH
How?	**Come?**
	KOH-meh
Which?	**Quale?**
	KWAH-leh
How many / much?	**Quanto -a? / Quanti -e?**
	KWAHN-toh -tah / KWAHN-tee -teh

THE ANSWERS: WHO

For full coverage of pronouns, see p19.

I	**Io**
	EE-oh
you	**Lei / tu**
	lay / too
him	**lui**
	LOO-ee
her	**lei**
	lay
us	**noi**
	NOH-ee
them	**loro**
	LOH-roh

THE ANSWERS: WHEN

For full coverage of time, see p12.

now	**ora** *OH-rah*
later	**più tardi** *PYOO TAHR-dee*
in a minute	**fra un minuto** *frah oon mee-NOO-toh*
today	**oggi** *OHD-jee*
tomorrow	**domani** *doh-MAH-nee*
yesterday	**ieri** *YEH-ree*
in a week	**fra una settimana** *frah oonah seht-tee-MAH-nah*
next week	**la settimana prossima** *lah set-tee-MAH-nah prohs-SEE-mah*
last week	**la settimana scorsa** *lah set-tee-MAH-nah SKOHR-sah*
next month	**il mese prossimo** *eel MEH-zeh prohs-SEE-moh*
At ____	**Alle ____** *AHL-leh*
ten o'clock this morning.	**dieci di stamattina.** *DYEH-chee dee stah-maht-TEE-nah*
two o'clock this afternoon.	**due di oggi pomeriggio.** *DOO-eh dee OHD-jee poh-meh-REED-joh*
seven o'clock this evening.	**sette di stasera.** *SEHT-teh dee stah-SEH-rah*

For full coverage of numbers, see p7.

THE ANSWERS: WHERE

here	**qui / qua**
	kwee / kwah
there	**lì / là**
	LEE / LAH
near	**vicino**
	vee-CHEE-noh
closer	**più vicino**
	PYOO vee-CHEE-noh
closest	**il più vicino**
	eel PYOO vee-CHEE-noh
far	**lontano**
	lohn-TAH-noh
farther	**più lontano**
	PYOO lohn-TAH-noh
farthest	**il più lontano**
	eel PYOO lohn-TAH-noh
across from	**di fronte a**
	dee FROHN-teh ah
next to	**di fianco a**
	dee FYAHN-koh ah
behind	**dietro a**
	DYEH-troh ah
straight ahead	**diritto**
	dee-REET-toh
left	**a sinistra**
	ah see-NEES-trah
right	**a destra**
	ah DEHS-trah
up	**su**
	soo
down	**giù**
	JOO
lower	**più giù**
	PYOO JOO

higher	**più su**
	PYOO soo
forward	**avanti**
	ah-VAHN-tee
back	**indietro**
	een-DYEH-troh
around	**attorno**
	aht-TOHR-noh
across the street	**dall'altra parte della strada**
	dahl-LAHL-trah PAHR-teh DEHL-la
	STRAH-dah
down the street	**più avanti**
	PYOO ah-VAHN-tee
on the corner	**all'angolo**
	ahl-LAHN-goh-loh
kittycorner	**all'angolo opposto**
	ahl-LAHN-goh-loh ohp-POHS-toh
____ blocks from here	**____ traverse più in là**
	____ trah-VEHR-seh PYOO een LAH

For a full list of numbers, see the next page.

THE ANSWERS: WHICH

this one	**questo -a**
	KWEHS-toh -tah
that	**quello -la**
	KWEHL-loh -lah
these	**questi -e**
	KWEHS-tee -teh
those	**quelli -le**
	KWEHL-lee -leh

NUMBERS & COUNTING

one	**uno** *OO-noh*	seventeen	**diciassette** *dee-chahs-SEHT-teh*
two	**due** *DOO-eh*	eighteen	**diciotto** *dee-CHOT-toh*
three	**tre** *treh*	nineteen	**diciannove** *dee-chahn-NOH-veh*
four	**quattro** *KWAHT-troh*	twenty	**venti** *VEHN-tee*
five	**cinque** *CHEEN-kweh*	twenty-one	**ventuno** *vehn-TOO-noh*
six	**sei** *SEH-ee*	thirty	**trenta** *TREHN-tah*
seven	**sette** *SEHT-teh*	forty	**quaranta** *kwah-RAHN-tah*
eight	**otto** *OHT-toh*	fifty	**cinquanta** *cheen-KWAN-tah*
nine	**nove** *NOH-veh*	sixty	**sessanta** *sehs-SAHN-tah*
ten	**dieci** *dee-EH-chee*	seventy	**settanta** *seht-TAHN-tah*
eleven	**undici** *OON-dee-chee*	eighty	**ottanta** *oht-TAHN-tah*
twelve	**dodici** *DOH-dee-chee*	ninety	**novanta** *noh-VAHN-tah*
thirteen	**tredici** *TREH-dee-chee*	one hundred	**cento** *CHEHN-to*
fourteen	**quattordici** *KWAHT-tohr-dee-chee*	two hundred	**duecentos** *DOO-eh-CHEHN-toh*
fifteen	**quindici** *KWEEN-dee-chee*	one thousand	**mill** *MEEL-leh*
sixteen	**sedici** *SEH-dee-chee*		

FRACTIONS & DECIMALS

one eighth	**un ottavo**
	oon oht-TAH-voh
one quarter	**un quarto**
	oon KWAHR-toh
three eighths	**tre ottavi**
	treh oht-TAH-vee
one third	**un terzo**
	oon TEHR-tsoh
one half	**mezzo**
	MEHD-dzoh
two thirds	**due terzi**
	DOO-eh TEHR-tsee
three quarters	**tre quarti**
	treh KWAHR-tee
double	**doppio**
	DOHP-pyoh
triple	**triplo**
	TREE-ploh
one-tenth	**un decimo**
	oon DEH-chee-moh
one-hundredth	**un centesimo**
	oon chehn-TEH-zee-moh
one-thousandth	**un millesimo**
	oon meel-LEH-zee-moh

MATH

addition	**addizione**
	ahd-deet-TSYOH-neh
2 + 1	**due più uno**
	DOO-eh PYOO OO-noh
subtraction	**sottrazione**
	soht-traht-TSYOH-neh
2 − 1	**due meno uno**
	DOO-eh MEH-noh OO-noh

multiplication	**moltiplicazione**
	mohl-tee-plee-kaht-TSYOH-neh
2×3	**due per tre**
	DOO-eh pehr treh
division	**divisione**
	dee-vee-ZYOH-neh
$6 \div 3$	**sei diviso tre**
	SEH-ee dee-VEE-zoh treh

ORDINAL NUMBERS

first	**primo -a**
	PREE-moh -mah
second	**secondo -a**
	sch KOHN-doh -dah
third	**terzo -a**
	TEHR-tsoh -tsah
fourth	**quarto -a**
	KWAHR-toh -tah
fifth	**quinto -a**
	KWEEN-toh -tah
sixth	**sesto -a**
	SEHS-toh -tah
seventh	**settimo -a**
	SEHT-tee-moh -mah
eighth	**ottavo -a**
	oht-TAH-voh -vah
ninth	**nono -a**
	NOH-noh -nah
tenth	**decimo -a**
	DEH-chee-moh -mah
last	**ultimo -a**
	OOL-tee-moh -mah

MEASUREMENTS

Measurements are usually metric, though you may need a few
Imperial measurement terms.

centimeter	**centimetro** *chehn-TEE-meh-troh*
meter	**metro** *MEH-troh*
kilometer	**chilometro** *kee-LOH-meh-troh*
millimeter	**millimetro** *meel-LEE-meh-troh*
hectares	**ettari** *EHT-tah-ree*
a distance squared is	**quadrato** *kwah-DRAH-toh*
short	**corto -a** *KOHR-toh -tah*
long	**lungo -a** *LOON-goh -gah*

VOLUME

milliliters	**millilitro** *meel-LEE-lee-troh*
liter	**litro** *LEE-troh*
cup	**tazza** *TAHT-sah*

QUANTITY

some (always singular)	**qualche** *KWAHL-keh*
none	**niente** *NYEHN-teh* **nessuno** *nehs-SOO-noh*

Dos and Don'ts

Italians measure foodstuffs by the kilogram or smaller 100g unit (**ettogrammo** abbreviated to *etto*: equivalent to just under 4oz). **Pizzerie al taglio** (pizza slice shops) generally run on this system, but hand gestures can suffice. A good server poises the knife, then asks for approval before cutting. **Più** (PYOO) is "more," **meno** (MEH-noh) "less." **Basta** (BAHS-tah) means "enough." To express "half" of something, do say **mezzo** (MEHD-zoh).

all	**tutto -a / tutti -e**
	TOOT-toh -tah / TOOT-tee -teh
much / many	**molto -a / molti -e**
	MOHL-toh -tah / MOHL-tee -teh
A little bit (can be used	**poco -a**
for quantity or for time)	*POH-koh -kah*
dozen	**dozzina**
	dot-SEE-nah

SIZE

small	**piccolo -a**
	PEEK-koh-loh-lah
the smallest (literally	**il / la più piccolo -a**
"the most small")	*eel / lah PYOO PEEK-koh-loh -lah*
medium	**medio -a**
	MEH-dyoh -dyah
big	**grande**
	GRAHN-deh
fat	**grasso -a**
	GRAHS-soh -sah
really fat	**molto grasso -a**
	MOHL-toh GRAHS-soh -sah

the biggest	**il / la più grande** *eel / lah PYOO GRAHN-deh*
wide	**largo -a** *LAHR-goh -gah*
narrow	**stretto -a** *STREHT-toh -tah*

TIME

Time in Italian is referred to, literally, by the hour. **Che ora è?** translates as "What's the hour?"

For full coverage of number terms, see p7.

HOURS OF THE DAY

What time is it?	**Che ora è?** *keh OH-rah EH*
At what time?	**A che ora?** *ah keh OH-rah*
For how long?	**Per quanto tempo?** *pehr KWAHN-toh TEHM-poh*

A little tip

By adding a diminutive suffix, **-ino -a**, **-etto -a**, or a combination of the two, you can make anything smaller or shorter. These endings replace the original -o and -a, respectively:

a really little bit	**pochino -a** (*poh-KEE-noh -nah*)
a really teeny tiny bit	**pochettino -a** (*poh-keht-TEE-noh -nah*)

It's one o'clock.	**È l'una.** *EH LOO-nah*
It's two o'clock.	**Sono le due.** *SOH-noh leh DOO-eh*
It's two thirty.	**Sono le due e mezzo.** *SOH-noh leh DOO-eh eh MEHD-dzoh*
It's two fifteen.	**Sono le due e un quarto.** *SOH-noh leh DOO-eh eh oon KWAHR-toh*
It's a quarter to three.	**Sono le tre meno un quarto. / Manca un quarto alle tre.** *SOH-noh leh treh MEH-noh oon KWAHR-toh / MAHN-kah oon KWAHR-toh AHL-leh treh*
It's noon.	**È mezzogiorno.** *EH mehd-dzoh -JOHR-noh*
It's midnight.	**È mezzanotte.** *EH mehd-dzah-NOHT-teh*
It's early.	**È presto.** *EH PREHS-toh*
It's late.	**È tardi.** *EH TAHR-dee*
in the morning	**al mattino** *ahl maht-TEE-noh*
in the afternoon	**al pomeriggio** *ahl poh-meh-REED-joh*
at night	**di notte** *dee NOHT-teh*
dawn	**l'alba** *LAHL-bah*

DAYS OF THE WEEK

Sunday	**domenica**
	doh-MEH-nee-kah
Monday	**lunedì**
	loo-neh-DEE
Tuesday	**martedì**
	mahr-teh-DEE
Wednesday	**mercoledì**
	mehr-koh-leh-DEE
Thursday	**giovedì**
	joh-veh-DEE
Friday	**venerdì**
	veh-nehr-DEE
Saturday	**sabato**
	SAH-bah-toh
today	**oggi**
	OHD-jee
tomorrow	**domani**
	doh-MAH-nee
yesterday	**ieri**
	YEH-ree
the day before yesterday	**avantieri**
	ah-vahn-TYEH-ree
these last few days	**questi ultimi giorni**
	KWEHS-tee OOL-tee-mee JOHR-nee
one week	**una settimana**
	OO-nah seht-tee-MAH-nah
next week	**la prossima settimana**
	lah PROHS-see-mah seht-tee-MAH-nah
last week	**la settimana scorsa**
	lah seht-tee-MAH-nah SKOHR-sah

MONTHS OF THE YEAR

January	**gennaio**
	jehn-NAH-yoh

February	**febbraio**
	fehb-BRAH-yoh
March	**marzo**
	MAHR-tso
April	**aprile**
	ah-PREE-leh
May	**maggio**
	MAHD-joh
June	**giugno**
	JEWN-nyo
July	**luglio**
	LOOL-lyo
August	**agosto**
	ah-GOHS-toh
September	**settembre**
	seht-TEHM-breh
October	**ottobre**
	oht-TOH-breh
November	**novembre**
	noh-VEHM-breh
December	**dicembre**
	dee-CHEHM-breh
one month	**un mese**
	oon MEH-zeh
next month	**il prossimo mese**
	eel PROHS-see-moh MEH-zeh
last month	**il mese scorso**
	eel MEH-zeh SKOHR-soh

SEASONS OF THE YEAR

spring	**la primavera**
	lah pree-mah-VEH-rah
summer	**l'estate**
	lehs-TAH-teh
autumn	**l'autunno**
	low-TOON-noh
winter	**l'inverno**
	leen-VEHR-noh

ITALIAN GRAMMAR BASICS

Classified as a Romance language, Italian is closely related to Latin, French, Spanish, Portuguese, and Romanian. It arose from the Vulgar Latin of the late Roman Empire.

THE ALPHABET

The Italian alphabet has 21 letters. The letters **h**, **j**, **k**, **w**, **x**, and **y** are used only in words taken from other languages (such as jazz). Certain combinations of letters have special sounds in Italian, just as **ch**, **sh**, **th**, and **ng** have special sounds in English.

Letter	Name	Pronunciation
a	a	**ah** as in *father* - **La Scala** *lah SKAH-lah*
b	bi	**b** as in *bud* - **bacio** *BAH-choh* (kiss)
c	ci	**ca, co, cu, che, chi:** hard **k** sound as in *car* - **cane** *KAH-neh* (dog)
		ce, ci: **ch** as in *cheap* - **ciao** *CHAH-oh*
d	di	**d** as in *day* - **dente** *DEHN-teh* (tooth)
e	e	**eh** as in *bell* - **bene** *BEH-neh* (good, well)
f	effe	**f** as in *fan* - **forte** *FOHR-teh* (strong, loud)
g	gi	**ga, go, gu, ghe, ghi:** hard **g** as in *good* - **gatto** *GAHT-toh* (cat)
		ge, gi: soft **j** as in *jelly* - **gelato** *jeh-LAH-toh* (ice cream)
		gli: **lly** close to *million* - **figlio** *FEEL-lyoh* (son)
		gn: **ny** as in *poignant* - **bagno** *BAHN-nyoh* (bathroom, restroom)
h	acca	silent before vowels, stresses **a** and **o:** **ho** *OH* (I have), **hai** *AH-ee* (you have)
i	i	**ee** as in *eel* - **ieri** *ee-EH-ree* (yesterday)
l	elle	**l** as in *lunch* - **letto** *LET-toh* (bed)
m	emme	**m** as in *Mary* - **mano** *MAH-noh* (hand)
n	enne	**n** as in *nail* - **nero** *NEH-roh* (black)
o	o	**oh** as in *pot* - **oggi** *OHD-jee* (today)
p	pi	**p** as in *pet* - **pasta** *PAHS-tah*
q	cu	**q** as in *quick* - **questo** *KWEHS-toh* (this)
r	erre	trilled, as in the Scottish **r** - **Roma**

Letter	Name	Pronunciation
s	esse	**s** as in *soon* - **sasso** *SAHS-soh* (rock)
		z as in *rose* between vowels - **casa** *KAH-zah* (house, home)
		sce, sci: sh as in *shop* - **pesce** *PEH-sheh* (fish)
		sche, schi: sk as in *skip* - **schifo** *SKEE-foh* (disgust)
t	ti	**t** as in *tea* - **Torino** *toh-REE-noh* (Turin)
u	u	**oo** as in *boom* - **uno** *OO-noh* (one)
v	vu	**v** as in *very* - **Verona** *veh-ROH-nah*
z	zeta	**dz** or **ts** as in *mezzo* and *matzo* **zucchero** *DZOOK-keh-roh* (sugar) **pizza** *PEET-sah*

Foreign letters

j	i lunga	**j** as *jazz*
k	kappa	**k** sound
w	doppia vu	**w** sound

PRONUNCIATION

Italian has few pitfalls like silent letters; a word's sound closely resembles its written form. Such straightforward pronunciation makes this melodious language accessible and appealing to even the most casual student.

Often **c** and **g** are stumbling blocks for beginners. Both have a soft sound before **e** or **i**, a hard sound before **a**, **o**, and **u**. Think **cubo** *KOO-boh* (cube) versus **arrivederci** *ahr-ree-veh-DEHR-chee* (bye) and **gala** *GAH-lah* versus **Luigi** *loo-EE-jee*.

Double consonants should be pronounced twice—or lengthened and intensified. English speakers are already familiar with this from phrases such as gra**b** **b**ag, bla**ck** **c**at, goo**d** **d**ay, hal**f** **f**ull, goo**d** **j**ob, ho**t** **t**ea and ki**ds** **z**one.

Enjoy the language's drama and richness, but don't slip into an operatic parody. Italians often accuse foreigners of doubling all consonants. Yet no native, when listening to an aria, would ever confuse **m'ama** (she loves me) with **mamma** (mom)!

GENDER, ADJECTIVES, MODIFIERS

The ending of an Italian noun reveals its gender (masculine or feminine) and number (singular and plural). Those ending in *o* are generally masculine and become *i* (plural); those ending in *a* are typically feminine and become *e* (plural). Ones that conclude in *e* can be masculine or feminine, and shift to *i* (plural). Adjectives agree in gender and number, and usually follow the nouns.

	Singular	Plural
Masculine	**il piatto bianco** (the white plate)	**i piatti bianch*i*** (the white plates)
	il cane grande (the large dog)	**i cani grand*i*** (the large dogs)
Feminine	**la pizza calda** (hot pizza)	**le pizze calde** (hot pizzas)
	la carne tenera (tender meat)	**le carni tenere** (tender meats)

Nouns often are accompanied by a masculine or feminine definite article (the): **il**, **lo**, **la** (singular); **i**, **gli**, **le** (plural). Indefinite articles (a, an, some)—**un**, **una** (singular) and **dei**, **delle** (plural)—must also correspond to the nouns they modify.

The Definite Article ("The")

	Masculine	Feminine
Singular	*il* **cane** (the dog) *lo* **stivale** (the boot)	*la* **tavola** (the table) *la* **rete** (the net)
Plural	*i* **cani** (the dogs) *gli* **stivali** (the boots)	*le* **tavole** (the tables) *le* **reti** (the nets)

The Indefinite Article ("A" or "An")

	Masculine	Feminine
Singular	*un* **cane** (a dog)	*una* **tavola** (a table)
Plural	*dei* **cani** (some dogs)	*delle* **tavole** (some tables)

PERSONAL PRONOUNS

English	Italian	Pronunciation
I	io	EE-oh
You (singular, familiar)	tu	TOO
He / She / You (singular, formal)	lui / lei / Lei	LOO-ee / lay / lay
We	noi	NOH-ee
You (plural, familiar)	voi	VOH-ee
They / You (plural, formal)	loro / Loro	LOH-roh

PRONOUNS

English	Italian	Pronunciation
This	questo -a	KWEHS-toh -tah
That	quello -a	KWEHL-loh -lah
These	questi -e	KWEHS-tee -teh
Those	quelli -e	KWEHL-lee -leh

Hey, You!

Italian has two words for "you"—**tu**, spoken among friends and familiars, and to address children; and **Lei / Loro**, used among strangers or as a sign of respect toward elders and authority figures. When speaking with a stranger, expect to use **Lei / Loro** unless you are invited to do otherwise. The trend is toward using the second person familiar form (**voi**) to replace the formal **Loro**.

REGULAR VERB CONJUGATIONS

Italian verb infinitives end in ARE (e.g. **parlare**, to speak), ERE (e.g. **vendere**, to sell), and IRE (e.g. **partire**, to leave). Drop the last three letters to determine the word's stem. Then add endings that reveal who did the action—and when. Following are the present-tense conjugations for regular verbs.

Present Tense

ARE Verbs	PARLARE "To Talk, To Speak"	
I talk.	Io parlo.	PAHR-loh
You (singular, familiar) talk.	Tu parli.	PAHR-lee
He / She talks. You (singular, formal) talk.	Lui / Lei / Lei parla.	PAHR-lah
We talk.	Noi parliamo.	pahr-LYAH-moh
You (plural, familiar) talk.	Voi parlate.	pahr-LAH-teh
They / You (plural, formal) talk.	Loro / Loro parlano.	PAHR-lah-noh

ERE Verbs	VENDERE "To Sell"	
I sell.	Io vendo.	VEHN-doh
You (singular, familiar) sell.	Tu vendi.	VEHN-dee
He / She sells. You (singular, formal) sell.	Lui / Lei / Lei vende.	VEHN-deh
We sell.	Noi vendiamo.	vehn-DYAH-moh
You (plural, familiar) sell.	Voi vendete.	vehn-DEH-teh
They / You (plural, formal) sell.	Loro / Loro vendono.	VEHN-doh-noh

IRE Verbs	PARTIRE "To Leave"	
I leave.	Io parto.	PAHR-toh
You (singular, familiar) leave.	Tu parti.	PAHR-tee
He / She leaves. You (singular, formal) leave.	Lui / Lei / Lei parte.	PAHR-teh
We leave.	Noi partiamo.	pahr-TYAH-moh
You (plural, familiar) leave.	Voi partite.	pahr-TEE-teh
They / You (plural, formal) leave.	Loro / Loro partono.	PAHR-toh-noh

Past Tense

Italian has five past tenses. The present perfect most often expresses the simple past (equivalent to the English "I have eaten" or "I ate"). The imperfect tense conveys an unfinished or continuing action ("I was eating"). So for verbs like **essere** (to be) we've supplied that form instead. Below are examples for regular verbs.

ARE Verbs	PARLARE "To Talk, To Speak"	
I talked.	Io ho parlato.	oh pahr-LAH-toh
You (singular, familiar) talked.	Tu hai parlato.	eye pahr-LAH-toh
He / She / You (singular, formal) talked.	Lui / Lei / Lei ha parlato.	AH pahr-LAH-toh
We talked.	Noi abbiamo parlato.	ahb-BYAH-moh pahr-LAH-toh
You (plural, familiar) talked.	Voi avete parlato.	ah-VEH-teh pahr-LAH-toh
They / You (plural, formal) talked.	Loro / Loro hanno parlato.	AHN-noh pahr-LAH-toh

ERE Verbs	VENDERE "To Sell"	
I sold.	Io *ho* ven*du*to.	oh vehn-DOO-toh
You (singular, familiar) **sold.**	Tu *hai* ven*du*to.	eye vehn-DOO-toh
He / She / You (singular, formal) **sold.**	Lui / Lei / Lei *ha* ven*du*to.	AH vehn-DOO-toh
We sold.	Noi *abbiamo* ven*du*to.	ahb-BYAH-moh vehn-DOO-toh
You (plural, familiar) **sold.**	Voi *avete* ven*du*to.	ah-VEH-teh vehn-DOO-toh
They / You (plural, formal) **sold.**	Loro / Loro *hanno* ven*du*to.	AHN-noh vehn-DOO-toh

IRE Verbs	PARTIRE "To Leave"	
I left.	Io *sono* par*ti*to.	SOH-noh pahr-TEE-toh
You (singular, familiar) **left.**	Tu *sei* par*ti*to.	SEH-ee pahr-TEE-toh
He / She / You (singular, formal) **left.**	Lui / Lei / Lei *è* par*ti*to.	EH pahr-TEE-toh
We left.	Noi *siamo* par*ti*ti.	SYAH-moh pahr-TEE-tee
You (plural, familiar) **left.**	Voi *siete* par*ti*ti.	SYEH-teh pahr-TEE-tee
They / You (plural, formal) **left.**	Loro / Loro *sono* par*ti*ti.	SOH-noh pahr-TEE-tee

The Future Tense
ARE Verbs

PARLARE "To Talk, To Speak"

I will talk.	Io parlerò.	pahr-leh-ROH
You (singular, familiar) will talk.	Tu parlerai.	pahr-leh-REYE
He / she / you (singular, formal) will talk.	Lui / Lei / Lei parlerà.	pahr-leh-RAH
We will talk.	Noi parleremo.	pahr-leh-REH-moh
You (plural, familiar) will talk.	Voi parlerete.	pahr-leh-REH-teh
They / You (plural, formal) will talk.	Loro / Loro parleranno.	pahr-leh-RAHN-noh

ERE Verbs

VENDERE "To Sell"

I will sell.	Io venderò.	vehn-deh-ROH
You (singular, familiar) will sell.	Tu venderai.	vehn-deh-REYE
He / She / You (singular, formal) will sell.	Lui / Lei / Lei venderà.	vehn-deh-RAH
We will sell.	Noi venderemo.	vehn-deh-REH-moh
You (plural, familiar) will sell.	Voi venderete.	vehn-deh-REH-teh
They / You (plural, formal) will sell.	Loro / Loro venderanno.	vehn-deh-RAHN-noh

IRE Verbs	PARTIRE "To Leave"	
I will leave.	Io partirò.	pahr-tee-ROH
You (singular, familiar) will leave.	Tu partirai.	pahr-tee-REYE
He / She / You (singular, formal) will leave.	Lui / Lei / Lei partirà.	pahr-tee-RAH
We will leave.	Noi partiremo.	pahr-tee-REH-moh
You (plural, familiar) will leave.	Voi partirete.	pahr-tee-REH-teh
They / You (plural, formal) will leave.	Loro / Loro partiranno.	pahr-tee-RAHN-noh

TO BE OR NOT TO BE

Italian has two verbs that mean "to be" (am, are, is, was, were). One is for physical location or temporary conditions (**stare**), and the other is for fixed qualities or conditions (**essere**). Stare is used in courtesy expressions with **bene** or **male** (well, unwell), e.g. **Come sta? Sto bene / male** (How are you? I'm fine / not well) and to express a progressive -ing action, e.g. **Sto mangiando** (I am eating). **Essere** is used most of the time to express fixed qualities or conditions (as in English) and health states other than **bene** or **male**, e.g. **Sono stanco** (I'm tired).

I am here. (temporary, stare)	**Io sto qua.**
What are you doing? (temporary, stare)	**Cosa sta facendo?**
The train is slow. (quality, essere)	**Il treno è lento.**

Stare "To Be, To Stay" (conditional)
Present Tense

I am.	Io sto.	stoh
You (singular, familiar) are.	Tu stai.	steye
He / She is. You (singular, formal) are.	Lui / Lei / Lei sta.	stah
We are.	Noi stiamo.	STYAH-moh
You (plural, familiar) are.	Voi state.	STAH-teh
They / You (plural, formal) are.	Loro / Loro stanno.	STAHN-noh

Past (imperfect) Tense

I was.	Io stavo.	STAH-voh
You (singular, familiar were.	Tu stavi.	STAH-vee
He / She was. You (singular, formal) were.	Lui / Lei / Lei stava.	STAH-vah
We were.	Noi stavamo.	stah-VAH-moh
You (plural, familiar) were.	Voi stavate.	stah-VAH-teh
They / You (plural, formal) were.	Loro / Loro stavano.	STAH-vah-noh

Essere "To Be" (permanent)
Present Tense

I am.	Io sono.	SOH-noh
You (singular, familiar) are.	Tu sei.	SEH-ee
He /She is. You (singular, formal) are.	Lui / Lei / Lei è.	EH
We are.	Noi siamo.	SYAH-moh
You (plural, familiar) are.	Voi siete.	SYEH-teh
They / You (plural, formal) are.	Loro / Loro sono.	SOH-noh

Past (imperfect) Tense

I was.	Io ero.	EH-roh
You (singular, familiar) were.	Tu eri.	EH-ree
He / She was. You (singular, formal) were.	Lui / Lei / Lei era.	EH-rah
We were.	Noi eravamo.	eh-rah-VAH-moh
You (plural, familiar) were.	Voi eravate.	eh-rah-VAH-teh
They / You (plural, formal) were.	Loro / Loro erano.	EH-rah-noh

IRREGULAR VERBS

Italian has numerous irregular verbs that stray from the standard -ARE, -ERE, and -IRE conjugations. Rather than bog you down with too much grammar, we're providing the present tense conjugations for the most common irregular verbs.

AVERE "To Have"

I have.	Io *ho.*	OH
You (singular, familiar) have.	Tu *hai.*	EYE
He / She has. You (singular, formal) have.	Lui / Lei / Lei *ha.*	AH
We have.	Noi *abbiamo.*	ahb-BYAH-moh
You (plural, familiar) have.	Voi *avete.*	ah-VEH-teh
They / You (plural, formal) have.	Loro / Loro *hanno.*	AHN-noh

ANDARE "To Go"

I go.	Io *vado.*	VAH-doh
You (singular, familiar) go.	Tu *vai.*	VAH-ee
He / She goes. You (singular, formal) go.	Lui / Lei / Lei *va.*	vah
We go.	Noi *andiamo.*	ahn-DYAH-moh
You (plural, familiar) go.	Voi *andate.*	ahn-DAH-teh
They / You (plural, formal) go.	Loro / Loro *vanno.*	VAHN-noh

DARE "To Give"

I give.	Io do.	DOH
You (singular, familiar) **give.**	Tu d*ai*.	DAH-ee
He / She gives. You (singular, formal) **give.**	Lui / Lei / Lei dà.	DAH
We give.	Noi d*iamo*.	DYAH-moh
You (plural, familiar) **give.**	Voi d*ate*.	DAH-teh
They / You (plural, formal) **give.**	Loro / Loro d*anno*.	DAHN-noh

FARE "To Do, To Make"

I do / make.	Io f*accio*.	FAHT-choh
You (singular, familiar) **do / make.**	Tu f*ai*.	FAH-ee
He / She does / makes. You (singular, formal) **do / make.**	Lui / Lei / Lei fa.	FAH
We do / make.	Noi f*acciamo*.	faht-CHAH-moh
You (plural, familiar) **do / make.**	Voi f*ate*.	FAH-teh
They / You (plural, formal) **do / make.**	Loro / Loro f*anno*.	FAHN-noh

Fare

The verb *fare* means to make or do. It's also used to describe the weather. For example:

Fa caldo. It's hot.
  (Literally: It makes hot.)
Fa freddo. It's cold.
  (Literally: It makes cold.)

Be careful not to say **Sono freddo**, as this translates "I'm a cold person" or "I'm sexually frigid". Instead, say **Ho freddo / caldo**. (Literally: I have cold / hot.) Likewise, **Sono caldo** can mean "hot to trot."

BERE "To Drink"

I drink.	Io be*vo*.	BEH-voh
You (singular, familiar) **drink.**	Tu be*vi*.	BEH-vee
He / She drinks. You (singular, formal) **drink.**	Lui / Lei / Lei be*ve*.	BEH-veh
We drink.	Noi be*viamo*.	beh-VYAH-moh
You (plural, familiar) **drink.**	Voi be*vete*.	beh-VEH-teh
They / You (plural, formal) **drink.**	Loro / Loro be*vono*.	BEH-voh-noh

DOVERE "Must, To Have To"

I must / have to.	Io de*vo.*	DEH-voh
You (singular, familiar) **must / have to.**	Tu de*vi.*	DEH-vee
He / She must / has to. You (singular, formal) **must / have to.**	Lui / Lei / Lei de*ve.*	DEH-veh
We must / have to.	Noi do*bbiamo.*	dohb-BYAH-moh
You (plural, familiar) **must / have to.**	Voi do*vete.*	doh-VEH-teh
They / You (plural, formal) **must / have to.**	Loro / Loro de*vono.*	DEH-voh-noh

POTERE "Can, To Be Able"

I can / am able.	Io po*sso.*	POHS-soh
You (singular, familiar) **can / are able.**	Tu pu*oi.*	poo-OH-ee
He / She can/ is able. You (singular, formal) **can / are able.**	Lui /Lei / Lei pu*ò.*	poo-OH
We can / are able.	Noi po*ssiamo.*	pohs-SYAH-moh
You (plural, familiar) **can / are able.**	Voi po*tete.*	poh-TEH-teh
They / You (plural, formal) **can / are able.**	Loro / Loro po*ssono.*	POHS-soh-noh

SAPERE "To Know"

I know.	Io so.	soh
You (singular, familiar) know.	Tu sai.	SAH-ee
He / She knows. You (singular, formal) know.	Lui / Lei / Lei sa.	SAH
We know.	Noi sappiamo.	sahp-PYAH-moh
You (plural, familiar) know.	Voi sapete.	sah-PEH-teh
They / You (plural, formal) know.	Loro / Loro sanno.	SAHN-noh

VOLERE "To Want"

I want.	Io voglio.	VOHL-lyoh
You (singular, familiar) want.	Tu vuoi.	VWOH-ee
He / She wants. You (singular, formal) want.	Lui / Lei / Lei vuole.	VWOH-leh
We want.	Noi vogliamo.	vohl-LYAH-moh
You (plural, familiar) want.	Voi volete.	voh-LEH-teh
They / You (plural, formal) want.	Loro / Loro vogliono.	VOHL-lyoh-noh

USCIRE "To Get Out"

I get out.	Io *esco*.	EHS-koh
You (singular, familiar) get out.	Tu *esci*.	EH-shee
He / She gets out. You (singular, formal) **get out.**	Lui / Lei / Lei *esce*.	EH-sheh
We get out.	Noi us*ciamo*.	oo-SHAH-moh
You (plural, familiar) get out.	Voi us*cite*.	oo-SHEE-teh
They / You (plural, formal) **get out.**	Loro / Loro *escono*.	EHS-koh-noh

VENIRE "To Come"

I come.	Io ven*go*.	VEHN-goh
You (singular, familiar) **come.**	Tu v*ieni*.	VYEH-nee
He / She comes. You (singular, formal) **come.**	Lui / Lei / Lei v*iene*.	VYEH-neh
We come.	Noi ven*iamo*.	veh-NYAH-moh
You (plural, familiar) **come.**	Voi ven*ite*.	veh-NEE-teh
They / You (plural, formal) **come.**	Loro / Loro ven*gono*.	VEHN-goh-noh

Piacere

The Italian for "to like" is *piacere*, which literally means to please. So, rather than "I like chocolate," Italians say, "Chocolate is pleasing to me."

Mi piace il cioccolato. I like chocolate.
(Literally: Chocolate is pleasing to me.)
Mi piacciono i dolci. I like sweets / desserts.
(Literally: Sweets are pleasing to me.)

Piacere "To Like"

Present Tense	Singular	Plural
I like.	*Mi* piace. PYAH-cheh	*Mi* piacciono. PYAHT-choh-noh
You (informal, singular) like.	*Ti* piace.	*Ti* piacciono.
He / She likes. You (formal, singular) like.	*Gli / Le / Le* piace.	*Gli / Le / Le* piacciono.
We like.	*Ci* piace.	*Ci* piacciono.
You (informal, plural) like.	*Vi* piace.	*Vi* piacciono.
They / You (formal, plural) like.	*Gli / Loro* piace.	*Gli / Loro* piacciono.

Past Tense	Singular	Plural
I liked.	*Mi* piaceva. pyah-CHEH-vah	*Mi* piacevano. pyah-CHEH-vah-noh
You (informal, singular) **liked.**	*Ti* piaceva.	*Ti* piacevano.
He / She/ You (formal, singular) **liked.**	*Gli / Le / Le* piaceva.	*Gli / le / Le* piacevano.
We liked.	*Ci* piaceva.	*Ci* piacevano.
You (informal, plural) **liked.**	*Vi* piaceva.	*Vi* piacevano.
They / You (formal, plural) **liked.**	*Gli / Loro* piaceva.	*Gli / Loro* piacevano.

REFLEXIVE VERBS

Italian has many more reflexive verbs than English. A verb is reflexive when both its subject and object refer to the same person or thing. For example: "Maria looks at herself in the mirror," **Maria si guarda allo specchio**. The following common verbs are used reflexively: **vestirsi** (to get dressed, literally to dress oneself), **bagnarsi** (to get oneself wet), and **svegliarsi** (to wake up, literally to wake oneself up).

VESTIRSI "To Get Dressed"		
I get dressed.	Io *mi* vesto.	mee VEHS-toh
You (singular, familiar) get dressed.	Tu *ti* vesti.	tee VEHS-tee
He / She gets dressed. You (singular, formal) get dressed.	Lui / Lei / Lei *si* veste.	see VEHS-teh
We get dressed.	Noi *ci* vestiamo.	chee vehs-TYAH-moh
You (plural, familiar) get dressed.	Voi *vi* vestite.	vee vehs-TEE-teh
They / You (plural, formal) get dressed.	Loro / Loro *si* vestono.	see VEHS-toh-noh

ESSENTIALS CHECK LIST

Do you have:

- A current **passport?** Make sure you leave a copy of the identification page (the one with your photo and passport number) with someone at home, or bring a copy with you and store it separately from your passport.

- The address and phone number of your country's **embassy or consulate?**

- A copy of your **itinerary,** with contact numbers, that you can leave with someone at home?

- Your health **insurance card?**

- Your **e-ticket documentation** (a printout of the reservation confirmation and your itinerary)?

- A current **ATM card?** Is your PIN (personal identification number) four digits? You need a four-digit PIN to use an ATM card in Italy. Ask your bank for one.

- A safe, accessible place to **store money?**

- Documentation for **traveler's checks** you might have purchased, stored separately from the checks?

- A **credit card** other than one issued by American Express? (Many establishments in Italy don't accept AmEx.)

- Enough **prescription medications** to last the duration of your trip? The generic names of medicines?

- An **adapter and/or transformer** for hair dryers, laptops, and other electrical appliances to use with Italian plugs?

- An extra pair of **glasses and/or contact lenses?**

- **Shoe and clothing sizes** of those you want to buy gifts for?

FUN FACTS

Area 116,314 sq. miles (301,253 sq. km), slightly larger than Arizona

Largest City Rome (population 2,459,776)

Life Expectancy 79 (only Japan is higher, at 80.7)

Longest River The Po flows 405 miles (652km) from the Alps to the Adriatic Sea

Median Age 41.4

Most Active Volcano Stromboli (several eruptions per hour); Europe's two other active volcanoes are also in Italy: Etna, in Sicily, and Vesuvius, outside Naples.

Neighbors Bordered on the northwest by France, on the north by Switzerland and Austria, and on the east by Slovenia (part of former Yugoslavia). The State of Vatican City, in Rome, and the Republic of San Marino, near Rimini, are completely surrounded by Italian territory.

Number of Annual Visitors 40 million

Number of Cellphones 56 million

Pasta Consumed Per Capita Per Year 55 pounds (25kg)

Population 58,057,477

Religion Roman Catholic (98%)

Tallest Dome St. Peter's Basilica, Rome 449 feet (136m); second tallest, Santa Maria del Fiore (the Duomo), Florence 300 feet (91m)

Tallest Mountain Mont Blanc (Monte Bianco; 15,771 feet (4,807m)

GREAT MOMENTS

Cruising Venice's Grand Canal From Piazza San Marco to the *ferrovia* (train station), the S-shaped Canal Grande flows alongside palaces, churches, and public buildings from the 14th through the 18th centuries. Casanova, Lord Byron, Richard Wagner, and legions of other travelers have gasped at the dreamlike panorama unfolding before them as they slipped along this historic waterway. You needn't spend a fortune to enjoy this experience; simply board a no. 1 *vaporetto* (public ferry) and, if the weather cooperates, take a seat in the open-air prow of the boat.

Taking in the Sights from Taormina's Teatro Greco-Romano in Sicily   The splendid theater the Greeks carved into the hillside in the 3rd century B.C. is today a ruin with a view: Mount Etna fumes in the background, the coastline far below seems to sweep away into infinity, and Sicily's legendary, flower-filled medieval resort clings to the cliff side as if it's about to plunge into the sea. The theater closes an hour before sunset, so settle for an almost-as-magnificent nighttime view from the balustrades of the Piazza IX Aprile.

Climbing Rome's Capitoline Hill in the Moonlight   Actually, you needn't wait for a cloudless sky—in any kind of weather, the view over the ruins of the forum, Colosseum, and other remnants of empire, set against a backdrop of Renaissance domes, is stunning.

Sipping a Glass of Wine in a Cafe on The Piazza del Campo in Siena   Montaigne adequately described the sloping, elliptical piazza—surrounded by Renaissance houses at the heart of Italy's most beautiful medieval city—as the "finest of any city in the world." The only times the square is less than enchanting is on July 2 and August 16, when half the population of Italy seems to congregate here to watch Il Palio, the city's famous bareback horse race. (Attend only if you don't mind standing in the sun for 6 or more hours without easy access to toilets or refreshments.)

Hiking in the Cinque Terre   The Five Lands (actually, the five seaside villages of Monterosso, Vernazza, Corniglia, Manarola, and Riomaggiore) are connected by a well-trodden path that dips and rises through vineyards and olive groves and provides a breathtaking view at every turn. Souvenir stands and backpackers are as thick on the ground as grapes, but avoid the crowds that descend in August and on weekends in warmer months and you'll get a sense of remote beauty. For the best experience, avoid crowded Monterosso and head for one of the other villages; Corniglia is the least-trammeled. *For information on rooms to rent, trails, and more, visit www.cinqueterre.com.*

Appreciating Art in the Vatican Museums   The Sistine Chapel is the show stealer, but Michelangelo's handiwork is just the icing on the cake in these rooms in the Vatican Palace. The Belvedere Torso (the Greek statue that inspired generations of Renaissance artists); Leonardo da Vinci's *St. Jerome with the Lion*; and Raphael's *Stanze* (the frescoes with which the artist decorated the apartments of Pope Julius II) are among the stunning treasures of classical and Renaissance art amassed by generations of popes. Choose one of four itineraries that last from 1 hour to 5 hours. *Open Mon–Sat daily except Jan 1 and 6, Easter, May 1 and 20, Nov 1, and Dec 8, 25, and 26. Nov–Feb 8:45am–12:20pm; Mar–Oct Mon–Fri 8:45am–3:20pm, Sat 8:45am–12:20pm. (Arrive early in summer to avoid lines.)*

Nibbling Your Way Through the Outdoor Food Market in Piazza Ghiaia in Parma   This market may yield the best food experience in all of Italy—and that's saying a lot. Parma's justifiably famous cheese (*Parmigiano-Reggiano*) and ham (*prosciutto di Parma*) fill the stalls, along with balsamic vinegar, Lambrusco wine, and other bounty of the Emilia-Romagna region. *Open Mon–Sat, 8am–1pm and 3pm–7pm.*

CHAPTER TWO

GETTING THERE & GETTING AROUND

This section deals with every form of transportation. Whether you've just reached your destination by plane or you're renting a car to tour the countryside, you'll find the necessary phrases in the next 30 pages.

AT THE AIRPORT

I am looking for ____	**Cerco** ____
	CHEHR-koh
a porter.	**un facchino.**
	oon fahk-KEE-noh
the check-in counter.	**il check-in.**
	eel check-in
the ticket counter.	**la biglietteria.**
	lah beel-lyeht-teh-REE-ah
arrivals.	**l'area arrivi.**
	LAH-reh-ah ahr-REE-vee
departures.	**l'area partenze.**
	LAH-reh-ah pahr-TEHN-tseh
gate number ____.	**l'uscita numero ____.**
	loo-SHEE-tah NOO-meh-roh

For full coverage of numbers, see p7.

the waiting area.	**l'area d'attesa.**
	LAH-reh-ah daht-TEH-zah
the men's restroom.	**la toilette uomini.**
	lah twa-LEHT WOH-mee-nee
the women's restroom.	**la toilette donne.**
	lah twa-LEHT DOHN-neh
the police station.	**la stazione di polizia.**
	lah stah-TSYOH-neh dee
	poh-lee-TSEE-ah

a security guard.	**una guardia di sicurezza.** *OOH-nah GWAHR-dyah dee* *see-koo-RET-sah*
the smoking area.	**l'area fumatori.** *LAH-reh-ah foo-mah-TOH-ree*
the information booth.	**l'ufficio informazioni.** *loof-FEE-choh een-FOHR-mah-* *TSYOH-nee*
a public telephone.	**un telefono pubblico.** *oon teh-LEH-foh-noh* *POOB-blee-koh*
an ATM / cashpoint.	**un bancomat.** *oon BAHN-koh-maht*
baggage claim.	**il ritiro bagagli.** *eel ree-TEE-roh bah-GAHL-lyee*
a luggage cart.	**un carrello portabagagli.** *oon kahr-REHL-loh* *POHR-tah- bah-GAHL-lyee*
a currency exchange.	**un cambiavalute.** *oon KAHM-byah-vah-LOO-teh*
a café.	**un caffè.** *oon kahf-FEH*
a restaurant.	**un ristorante.** *oon ree-stoh-RAHN-teh*
a bar.	**un bar.** *oon bar*
a bookstore or newsstand.	**una libreria o un'edicola.** *OO-nah lee-breh-REE-ah oh* *oon eh-DEE-koh-lah*
a duty-free shop.	**un duty-free.** *oon duty-free*

Is there Internet access here?	**C'è un accesso a Internet qui?**
	ch-EH oon atch-CHESS-oh ah Internet kwee
I'd like to page someone.	**Vorrei far chiamare qualcuno.**
	vohr-RAY fahr kyah-MAH-reh kwahl-KOO-noh
Do you accept credit cards?	**Prendete la carta di credito?**
	prehn-DEH-teh lah KAHR-tah dee KREH-dee-toh

CHECKING IN

I would like a one-way ticket to ____.	**Vorrei un biglietto di andata per ____.**
	vohr-RAY oon beel-LYEHT-toh dee ahn-DAH-tah pehr
I would like a round trip ticket to ____.	**Vorrei un biglietto di andata e ritorno per ____.**
	vohr-RAY oon beel-LYEHT-toh dee ahn-DAH-tah eh ree-TOHR-noh pehr
How much are the tickets?	**Quanto costano i biglietti?**
	KWAHN-toh KOHS-tah-noh ee beel-LYEHT-tee
Do you have anything less expensive?	**C'è qualcosa di meno caro?**
	ch-EH kwahl-KOH-zah dee MEH-noh KAH-roh
What time does flight ____ leave?	**A che ora parte il volo ____?**
	ah keh OH-rah PAHR-teh eel VOH-loh
What time does flight ____ arrive?	**A che ora arriva il volo ____?**
	ah keh OH-rah ahr-REE-vah eel VOH-loh

For full coverage of numbers, see p7.
For full coverage of time, see p12.

Common Airport Signs

Arrivi	Arrivals
Partenze	Departures
Terminal	Terminal
Uscita	Gate
Emissione biglietti	Ticketing
Dogana	Customs
Ritiro bagagli	Baggage Claim
Spingere	Push
Tirare	Pull
Vietato fumare	No Smoking
Entrata	Entrance
Uscita	Exit
Uomini	Men's
Donne	Women's
Bus navetta	Shuttle Buses
Taxi	Taxis

GETTING THERE

How long is the flight?	**Quanto dura il volo?** *KWAHN-toh DOO-rah eel VOH-loh*
Do I have a connecting flight?	**C'è una coincidenza?** *ch-EH OO-nah koh-een-chee-DEHN-tsa*
Do I need to change planes?	**Devo cambiare aereo?** *DEH-voh kahm-BYAH-reh ah-EH-reh-oh*
My flight leaves at __:__.	**Il mio aereo parte alle __:__.** *eel MEE-oh ah-EH-reh-oh PAHR-teh ahl-leh*
What time will the flight arrive?	**A che ora arriva l'aereo?** *ah keh OH-rah ahr-REE-vah lah-EH-reh-oh*

Is the flight on time?	**Il volo è in orario?** *eel VOH-loh EH een oh-RAH-ryoh*
Is the flight delayed?	**Il volo è in ritardo?** *eel VOH-loh EH een ree-TAHR-doh*
From which terminal is flight ____ leaving?	**Da che terminal parte il volo ____?** *dah keh TEHR-mee-nahl PAHR-teh eel VOH-loh*
From which gate is flight ____ leaving?	**Da che uscita parte il volo ____?** *dah keh oo-SHEE-tah PAHR-teh eel VOH-loh*

For full coverage of numbers, see p7.

How much time do I need for check-in?	**Quanto tempo ci vuole per fare il check-in?** *KWAHN-toh TEHM-poh chee VWOH-leh pehr FAH-reh eel check-in*
Is there an express check-in line?	**C'è una fila rapida per il check-in?** *ch-EH OO-nah FEE-lah RAH-pee-dah pehr eel check-in*
Is there electronic check-in?	**C'è un check-in elettronico?** *ch-EH oon check-in eh-leht-TROH-nee-koh*

Seat Preferences

I would like _____ ticket(s) in _____	**Vorrei _____ biglietto -i in _____** *vohr-RAY _____ beel-LYEHT- toh -ee een*
first / business class.	**prima classe.** *PREE-mah KLAHS-seh*
economy class.	**classe turistica.** *KLAHS-seh too-REES-tee-kah*
I would like _____	**Vorrei _____** *vohr-RAY*
Please don't give me _____	**Per favore non mi dia _____** *pehr fah-VOH-reh nohn mee DEE-ah*
a window seat.	**un posto vicino al finestrino.** *oon POHS-toh vee-CHEE-noh ahl fee-nehs-TREE-noh*
an aisle seat.	**un posto sul corridoio.** *oon POHS-toh sool kohr-ree-DOH-yoh*
an emergency exit row seat.	**un posto vicino all'uscita di sicurezza.** *oon POHS-toh vee-CHEE-noh ahl-loo-SHEE-tah dee see-koo-RET-sah*
a bulkhead seat.	**un posto in prima fila.** *oon POHS-toh een PREE-mah FEE-lah*
a seat by the restroom.	**un posto vicino alle toilette.** *oon POHS-toh vee-CHEE-noh AHL-leh twa-LEHT*
a seat near the front.	**un posto nella parte anteriore.** *oon POHS-toh NEHL-lah PAHR-teh ahn-teh-RYOH-reh*

a seat near the middle.	**un posto nella zona centrale.** *oon POHS-toh NEHL-lah* *DZOH-nah chehn-TRAH-leh*
a seat near the back.	**un posto verso il retro.** *oon POHS-toh VEHR-soh eel* *REH-troh*
Is there a meal on the flight?	**Viene servito un pasto durante il volo?** *VYEH-neh sehr-VEE-toh oon PAHS-toh doo-RAHN-teh eel VOH-loh*
I'd like to order ____	**Vorrei ordinare ____** *vohr-RAY ohr-dee-NAH-reh*
a vegetarian meal.	**un pasto vegetariano.** *oon PAHS-toh* *veh-jeh-tah-RYAH-noh*
a kosher meal.	**un pasto kasher.** *oon PAHS-toh KAH-shehr*
a diabetic meal.	**un pasto per diabetici.** *oon PAHS-toh pehr dyah-BEH-tee-chee*
I am traveling to ____.	**Sto andando a ____.** *stoh ahn-DAHN-doh ah*
I am coming from ____.	**Vengo da ____.** *VEHN-goh dah*
I arrived from ____.	**Arrivo da ____.** *ahr-REE-voh dah*

For full coverage of country terms, see English / Italian dictionary.

I'd like to change / cancel / confirm my reservation.	**Vorrei cambiare / annullare / confermare la mia prenotazione.** *vohr-RAY kahm-BYAH-reh / ahn-nool-LAH-reh / kohn-fehr-MAH-reh lah MEE-ah preh-noh-tah-TSYOH-neh*

I have ___ bags to check.	**Ho ___ bagagli da registrare.** *OH ___ bah-GAHL-lyee dah reh-jees-TRAH-reh*

For full coverage of numbers, see p7.

Passengers with Special Needs

Is that handicap accessible?	**C'è accesso ai disabili?** *ch-EH atch-CHESS-oh eye dee-ZAH-bee-lee*
May I have a wheelchair / a walker please?	**Posso avere una sedia a rotelle / un deambulatore, per favore?** *POHS-soh ah-VEH-reh OO-nah SEH-dyah ah roh-TEHL-leh / oon deh-ahm-boo-lah-TOH-reh pehr fah-VOH-reh*
I need some assistance boarding.	**Ho bisogno di assistenza all'imbarco.** *OH bee-ZOHN-nyoh dee ahs-sees-TEHN-tsa ahl-leem-BAHR-koh*
I need to bring my service dog.	**Devo portare il mio cane d'assistenza.** *DEH-voh pohr-TAH-reh eel MEE-oh KAH-neh dahs-sees-TEHN-tsa*
Do you have services for the hearing impaired?	**Ci sono servizi per ipoudenti?** *chee SOH-noh sehr-VEE-tsee pehr EE-poh-oo-DEHN-tee*
Do you have services for the visually impaired?	**Ci sono servizi per ipovedenti?** *chee SOH-noh sehr-VEE-tsee pehr EE-poh-oo-veh-DEHN-tee*

Trouble at Check-In

How long is the delay?	**Di quanto è il ritardo?**
	dee KWAHN-toh EH eel ree-TAHR-doh
My flight was late.	**Il mio volo era in ritardo.**
	eel MEE-oh VOH-loh EH-rah een ree-TAHR-doh
I missed my flight.	**Ho perso il volo.**
	OH PEHR-soh eel VOH-loh
When is the next flight?	**Quand'è il prossimo volo?**
	kwahn-DEH eel PROHS-see-moh VOH-loh
May I have a meal voucher?	**Posso avere un buono pasto?**
	POHS-soh ah-VEH-reh oon BWOH-noh PAHS-toh
May I have a room voucher?	**Posso avere un buono stanza?**
	POHS-soh ah-VEH-reh oon BWOH-noh STAHN-tsah

AT CUSTOMS / SECURITY CHECKPOINTS

I'm traveling with a group.	**Viaggio con un gruppo.**
	VYAHD-joh kohn oon GROOP-poh
I'm on my own.	**Viaggio da solo -a.**
	VYAHD-joh dah SOH-loh -ah
I'm traveling on business.	**Sono in viaggio d'affari.**
	SOH-noh een VYAHD-joh dahf-FAH-ree
I'm on vacation.	**Sono in vacanza.**
	SOH-noh een vah-KAHN-tsah
I have nothing to declare.	**Non ho nulla da dichiarare.**
	nohn OH NOOL-lah dah dee-kyah-RAH-reh
I would like to declare ____.	**Vorrei dichiarare ____.**
	vohr-RAY dee-kyah-RAH-reh
I have some liquor.	**Ho un po' di liquore.**
	OH oon POH dee lee-KWOH-reh

I have some cigars.	**Ho dei sigari.**
	OH day SEE-gah-ree
They are gifts.	**Sono regali.**
	SOH-noh reh-GAH-lee
They are for personal use.	**Sono per uso personale.**
	SOH-noh pehr OO-zoh pehr-soh-NAH-leh
That is my medicine.	**È la mia medicina.**
	EH lah MEE-ah meh-dee-CHEE-nah
I have my prescription.	**Ho la mia ricetta.**
	OH lah MEE-ah ree-CHET-tah
My children are traveling on the same passport.	**I miei bambini viaggiano con lo stesso passaporto.**
	ee mee-EH-ee bahm-BEE-nee VYAHD-jah-noh kohn loh STEHS-soh pahs-sah-POHR-toh
I'd like a female / male officer to conduct the search.	**Vorrei un agente donna / uomo per la perquisizione.**
	vohr-RAY oon ah-JEN-teh DOHN-nah / WOH-moh pehr lah pehr-kwee-zee-TSYOH-neh

GETTING THERE

Listen Up: Security Lingo

Per favore, ____	Please ____
si tolga le scarpe.	remove your shoes.
si tolga la giacca / la maglia.	remove your jacket / sweater.
si tolga i gioielli.	remove your jewelry.
metta le borse sul trasportatore.	place your bags on the conveyor belt.
Si sposti di qua.	Step to the side.
Dobbiamo fare un'ispezione manuale.	We have to do a hand search.

Trouble at Security

Help me. I've lost ____	**Mi aiuti. Ho perso ____** *mee ah-YOO-tee OH PEHR-soh*
my passport.	**il passaporto.** *eel pahs-sah-POHR-toh*
my boarding pass.	**la carta d'imbarco.** *lah KAHR-tah deem-BAHR-koh*
my identification.	**il documento d'identità.** *eel doh-koo-MEHN-toh dee-dehn-tee-TAH*
my wallet.	**il portafoglio.** *eel pohr-tah-FOHL-lyoh*
my purse.	**la borsa.** *lah BOHR-sah*
Someone stole my purse / wallet!	**Mi hanno rubato la borsa / il portafoglio!** *mee AHN-noh roo-BAH-toh lah BOHR-sah / eel pohr-tah-FOHL-lyoh*

IN-FLIGHT

It's unlikely you'll need much Italian on the plane, but these phrases will help if a bilingual flight attendant is unavailable or if you need to talk to an Italian-speaking neighbor.

I think that's my seat.	**Credo che quello sia il mio posto.** *KREH-doh keh KWEHL-loh SEE-ah eel MEE-oh POHS-toh*
May I have ____	**Posso avere ____** *POHS-soh ah-VEH-reh*
water?	**dell'acqua?** *dehl-LAHK-wah*
sparkling water?	**gassata?** *gas-SAH-tah*
orange juice?	**del succo d'arancia?** *dehl SOOK-koh dah-RAHN-chah*

soda?	**una bibita?**
	OO-nah BEE-bee-tah
diet soda?	**una bibita light?**
	OO-nah BEE-bee-tah light
a beer?	**una birra?**
	OO-nah BEER-rah
wine?	**del vino?**
	dehl VEE-noh

For a complete list of drinks, see p100.

a pillow?	**un cuscino?**
	oon koo-SHEE-noh
a blanket?	**una coperta?**
	OO-nah koh-PEHR-tah
headphones?	**le cuffie?**
	leh KOOF-fyeh
a magazine or newspaper?	**una rivista o un giornale?**
	OO-nah ree-VEES-tah oh oon johr-NAH-leh
When will the meal be served?	**Quando sarà servito il pasto?**
	KWAHN-doh sah-RAH sehr-VEE-toh eel PAHS-toh
How long until we land?	**Quanto manca all'atterraggio?**
	KWAHN-toh MAHN-kah ahl-laht-tehr-RAHD-joh
May I move to another seat?	**Posso cambiare posto?**
	POHS-soh kahm-BYAH-reh POHS-toh
How do I turn the light on / off?	**Come si accende / spegne la luce?**
	KOH-meh see atch-CHEN-deh / SPEHN-nyeh lah LOO-cheh

Trouble In-Flight

These headphones are broken.	**Queste cuffie sono guaste.**
	KWEHS-teh KOOF-fyeh SOH-noh GWAHS-teh

I spilled.	**Mi si è rovesciato.**
	mee see EH roh-veh-SHAH-toh
My child spilled.	**Si è rovesciato al bambino.**
	see EH roh-veh-SHAH-toh ahl
	bahm-BEE-noh
My child is sick.	**Il mio bambino / la mia bambina**
	sta male.
	eel MEE-oh bahm-BEE-noh / lah
	MEE-ah bahm-BEE-nah stah
	MAH-leh
I need an airsickness bag.	**Mi serve un sacchetto per il mal d'aria.**
	mee SEHR-veh oon sahk-KEHT-toh
	perh eel mahl DAHR-yah
I smell something strange.	**Sento uno strano odore.**
	SEHN-toh OO-noh STRAH-noh
	oh-DOH-reh
That passenger is behaving suspiciously.	**Quel passeggero si comporta in modo sospetto.**
	kwehl pahs-sed-JEH-roh see
	kohm-POHR-tah een MOH-doh
	sohs-PEHT-to

BAGGAGE CLAIM

Where is baggage claim for flight ____?	**Dov'è il ritiro bagagli per il volo ____?**
	doh-VEH eel ree-TEE-roh
	bah-GAHL-lyee pehr eel VOH-loh
Would you please help with my bags?	**Può aiutarmi con i bagagli?**
	PWOH ah-yoo-TAHR-mee
	kohn ee bah-GAHL-lyee
I am missing ____ bags.	**Mi mancano ____ borse.**
	mee MAHN-kah-noh ____
	BOHR-seh

For full coverage of numbers, see p7.

My bag is _____	**La mia borsa è _____**
	lah MEE-ah BOHR-sah EH
lost.	**smarrita.**
	zmahr-REE-tah
damaged.	**danneggiata.**
	dahn-ned-JAH-tah
stolen.	**stata rubata.**
	STAH-tah roo-BAH-tah
a suitcase.	**una valigia.**
	OO-nah vah-LEE-jah
a briefcase.	**una valigetta.**
	OO-nah vah-lee-JEHT-tah
a carry-on.	**un bagaglio a mano.**
	oon bah-GAHL-lyoh ah
	MAH-noh
a suit bag.	**una borsa portabiti.**
	OO-nah BOHR-sah
	pohr-TAH-bee-tee
a trunk.	**un baule.**
	oon bah-OO-leh
golf clubs.	**mazze da golf.**
	MAHT-seh dah golf

For colors terms, see English / Italian Dictionary.

hard.	**rigido -a.**
	REE-jee-doh -ah
made out of _____	**fatto -a di _____**
	FAHT-toh -ah dee
canvas.	**tela.**
	TEH-lah
vinyl.	**vinile.**
	vee-NEE-leh
leather.	**pelle.**
	PEHL-leh

hard plastic.	**plastica dura.**
	PLAHS-tee-kah DOO-rah
aluminum.	**alluminio.**
	ahl-loo-MEE-nyoh

RENTING A VEHICLE

Is there a car rental agency in the airport?

C'è un'agenzia di autonoleggio in aeroporto?
ch-EH oon-ah-jehn-TSEE-ah dee ow-toh-noh-LEHD-joh een ah-EH-roh-POHR-toh

I have a reservation.

Ho una prenotazione.
OH OO-nah preh-noh-tah-TSYOH-neh

Vehicle Preferences

I would like to rent _____

Vorrei noleggiare _____
vohr-RAY noh-lehd-JAH-reh

an economy car.	**un'auto economica.**
	oon-OW-toh eh-koh-NOH-mee-kah
a midsize car.	**un'auto di media dimensione.**
	oon-OW-toh dee MEH-dyah dee-mehn-SYOH-neh
a sedan.	**una berlina.**
	OO-nah berh-LEE-nah
a convertible.	**un'auto convertibile.**
	oon-OW-toh kohn-vehr-TEE-bee-leh
a van.	**un furgoncino.**
	oon foor-gohn-CHEE-noh
a sports car.	**un'auto sportiva.**
	oon-OW-toh spohr-TEE-vah
a 4-wheel-drive vehicle.	**una quattro per quattro.**
	OO-nah KWAHT-troh pehr KWAHT-troh

a motorcycle.	**una moto.**
	OO-nah MOH-toh
a scooter.	**uno scooter.**
	OO-noh scooter
Do you have one with ____	**C'è un'auto con ____**
	ch-EH oon-OW-toh kohn
air conditioning?	**climatizzatore?**
	klee-mah-teed-zsah-TOH-reh
a sunroof?	**tettuccio apribile?**
	teht-TOOT-choh ah-PREE-bee-leh
a CD player?	**lettore di CD?**
	leht-TOH-reh dee chee-DEE
satellite radio?	**radio satellitare?**
	RAH-dyoh sah-tehl-lee-TAH-reh
satellite tracking?	**navigazione satellitare?**
	nah-vee-gah-TZYOH-neh
	sah-tehl-lee-TAH-reh
an onboard map?	**sistema di navigazione?**
	see-STEH-mah dee
	nah-vee-gah-TSYOH-neh
a DVD player?	**lettore di DVD?**
	leht-TOH-reh dee dee-voo-DEE
child seats?	**sedili per bambini?**
	seh-DEE-lee pehr bahm-BEE-nee
Do you have a ____	**C'è ____**
	ch-EH
smaller car?	**un'auto più piccola?**
	oon-OW-toh PYOO PEEK-koh-lah
bigger car?	**un'auto più grande?**
	oon-OW-toh PYOO GRAHN-deh
cheaper car?	**un'auto più economica?**
	oon-OW-toh PYOO
	eh-koh-NOH-mee-kah

GETTING THERE

Do you have a non-smoking car?	**C'è un'auto per non fumatori?** *ch-EH oon-OW-toh pehr nohn foo-mah-TOH-ree*
I need an automatic transmission.	**Mi serve un'auto con cambio automatico.** *mee SEHR-veh oon-OW-toh kohn KAHM-byoh ow-toh-MAH-tee-koh*
A standard transmission is okay.	**Con cambio manuale va bene.** *kohn KAHM-byoh mah-NWAH-leh vah BEH-neh*
May I have an upgrade?	**Posso avere una categoria superiore?** *POHS-soh ah-VEH-reh OO-nah kah-teh-goh-REE-ah soo-peh-RYOH-reh*

Money Matters

What's the daily / weekly / monthly rate?	**Qual è la tariffa giornaliera / settimanale / mensile?** *kwah-LEH lah tah-REEF-fah johr-nah-LYEH-rah / seht-tee-mah-NAH-leh / mehn-SEE-leh*
What is the mileage rate?	**Qual è la tariffa chilometrica?** *kwah-LEH lah tah-REEF-fah kee-loh-MEH-tree-kah*
How much is insurance?	**Quanto costa l'assicurazione?** *KWAHN-toh KOHS-tah lahs-see-koo-raht-SYOH-neh*
Are there other fees?	**Ci sono altri costi?** *chee SOH-noh AHL-tree KOHS-tee*
Is there a weekend rate?	**C'è una tariffa per il weekend?** *ch-EH OO-nah tah-REEF-fah pehr eel weekend*

Technical Questions

What kind of gas does it take?
Che tipo di benzina prende?
keh TEE-poh dee behn-DZEE-nah PREHN-deh

Do you have the manual in English?
Ha il manuale in inglese?
AH eel mah-NWA-leh een een-GLEH-zeh

Do you have an English booklet with the local traffic laws?
Ha un codice della strada in inglese?
AH oon KOH-dee-cheh DEHL-lah STRAH-dah een een-GLEH-zeh

Car Troubles

The ____ doesn't work.
____ non funziona.
nohn foon-TSYOH-nah

See diagram on p58 for car parts.

It is already dented.
È già ammaccata.
EH JAH ahm-mahk-KAH-tah

It is scratched.
È graffiata.
EH grahf-FYAH-tah

The windshield is cracked.
Il parabrezza è crepato.
eel pah-rah-BREHT-sah EH kreh-PAH-toh

The tires look low.
Le gomme sembrano sgonfie.
leh GOHM-meh SEHM-brah-noh SGOHN-fyeh

It has a flat tire.
Ha una gomma a terra.
AH OO-nah GOHM-mah ah TEHR-rah

Whom do I call for service?
Chi chiamo per l'assistenza?
kee KYAH-moh pehr lahs-sees-TEHN-tsa

It won't start.
Non parte.
nohn PAHR-teh

GETTING THERE

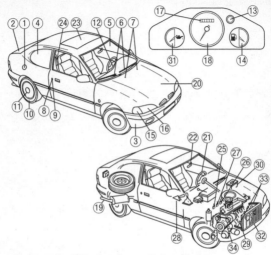

1. lo sportello del serbatoio
2. il portabagagli
3. il paraurti
4. il finestrino
5. il parabrezza
6. I tergicristalli
7. Il liquido tergicristalli
8. la serratura
9. la serratura automatica
10. I pneumatici
11. le ruote
12. l'accensione
13. la spia
14. l'indicatore di livello di carburante
15. gli indicatori di direzione
16. I fanali
17. il contachilometri
18. il tachimetro
19. la marmitta
20. il cofano
21. il volante
22. lo specchietto retrovisore
23. il tettuccio apribile
24. la cintura di sicurezza
25. l'acceleratore
26. la frizione
27. il freno
28. il freno d'emergenza
29. il motore
30. la batteria
31. l'indicatore di livello dell'olio
32. il radiatore
33. il tubo del radiatore
34. la cinghia del ventilatore

It's out of gas.	**È a secco.**
	EH ah SEHK-koh
The Check Engine light is on.	**La spia del motore è accesa.**
	lah SPEE-ah dehl moh-TOH-reh
	EH aht-CHEH-zah
The oil light is on.	**La spia dell'olio è accesa.**
	lah SPEE-ah dehl-LOH-lyoh EH
	aht-CHEH-zah
The brake light is on.	**La spia dei freni è accesa.**
	lah SPEE-ah day FREH-nee EH
	aht-CHEH-zah
It runs rough.	**Non va bene, fa rumore.**
	nohn vah BEH-neh fah roo-MOH-reh
The car is over-heating.	**L'auto si surriscalda.**
	LOW-toh see soor-ree-SKAHL-dah

Asking for Directions

Excuse me.	**Mi scusi.**
	mee SKOO-zee
How do I get to _____?	**Come si arriva a _____?**
	KOH-meh see ahr-REE-vah ah
Go straight.	**Vada dritto.**
	VAH-dah DREET-toh
Turn left.	**Giri a sinistra.**
	JEE-ree ah see-NEES-trah
Continue right.	**Continui a destra.**
	kohn-TEE-nwee ah DEHS-trah
It's on the right.	**E' sulla destra.**
	EH SOOL-lah DEHS-trah
Can you show me on the map?	**Può mostrarmi sulla cartina?**
	PWOH mohs-TRAHR-mee SOOL-lah
	kahr-TEE-nah
How far is it from here?	**Quanto dista da qui?**
	KWAHN-toh DEES-tah dah kwee
Is this the right road for _____?	**Questa è la strada giusta per _____?**
	KWEHS-tah EH lah STRAH-dah
	JOOS-tah pehr

I've lost my way.	**Mi sono perso -a.** *mee SOH-noh PEHR-soh -sah*
Would you repeat that, please?	**Può ripetere, per favore?** *PWOH ree-PEH-teh-reh pehr fah-VOH-reh*
Thanks for your help.	**Grazie per l'aiuto.** *GRAH-tsyeh pehr lah-YOO-toh*

For full coverage of direction-related terms, see p5.

Sorry, Officer

What is the speed limit?	**Qual è il limite di velocità?** *kwah-LEH eel LEE-mee-teh dee veh-loh-chee–TAH*
I wasn't going that fast.	**Non andavo così veloce.** *nohn ahn-DAH-voh koh-ZEE veh-LOH-cheh*
How much is the fine?	**Quant'è la multa?** *kwahn-TEH lah MOOL-tah*
Where do I pay the fine?	**Dove si paga la multa?** *DOH-veh see PAH-gah lah MOOL-tah*

Road Signs

Limite di velocità	Speed Limit
Stop	Stop
Dare la precedenza	Yield
Pericolo	Danger
Strada senza sbocco	No Exit
Senso unico	One Way
Vietato l'accesso	Do Not Enter
Strada chiusa	Road Closed
Pagamento pedaggio	Toll
Solo contanti	Cash Only
Parcheggio vietato	No Parking
Tariffa di parcheggio	Parking fee
Parcheggio	Parking garage

Do I have to go to court?	**Devo andare in tribunale?** *DEH-voh ahn-DAH-reh een tree-boo-NAH-leh*
I had an accident.	**Ho avuto un incidente.** *OH ah-VOO-toh oon een-chee-DEHN-teh*
The other driver hit me.	**L'altro autista mi ha investito -a.** *LAHL-troh ow-TEES-tah mee AH een-vehs-TEE-toh -tah*
I'm at fault.	**È colpa mia.** *EH KOHL-pah MEE-ah*

BY TAXI

Where is the taxi stand?	**Dov'è la fermata dei taxi?** *doh-VEH lah fehr-MAH-tah day taxi*
Is there a limo / bus / van for my hotel?	**C'è un servizio di limousine / bus / navetta per il mio hotel?** *ch-EH oon sehr-VEE-tsyoh dee limousine / boos / nah-VEHT-tah pehr eel MEE-oh hotel*
I need to get to _____.	**Devo andare a _____.** *DEH-voh ahn-DAH-reh ah*
How much will that cost?	**Quanto mi costa?** *KWAHN-toh mee KOHS-tah*
How long will it take?	**Quanto tempo ci vuole?** *KWAHN-toh TEHM-poh chee VWOH-leh*

Listen Up: Taxi Lingo

Salga!	Get in!
Lasci i bagagli, faccio io.	Leave your luggage, I got it.
Sono cinque euro al pezzo.	It's 5 Euros for each bag.
Quanti passeggeri?	How many passengers?
Ha fretta?	Are you in a hurry?

Can you take me / us to the train / bus station?	**Può portarmi / portarci alla stazione dei treni / degli autobus?** *PWOH pohr-TAHR-mee / chee AHL-lah stah-TSYOH-neh day TREH-nee / DEHL-lye OW-toh-boos*
I am in a hurry.	**Ho fretta.** *OH FREHT-tah*
Slow down.	**Rallenti.** *rahl-LEHN-tee*
Am I close enough to walk?	**Sono abbastanza vicino da andarci a piedi?** *SOH-noh ahb-bahs-TAHN-tsah vee-CHEE-noh dah ahn-DAHR-chee ah PYEH-dee*
Let me out here.	**Mi lasci qui.** *mee LAH-shee kwee*
That's not the correct change.	**Il resto non è giusto.** *eel REH-stoh nohn EH JOOS-toh*

BY TRAIN

How do I get to the train station?	**Come si arriva alla stazione ferroviaria?** *KOH-meh see ahr-REE-vah AHL-lah stah-TSYOH-neh fehr-roh-VYAH-ryah*
Would you take me to the train station?	**Può portarmi alla stazione ferroviaria?** *PWOH pohr-TAHR-mee AHL-lah stah-TSYOH-neh fehr-roh-VYAH-ryah*
How long is the trip to ____?	**Quanto ci vuole fino a ____?** *KWAHN-toh chee VWOH-leh FEE-noh ah*
When is the next train?	**Quand'è il prossimo treno?** *kwahn-DEH eel PROHS-see-moh TREH-noh*

Do you have a schedule / timetable?	**Ha un orario?** *AH oon oh-RAH-ryoh*
Do I have to change trains?	**Devo cambiare treni?** *DEH-voh kahm-BYAH-reh TREH-nee*
a one-way ticket	**un biglietto di sola andata** *oon beel-LYEHT-toh dee SOH-lah ahn-DAH-tah*
a round-trip ticket	**un biglietto di andata e ritorno** *oon beel-LYEHT-toh dee ahn-DAH-tah eh ree-TOHR-noh*
Which platform does it leave from?	**Da che binario parte?** *dah keh bee-NAH-ryoh PAHR-teh*
Is there a bar car?	**C'è una carrozza bar?** *ch-EH OO-nah kahr-ROHT-sah bar*
Is there a dining car?	**C'è una carrozza ristorante?** *ch-EH OO-nah kahr-ROHT-sah ree-stoh-RAHN-teh*
Which car is my seat in?	**In quale carrozza è il mio posto?** *een KWAH-leh kahr-ROHT-sah EH eel MEE-oh POHS-toh*
Is this seat taken?	**È occupato questo posto?** *EH ohk-koo-PAH-toh KWEHS-toh POHS toh*
Where is the next stop?	**Dov'è la prossima fermata?** *doh-VEH lah PROHS-see-mah fehr-MAH-tah*
How many stops to ____?	**Quante fermate fino a ____?** *KWAHN-teh fehr-MAH-teh FEE-noh ah*
What's the train number and destination?	**Qual è il numero del treno e la destinazione?** *kwah-LEH eel NOO-meh-roh dehl TREH-noh eh lah dehs-tee-nah-TSYOH-neh*

BY BUS

How do I get to the bus station?	**Come si arriva alla stazione degli autobus?** *KOH-meh see ahr-REE-vah ahl-LAH stah-TSYOH-neh DEHL-lye OW-toh-boos*
Would you take me to the bus station?	**Può portarmi alla stazione degli autobus?** *PWOH pohr-TAHR-mee ahl-LAH stah-TSYOH-neh DEHL-lye OW-toh-boos*
May I have a bus schedule?	**Posso avere un orario degli autobus?** *POHS-soh ah-VEH-reh oon oh-RAH-ryoh DEHL-lye OW-toh-boos*
Which bus goes to ____?	**Quale autobus va a ____?** *KWAH-leh OW-toh-boos vah ah*
Where does it leave from?	**Da dove parte?** *dah DOH-veh PAHR-teh*
How long does the bus take?	**Quanto tempo ci impiega l'autobus?** *KWAHN-toh TEHM-poh chee eem-PYEH-gah LOW-toh-boos*
How much is it?	**Quanto costa?** *KWAHN-toh KOHS-tah*
Is there an express bus?	**C'è un autobus espresso?** *ch-EH oon OW-toh-boos ehs-PREHS-soh*

Does it make local stops?	**Fa fermate locali?**
	fah fehr-MAH-teh loh-KAH-lee
Does it run at night?	**Fa servizio notturno?**
	fah sehr-VEE-tsyoh noht-TOOR-noh
When is the next bus?	**Quand'è il prossimo autobus?**
	kwahn-DEH eel PROHS-see-moh
	OW-toh-boos
a one-way ticket	**un biglietto di sola andata**
	oon beel-LYEHT-toh dee SOH-lah
	ahn-DAH-tah
a round-trip ticket	**un biglietto di andata e ritorno**
	oon beel-LYEHT-toh dee ahn-DAH-
	tah eh ree-TOHR-noh
How long will the bus be stopped?	**Quanto tempo sta fermo l'autobus?**
	KWAHN-toh TEHM-poh stah
	FEHR-moh LOW-toh-boos
Is there an air conditioned bus?	**C'è un autobus con aria condizionata?**
	ch-EH oon OW-toh-boos kohn
	AH-ryah kohn-dee-tsyoh-NAH-tah
Is this seat taken?	**È occupato questo posto?**
	EH ohk-koo-PAH-toh KWEHS-toh
	POHS-toh

Ticket etiquette

Travelers in Italy often need to validate their tickets before embarking. In a train station, search for a yellow **macchina obliteratrice** (stamping machine), which prints the time and date in the space marked **convalida** (validation). These usually stand at the end of each **binario** (platform). Many subways have a similar system, but buses validate onboard. If you forget—or can't reach the machine in a crowd—write the details in pen.

Where is the next stop?	**Dov'è la prossima fermata?**
	doh-VEH lah PROHS-see-mah
	fehr-MAH-tah
Please tell me when we reach ____.	**Mi dice quando arriviamo a ____, per favore.**
	mee DEE-cheh KWAHN-doh ahr-ree-VYAH-moh ah pehr fah-VOH-reh
Let me off here.	**Mi lasci qui.**
	mee LAH-shee kwee

BY BOAT OR SHIP

Would you take me to the port?	**Può portarmi al porto?**
	PWOH pohr-TAHR-mee ahl POHR-toh
When does the ship sail?	**Quando salpa la nave?**
	KWAHN-doh SAHL-pah lah NAH-veh
How long is the trip?	**Quanto dura il viaggio?**
	KWAHN-toh DOO-rah eel VYAHD-joh
Where are the life preservers?	**Dove sono i salvagenti?**
	DOH-veh SOH-noh ee sahl-vah-JEHN-tee
I would like a private cabin.	**Vorrei una cabina privata.**
	vohr-RAY OO-nah kah-BEE-nah pree-VAH-tah
Is the trip rough?	**È una traversata agitata?**
	EH OO-nah trah-vehr-SAH-tah ah-jee-TAH-tah
I feel seasick.	**Ho mal di mare.**
	OH eel mahl dee MAH-reh
I need some seasick pills.	**Ho bisogno di pastiglie antinausea.**
	OH bee-ZOHN-nyoh dee pahs-TEEL-lyeh ahn-tee-NOW-seh-ah
Where is the bathroom?	**Dov'è la toilette?**
	doh-VEH lah twah-LEHT

Does the ship have a casino?	**C'è un casinò sulla nave?** *ch-EH oon kah-zee-NOH SOOL-lah NAH-veh*
Will the ship stop at ports along the way?	**La nave si ferma nei porti lungo il tragitto?** *lah NAH-veh seeFEHR-mah NAY POHR-tee LOON-goh eel trah-JEET-oh*

BY SUBWAY

Where's the subway station?	**Dov'è la stazione del metrò?** *doh-VEH lah stah-TSYOH-neh dehl meh-TROH*
Where can I buy a ticket?	**Dove si comprano i biglietti?** *DOH-veh see KOHM-prah-noh ee beel-LYEHT-tee*

GETTING THERE

SUBWAY TICKETS

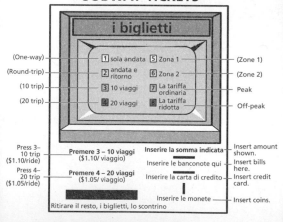

i biglietti

(One-way) — 1 sola andata
(Round-trip) — 2 andata e ritorno
(10 trip) — 3 10 viaggi
(20 trip) — 4 20 viaggi

5 Zona 1 — (Zone 1)
6 Zona 2 — (Zone 2)
7 La tariffa ordinaria — Peak
8 La tariffa ridotta — Off-peak

Press 3– 10 trip ($1.10/ride) — **Premere 3 – 10 viaggi** ($1.10/ viaggio)
Press 4– 20 trip ($1.05/ride) — **Premere 4 – 20 viaggi** ($1.05/ viaggio)

Inserire la somma indicata — Insert amount shown.
Inserire le banconote qui — Insert bills here.
Inserire la carta di credito — Insert credit card.
Inserire le monete — Insert coins.

Ritirare il resto, i biglietti, lo scontrino

Could I have a map of the subway?	**Mi da' una cartina del metrò?** *mee DAH OO-nah kahr-TEE-nah dehl meh-TROH*
Which line should I take for ____?	**Che linea devo prendere per ____?** *keh LEE-neh-ah DEH-voh PREHN-deh-reh pehr*
Is this the right line for ____?	**Questa è la linea giusta per ____?** *KWEHS-tah EH lah LEE-neh-ah JOOS-tah pehr*
Which stop is it for ____?	**Qual è la fermata per ____?** *kwah-LEH lah fehr-MAH-tah pehr*
How many stops is it to ____?	**Quante fermate per ____?** *KWAHN-teh fehr-MAH-teh pehr*
Is the next stop ____?	**La prossima fermata è ____?** *lah PROHS-see-mah fehr-MAH-tah EH*
Where are we?	**Dove siamo?** *DOH-veh see-AH-moh*
Where do I change to ____?	**Dove devo cambiare per ____?** *DOH-veh DEH-voh kahm-BYAH-reh pehr*
What time is the last train to ____?	**A che ora parte l'ultimo treno per ____?** *ah keh OH-rah PAHR-teh LOOL-tee-moh TREH-noh pehr*

TRAVELERS WITH SPECIAL NEEDS

Do you have wheelchair access?	**C'è accesso alle sedie a rotelle?** *ch-EH atch-CHESS-oh ALH-leh SEH-dyeh ah roh-TEHL-leh*
Do you have elevators? Where?	**Ci sono ascensori? Dove?** *chee SOH-noh ah-shehn-SOH-ree DOH-veh*

Do you have ramps? Where?

Are the restrooms wheelchair accessible?

Ci sono rampe? Dove?
chee SOH-noh RAHM-peh DOH-veh

Le toilettes hanno accesso alle sedie a rotelle?
leh twa-LEHT AHN-noh atch-CHESS-oh ALH-leh SEH-dyeh ah roh-TEHL-leh

Do you have audio assistance for the hearing impaired?

I am deaf.

C'è assistenza audio per ipoudenti?
ch-EH ahs-sees-TEHN-tsa OW-dyoh pehr EE-poh-oo-DEHN-tee

Sono ipoudente.
SOH-noh ee-poh-oo-DEHN-teh

May I bring my service dog?

Posso portare il mio cane di assistenza?
POHS-soh pohr-TAH-reh eel MEE-oh KAH-neh dee ahs-sees-TEHN-tsa

I am blind.

Sono ipovedente.
SOH-noh ee-poh-veh-DEHN-teh

I need to charge my power chair.

Devo caricare la mia sedia a rotelle.
DEH-voh kah-ree-KAH-reh lah MEE-ah SEH-dyah ah roh-TEHL-leh

UNFORGETTABLE SIGHTS BY REGION

Lazio (Latium)   Rome, center of the ancient world, capital of modern Italy, with a rich past remembered in ancient, medieval, Renaissance, and baroque monuments. Vatican City, center of the Roman Catholic Church, home to St. Peter's Cathedral and the Vatican Museums.

Liguria   The Italian Riviera. Genoa, Italy's largest port, with a warren of Renaissance palaces and alleys sloping down to the sea. Some of Europe's most pleasant seaside resort towns: Portofino, San Remo, Rapallo, Santa Margherita Ligure. Cinque Terre, a string of five fishing villages along a relatively remote stretch of coast.

Lombardy   Milan, famous for high fashion, La Scala opera house, Europe's third-largest cathedral, Leonardo's *Last Supper*, and other masterpieces. The Italian Lakes (Como, Garda, Maggiore, Orta), backed by Alpine peaks.

Sicily   Unforgettable Greek ruins, Norman cathedrals, and Moorish palaces. Palermo, a diamond in the rough. Catania, a city of baroque domes in the shadow of Mount Etna. Agrigento, Selinunte, and Siracusa—well-preserved remnants of the ancient world. Taormina, glamorous hilltop resort.

Trentino-Alto Adige   The craggy Dolomites. Cortina d'Ampezzo, Italy's most famous ski resort. Trieste, a moody port city with a Viennese flair (a remnant of the Austro-Hungarian Empire).

Tuscany   Florence, the world's greatest repository of Renaissance art. Chianti, region of rolling vineyards and medieval villages. Lucca, surrounded by Renaissance walls. Pisa, famous for its leaning tower. Siena, the world's most beautiful medieval city. Dozens of other art-filled hill towns.

Umbria   All the beauty of Tuscany but with fewer tourists. Perugia, medieval hill town and bustling modern metropolis.

Assisi, home of St. Francis, with celebrated frescoes by Giotto. Orvieto, mountaintop citadel topped with a magnificent cathedral. Spoleto, famous for its annual arts festival.

Valle d'Aosta The Matterhorn and Mont Blanc (Monte Bianco), Europe's two tallest mountain peaks. Courmayeur and Breuil-Cervinia, two of Europe's most famous ski resorts.

The Veneto A treasure trove of art and architecture. Venice, world's most beautiful and intriguing city. Verona, home to legendary Romeo and Juliet and the best-preserved Roman amphitheater in the world. Vincenza, where Andrea Palladio built Renaissance villas. Padua, graced with Giotto frescoes.

FLYING TIMES

To Rome
. . . from New York and Newark, 8.25 hours (nonstop)
. . . from Chicago, 12 hours (one stop)
. . . from Los Angeles, 13.5 hours (one stop)

To Milan
. . . from New York and Newark, 8 hours (nonstop)
. . . from Chicago, 10.75 hours (one stop)
. . . from Los Angeles, 14.5 hours (one stop)

HOW TO FIND THE BEST AIRFARE

- **Travel midweek** Fares for travel on Tuesday, Wednesday, and Thursday are often much less expensive than they are on peak weekend travel days.

- **Be flexible with your travel dates** Leaving or returning a day or two earlier or later may save you hundreds of dollars.

- **Be flexible with routing** Rather than flying directly to Italy from North America, you might find it's cheaper to fly into London, and continue from there, perhaps on a low-cost European airline. You might also find it's cheaper to fly into Pisa than into Florence; or to fly into Milan or even Lugano, Switzerland, rather than Venice.

GETTING THERE

- **Avoid the busiest holiday periods**   Christmas and Easter are especially expensive times to travel to Italy. Be creative with your scheduling to avoid the days when most people want to travel—consider traveling on Christmas Day, for example.

- **Be a low-season traveler**   You'll spend less and have sparser crowds to compete with if you visit October through November or January through March.

- **Check out travel websites**   You don't necessarily have to book online, but these sites provide a handy way to do comparison shopping. Type in various dates and various departure and arrival cities and see what you come up with. Some sites to check: www.frommers.com; www.travelocity. com; www.lowestfare.com; www.expedia.com; www.smarterliving.com.

GETTING AROUND BY CAR

A rental car is the easiest means of exploring the Italian countryside, but it's unnecessary if your itinerary includes only the major cities. In general:

- **Italian roads** are well marked and very well-maintained, and you can easily speed from city to city on the *autostrade* (national express highways).

- **Driving in towns and cities** can be a nightmare of traffic jams and one-way streets. In some towns, driving is illegal for nonresidents unless you're just dropping off your bags at a hotel.

- **Street parking** is highly restricted in many towns (often reserved for residents), but many municipalities provide car parks. We highly recommend that you find one upon arrival, leave your car, and explore on foot or by public transportation.

- U.S. and Canadian drivers need only a valid **driver's license** to drive a rental car in Italy. To drive a private car, however, you must have an International Driver's License (accompanied by your regular driver's license); obtain one at any **American Automobile Association (AAA)** branch (© 800/222-4357 or 407/444-4300; www.aaa.com). In Canada, you can get the address of the **Canadian Automobile Association** closest to you by calling © 613/247-0117 or checking the website www.caa.ca.

- Rental car rates are fairly steep—about 200€ a week for a small car. The three major rental companies in Italy are **Avis** (© 800/331-1212; www.avis.com), **Budget** (© 800/472-3325; www.budget.com), and **Hertz** (© 800/654-3131; www.hertz.com). Also try **Autoeurope** at © 1-888/223-5555 (www.autoeurope.com).

- **Gasoline** (known as *benzina*) is expensive in Italy—at press time, about 1.02€ per liter (3.86€ per gallon). Gas stations on the *autostrade* are open 24 hours, but elsewhere gas stations are often closed from noon to 3pm for lunch, and after 7pm.

- **Speed limit** is 50kmph (31 mph) in cities and towns; 90kmph (56 mph) on main roads and local roads; and 130kmph (81 mph) on the *autostrade*. Use of seat belts is compulsory.

- In case of **car breakdown** or for any tourist information, foreign motorists can call © 803-116 (24-hr. nationwide telephone service). For road information, itineraries, and all sorts of travel assistance, call © 06-514971.

GETTING AROUND BY BUS

You'll probably travel by bus only to reach small towns not serviced by trains. Italy has no central bus network, so you'll need to pick up timetables from local companies or try **SITA** (© 055-4721; www.sita-on-line.it), a Florence-based company that covers many parts of the country. Note that many buses do not run on weekends.

CHAPTER THREE

LODGING

This chapter will help you find the right accommodations, at the right price—and the amenities you might need during your stay.

ROOM PREFERENCES

Please recommend ____	**Per favore, mi consigli ____** *pehr fah-VOH-reh mee kohn-SEEL-lyee*
a clean hostel.	**una locanda pulita.** *OO-nah loh-KAHN-dah poo-LEE-tah*
a moderately priced hotel.	**un albergo non caro.** *oon ahl-BEHR-goh nohn KAH-roh*
a moderately priced B&B.	**una pensione non cara.** *OO-nah pehn-SYOH-neh nohn KAH-rah*
a good hotel / motel.	**un buon hotel / motel.** *oon BWON hotel / motel*
Does the hotel have ____	**L'hotel ha ____** *loh-TEL AH*
a pool?	**una piscina?** *OO-nah pee-SHEE-nah*
a casino?	**un casinò?** *oon kah-zee-NOH*
suites?	**delle suite?** *DEHL-leh suite*
a balcony?	**un balcone?** *oon bahl-KOH-neh*
a fitness center?	**una palestra?** *OO-nah pah-LEHS-trah*
a spa ?	**un centro fitness?** *oon CHEN-troh fitness*

a private beach?	**una spiaggia privata?**
	OO-nah SPYAD-jah pree-VAH-tah
a tennis court?	**un campo da tennis?**
	oon KAHM-poh dah tennis
I would like a room	**Vorrei una stanza per ____**
for ____	*vohr-RAY OO-nah STAHN-tsah pehr*

For full coverage of numbers, see p7.

I would like ____	**Vorrei ____**
	vohr-RAY
a king-sized bed.	**un letto matrimoniale king size.**
	oon LET-toh mah-tree-moh-NYAH-leh (king size)
a double bed.	**un letto matrimoniale.**
	oon LET-toh mah-tree-moh-NYAH-leh
twin beds.	**due letti singoli.**
	DOO-eh LET-tee SEEN-goh-lee
adjoining rooms.	**stanze adiacenti.**
	STAHN-tseh ah-dyah-CHEN-tee
a smoking room.	**una stanza per fumatori.**
	OO-nah STAHN-tsah pehr foo-mah-TOH-ree

Listen Up: Reservations Lingo

Non abbiamo stanze libere.	We have no vacancies.
Quanto si ferma?	How long will you be staying?
Per fumatori o non fumatori?	Smoking or non smoking?
Abbiamo solo mezza pensione / pensione completa.	We only have full / half board.
Devo tenere il passaporto fino a domani.	I need to keep your passport overnight.

LODGING

a nonsmoking room.	**una stanza per non fumatori.**
	OO-nah STAHN-tsah pehr nohn foo-mah-TOH-ree
a private bathroom.	**un bagno privato.**
	oon BAHN-nyoh pree-VAH-toh
a shower.	**la doccia.**
	lah DOT-chah
a bathtub.	**la vasca da bagno.**
	lah VAHS-kah dah BAHN-nyoh
air conditioning.	**l'aria condizionata.**
	LAH-ryah kohn-dee-tsyoh-NAH-tah
television.	**la televisione.**
	lah teh-leh-vee-ZYOH-neh
cable.	**la televisione via cavo.**
	lah teh-leh-vee-ZYOH-neh VEE-ah KAH-voh
satellite TV.	**la TV satellitare.**
	lah tee-VOO sah-tehl-lee-TAH-reh
a telephone.	**un telefono.**
	oon teh-LEH-foh-noh
Internet access.	**accesso a Internet.**
	atch-CHESS-oh ah internet
high-speed Internet access.	**accesso ad Internet ad alta velocità.**
	atch-CHESS-oh ah internet ahd AHL-tah veh-loh-chee-TAH
a refrigerator.	**un frigorifero.**
	oon free-goh-REE-feh-roh
a beach view.	**una vista sulla spiaggia.**
	OO-nah VEES-tah SOOL-lah SPYAD-jah
a city view.	**una vista sulla città.**
	OO-nah VEES-tah SOOL-lah cheet-TAH

a kitchenette.	**un angolo cottura.**
	oon AHN-goh-loh koht-TOO-rah
a balcony.	**un balcone.**
	oon bahl-KOH-neh
a suite.	**una suite.**
	OO-nah suite
a penthouse.	**un attico.**
	oon AHT-tee-koh
I would like a room _____	**Vorrei una stanza _____**
	vohr-RAY OO-nah STAHN-tsah
on the ground floor.	**sul pianterreno.**
	SOOL pyahn-tehr-REH-noh
near the elevator.	**vicino all'ascensore.**
	vee-CHEE-noh ahl-ash-ehn-SOH-reh
near the stairs.	**vicino alle scale.**
	vee-CHEE-noh AHL-leh SKAH-leh
near the pool.	**vicino alla piscina.**
	vee-CHEE-noh AHL-lah pee-SHEE-nah
away from the street.	**lontano dalla strada.**
	lohn-TAH-noh DAHL-lah STRAH-dah
I would like a corner room.	**Vorrei una stanza d'angolo.**
	vohr-RAY OO-nah STAHN-tsah DAHN-goh-loh
Do you have _____	**C'è _____**
	ch-EH
a crib?	**una culla?**
	OO-nah KOOL-lah
a foldout bed?	**un lettino pieghevole?**
	oon leht-TEE-noh pyeh-GHE-voh-leh

FOR GUESTS WITH SPECIAL NEEDS

I need a room with ____	**Mi serve una stanza con ____** *mee SEHR-veh OO-nah STAHN-tsah kohn*
wheelchair access.	**accesso a sedia a rotelle.** *atch-CHESS-oh ah SEH-dyah ah roh-TEHL-leh*
services for the visually impaired.	**servizi per ipovedenti.** *sehr-VEET-see pehr ee-poh-veh-DEHN-tee*
services for the hearing impaired.	**servizi per ipoudenti.** *sehr-VEET-see pehr ee-poh-oo-DEHN-tee*
I am traveling with a service dog.	**Viaggio con un cane di assistenza.** *VYAHD-joh kohn oon KAH-neh dee ahs-sees-TEHN-tsa*

MONEY MATTERS

I would like to make a reservation.	**Vorrei fare una prenotazione.** *vohr-RAY FAH-reh OO-nah preh-noh-tah-TSYOH-neh*
How much per night?	**Quanto costa per notte?** *KWAHN-toh KOHS-tah pehr NOHT-teh*
Is breakfast included?	**È compresa la colazione?** *EH kohm-PREH-zah lah koh-lah-TSYOH-neh*
Do you have a ____	**C'è una tariffa ____** *ch-EH OO-nah tah-REEF-fah*
weekly / monthly rate?	**settimanale / mensile?** *seht-tee-mah-NAH-leh / mehn-SEE-leh*
a weekend rate?	**per il weekend?** *pehr eel weekend*

We will be staying for ____ days / weeks.	**Staremo per ____ giorni / settimane.**
	stah-REH-moh pehr ____ JOHR-nee / seht-tee-MAH-neh

For full coverage of number terms, see p7.

When is checkout time?	**A che ora è il check-out?**
	ah keh OH-rah EH eel check-out

For full coverage of time-related terms, see p12.

Do you accept credit cards / travelers checks?	**Prendete la carta di credito / i traveller's cheques?**
	PREHN-deh-teh lah KAHR-tah dee KREH-dee-toh / ee traveller's cheques
May I see a room?	**Posso vedere la stanza?**
	POHS-soh veh-DEH-reh lah STAHN-tsah

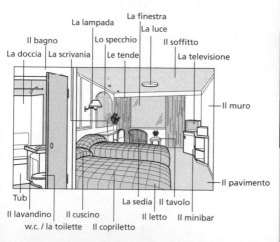

La lampada
La finestra
Il bagno
Lo specchio
La luce
La doccia
La scrivania
Le tende
Il soffitto
La televisione
Il muro
Il pavimento
Tub
La sedia
Il tavolo
Il lavandino
Il cuscino
Il letto
Il minibar
w.c. / la toilette
Il copriletto

LODGING

Is there a service charge?	**C'è una tariffa per il servizio?**
	ch-EH OO-nah tah-REEF-fah pehr eel sehr-VEE-tsyoh
I'd like to speak with the manager.	**Vorrei parlare con il direttore.**
	vohr-RAY pahr-LAH-reh kohn eel dee-reht-TOH-reh

IN-ROOM AMENITIES

I'd like _____	**Vorrei _____**
	vohr-RAY
to place an international call.	**fare una chiamata internazionale.**
	FAH-reh OO-nah KYAH-mah-tah een-tehr-nah-tsyoh-NAH-leh
to place a long-distance call.	**fare una chiamata interurbana.**
	FAH-reh OO-nah KYAH-mah-tah een-tehr-oor-BAH-nah
directory assistance in English.	**l'assistenza abbonati in inglese.**
	lahs-sees-TEHN-tsa ahb-boh-NAH-tee een een-GLEH-zeh

Instructions for dialing the hotel phone

Per chiamare un'altra stanza, comporre il numero di stanza.	To call another room, dial the room number.
Per chiamate locali, comporre prima il 9.	To make a local call, dial 9 first.
Per chiamare il centralinista, comporre lo 0.	To call the operator, dial 0.

room service.	**il servizio in camera.** *eel sehr-VEE-tsyoh een KAH-meh-rah*
maid service.	**il servizio di pulizia.** *eel sehr-VEE-tsyoh dee poo-lee-TSEE-ah*
the front desk operator	**il centralinista alla reception** *eel chen-trah-lee-NEES-tah AHL-lah reception*
Do you have room service?	**Offrite il servizio in camera?** *ohf-FREE-teh eel sehr-VEE-tsyoh een KAH-meh-rah*
When is the kitchen open?	**Quando apre la cucina?** *KWAHN-doh AH-preh lah koo-CHEE-nah*
When is breakfast served?	**A che ora servite la colazione?** *ah keh OH-rah sehr-VEE-teh lah koh-lah-TSYOH-neh*

For time-related terms, see p12.

Do you offer massages?	**Offrite il servizio massaggi?** *ohf-FREE-teh eel sehr-VEE-tsyoh mahs-SAHD-jee*
Do you have a lounge?	**Avete un salotto?** *ah-VEH-teh oon sah-LOHT-toh*
Do you have a business center?	**Avete un centro d'affari?** *ah-VEH-teh oon CHEN-troh dahf-FAH-ree*
Do you serve breakfast?	**Servite la colazione?** *sehr-VEE-teh lah koh-lah-TSYOH-neh*
Do you have Wi-Fi?	**Avete il wi-fi?** *ah-VEH-teh eel wi-fi*

LODGING

May I have a newspaper in the morning?	**Posso avere il giornale al mattino?** *POHS-soh ah-VEH-reh eel johr-NAH-leh ahl maht-TEE-noh*
Do you offer a laundry service?	**Offrite il servizio di lavanderia?** *ohf-FREE-teh eel sehr-VEE-tsyoh dee lah-vahn-deh-REE-ah*
Do you offer dry cleaning?	**Offrite il sevizio di lavasecco?** *ohf-FREE-the-eel-sehr-VEE-tsyoh dee lah-vah-SEHK-koh*
May we have ____	**Possiamo avere ___** *pohs-SYAH-moh ah-VEH-reh*
clean sheets today?	**lenzuola pulite oggi?** *lehn-TSWO-lah poo-LEE-tee OHD-jee*
more towels?	**altri asciugamani?** *AHL-tree ah-shoo-gah-MAH-nee*
more toilet paper?	**altra carta igienica?** *AHL-trah KAHR-tah ee-JEH-nee-kah*
extra pillows?	**altri cuscini?** *AHL-tree koo-SHEE-nee*
Do you have an ice machine?	**C'è un distributore di ghiaccio?** *ch-EH oon dees-tree-boo-TOH-reh dee GYAT-choh*

Did I receive any _____	**Ho ricevuto** _____
	OH ree-cheh-VOO-toh
messages?	**messaggi?**
	mehs-SAHD-jee
mail?	**posta?**
	POHS-ta
faxes?	**fax?**
	fax
A spare key, please.	**Una chiave di scorta, per favore.**
	OO-nah KYAH-veh dee SKOHR-tah
	pehr fah-VOH-reh
I'd like a wake up call.	**Vorrei un servizio di sveglia.**
	vohr-RAY oon sehr-VEE-tsyoh dee
	ZVEHL-lyah

For time-related terms, see p12.

Do you have alarm clocks?	**C'è un orologio sveglia?**
	ch-EH oon oh-roh-LOD-joh
	ZVEHL-lyah
Is there a safe in the room?	**C'è una cassaforte in camera?**
	ch-EH OO-nah kahs-sah-FOHR-teh
	een KAH-meh-rah
Does the room have a hair dryer?	**C'è un asciugacapelli in camera?**
	ch-EH oon ah-SHOO-gah kah-
	PEHL-lee een KAH-meh-rah

HOTEL ROOM TROUBLE

May I speak with the manager?	**Posso parlare con il direttore?** *POHS-soh pahr-LAH-reh kohn eel dee-REHT-toh-reh*
The ____ does not work.	**____ non funziona.** *nohn foon-TSYOH-nah*
television	**Il televisore** *eel teh-leh-vee-ZOH-reh*
telephone	**Il telefono** *eel teh-LEH-foh-noh*
air conditioning	**Il condizionatore d'aria** *eel kohn-dee-tsyoh-nah-TOH-reh DAH-ryah*
Internet access	**L'accesso a Internet** *laht-CHESS-oh ah internet*
cable TV	**La TV via cavo** *lah TV VEE-ah KAH-voh*
There is no hot water.	**Non c'è acqua calda.** *nohn ch-EH AHK-wah KAHL-dah*
The toilet is overflowing!	**Il water è l'acqua trabocca!** *eel VAH-tehr EH LAHK-wah trah-BOHK-kah*

This room is ____
Questa stanza è ____
KWEHS-tah STAHN-tsah EH

too noisy.
troppo rumorosa.
TROHP-poh roo-moh-ROH-zah

too cold.
troppo fredda.
TROHP-poh FREHD-dah

too warm.
troppo calda.
TROHP-poh KAHL-dah

This room has ____
In questa stanza ci sono ____
een KWEHS-tah STAHN-tsah chee SOH-noh

bugs.
degli insetti.
DEHL-lyee een-SEHT-tee

mice.
dei topi.
day TOH-pee

I'd like a different room.
Vorrei un'altra stanza.
vohr-RAY oo-NAHL-trah STAHN-tsah

Do you have a bigger room?
C'è una stanza più grande?
ch-EH OO-nah STAHN-tsah PYOO GRAHN-deh

I locked myself out of my room.
Ho lasciato le chiavi nella stanza.
OH lah-SHAH-toh leh KYAH-vee NEHL-lah STAHN-tsah

Do you have any fans?
Ci sono dei ventilatori?
chee SOH-noh day vehn-tee-lah-TOH-ree

The sheets are not clean.
Le lenzuola non sono pulite.
leh lehn-TSWOH-lah nohn SOH-noh poo-LEE-teh

The towels are not clean.
Gli asciugamani non sono puliti.
lyee ah-shoo-gah-MAH-nee nohn SOH-noh poo-LEE-tee

The room is not clean.
La stanza non è pulita.
lah STAHN-tsah nohn EH poo-LEE-tah

LODGING

The guests next door / above / below are being very loud.

Gli ospiti a fianco / di sopra / di sotto fanno molto rumore.
lyee OHS-pee-tee ah FYAHN-koh / dee SOH-prah / dee SOHT-toh FAHN-noh MOHL-toh roo-MOH-reh

CHECKING OUT

I think this charge is a mistake.

Credo questo addebito sia errato.
KREH-doh KWEHS-toh ahd-DEH-bee-toh SEE-ah ehr-RAH-to

Please explain this charge to me.

Mi spieghi questo addebito, per favore.
mee SPYEH-ghee KWEHS-toh ahd-DEH-bee-toh pehr fah-VOH-reh

Thank you, we enjoyed our stay.

Grazie, siamo stati contenti del soggiorno.
GRAH-tsyeh see-AH-moh STAH-tee kohn-TEHN-tee dehl sohd-JOHR-noh

The service was excellent.

Il servizio è stato ottimo.
eel sehr-VEE-tsyoh EH STAH-toh OHT-tee-moh

The staff is very professional and courteous.

Il personale è molto professionale e cortese.
eel pehr-soh-NAH-leh EH MOHL-toh proh-fehs-syo-NAH-leh eh kohr-TEH-zeh

Please call a cab for me.

Mi chiama un taxi, per favore?
mee KYAH-mah oon taxi pehr fah-VOH-reh

Would someone please get my bags?

Qualcuno può prendere le mie borse?
kwahl-KOO-noh PWOH PREHN-deh-reh leh MEE-eh BOHR-seh

HAPPY CAMPING

I'd like a site for ____
Vorrei un posto per____
vohr-RAY oon POHS-toh pehr

  a tent.
  una tenda.
  OO-nah TEHN-dah

  a camper.
  un camper.
  oon KAHM-pehr

Are there ____
Ci sono____
chee SOH-noh

  bathrooms?
  i bagni?
  ee BAHN-nyee

  showers?
  le docce?
  leh DOHT-cheh

Is there running water?
C'è acqua corrente?
ch-EH AHK-wah kohr-REHN-teh

Is the water drinkable?
L'acqua è potabile?
LAHK-wah EH poh-TAH-bee-leh

Where is the electrical hookup?
Dove sono gli attacchi elettrici?
DOH-veh SOH-noh lyee aht-TAH-kee eh-LEHT-tree-keh

ITALIAN HOTEL BASICS

Breakfast   More Italian hotels, especially those catering to international business travelers, are offering breakfast buffets—some quite lavish, with a choice of pastries, breads, and hot dishes. For the most part, though, the roll-and-coffee routine prevails, and you'll get better coffee and fresher pastry at the bar down the street; ask your hotel if you can get a reduced rate if you opt out of breakfast.

Confirmation   Get one. A verbal *va bene* doesn't necessarily guarantee your lodgings; Italian hoteliers are notorious for giving away reserved rooms. Secure a reservation with a credit card and ask for a confirmation via e-mail or fax.

Lodging Types   In general, an *albergo* is a hotel, a *locanda* is a rustic inn, and a *pensione* is a simple establishment that is often family-run. Some relatively recent terms in the lexicon are *Il bed and breakfast* and *agriturismo*, the latter being a working farm that takes in guests.

Seasons   High season is usually Easter through September, especially in Florence, Rome, and Venice. In many places, April, May, and September are also considered colder-season months, with lower rates. Christmas through mid-March is high season in the ski resorts. Christmas through New Year is high season in Rome, Venice, Taormina (Sicily), and other places where Italians like to spend their holidays.

Star System   Italian hotels are rated by government regional boards on a scale of one to five stars. The number of stars reflects amenities but doesn't account for other important factors, such as charm and location. Nor do stars necessarily reflect price: A five-star hotel in Parma may cost less than a two-star hotel in Florence. While the government rating system can provide meaningful comparisons of services and comfort, guidebook ratings are more comprehensive.

ITALY'S BEST HOTELS

If you can afford the very best, set your sights on the following hotels throughout the country. For exceptional apartments and farmhouse rentals, visit **www.untours.com**. For more extensive listings, see *Frommer's Italy.*

Cernobio
Grand Hotel Villa d'Este   This 16th-century palace is surrounded by acres of gardens on the shores of Lake Como. Guests are pampered with frescoed salons, antiques-filled accommodations, a swimming pool that floats in the lake, golf, spa treatments, and other amenities. (Cernobio; ✆ **031-3481**; www.villadeste.it)

Fiesole
Villa San Michele   Much about this luxurious hideaway in the hills above Florence is extraordinary: Michelangelo designed the facade, the former chapel is now the honeymoon suite, and a fresco by Ferrucci adorns the dining rooms. (Fiesole, outside Florence; ✆ **055-567-8200**; www.orientexpresshotels.com)

Portofino
Hotel Splendido   This former monastery set in hillside gardens has stunning sea views, visible from the balcony or terrace off every one of the comfortable guest rooms and suites. (Portofino; ✆ **0185-267801**; www.hotelsplendido.com)

Positano
Hotel Sirenuse   For 50 years, the Sersale family has opened their villa by the sea to guests. Colorful ceramic tiles and family antiques fill spacious guest rooms that, like the terraces, overlook the Mediterranean and the stunning domes and hillside houses of Positano. (Positano; ✆ **089-875066**; www.sirenuse.it)

Rome
Hotel Eden   Of the Eternal City's many luxury lodgings, the Eden is the most sumptuous and the most laid-back; this place is all about comfort, not ostentation. The service is flawless, the

Spanish Steps and Via Veneto are just outside the door, and the views are terrific. (Rome; ✆ **06-478121**; www.hotel-eden.it)

Taormina
Palazzo San Domenico   The highlight of the grand tour of **Sicily** is a stay at this 14th-century Dominican monastery. Cloisters, chapels, and vaulted hallways lend an otherworldly air to the opulent accommodations, set amid terraced gardens. (Taormina; ✆ **0942-613111**; www.sandomenico.thi.it)

Venice
Gritti Palace   Live like royalty in the former palace of Doge Andrea Gritti. These elegant, refined quarters on the banks of the Grand Canal inspired Ernest Hemingway, one of many celebrity guests, to praise the Gritti as "the best in a city of great hotels." (Venice; ✆ **041-794611**; www.hotelgrittivenice.com)

ITALY'S BEST BUDGET HOTELS

With doubles from around 60€ ($) to 150€ ($$$), here are some of Italy's best-value hotels. All provide comfort and atmospheric surroundings at a reasonable price:

Camogli (Liguria)
La Camogliese   Bedrooms are large and bright here, in the heart of the Italian Riviera's prettiest town. They're not right on the sea, but lean out the window and you'll catch a view. (Camogli, Liguria; ✆ **0185-771402**; www.lacamogliese.it) $$

Corniglia (Cinque Terre)
De Cecio   This delightful stone house is a find in the Cinque Terre, where decent lodging is scarce. Plain, comfortable rooms overlook the sea and olive groves, the terrace is a great place to rest after a long hike, and pretty Corniglia is quieter than its neighbors. (Corniglia, Cinque Terre; ✆ **0187-812043**) $

Cortina d'Ampezzo
Hotel Menardi   Italy's most famous and expensive ski resort is more affordable thanks to this charming family-run inn. Beds are covered with eiderdown quilts, fires blaze in the sit-

ting room hearths, and excellent meals are served in a paneled dining room (opt for the half-board plan here). (Cortina d'Ampezzo; ☎ **0436-2400**; www.hotelmenardi.it) $$$

Ferrara
Borgonuovo Bed and Breakfast The rooms in this medieval palace are the most charming accommodations in beautiful, art-filled Ferrara. The price includes a hearty breakfast, access to a lovely rear garden, and use of bicycles. (Ferrara, Emilia-Romagna; ☎ **0532-211100**; www.borgonuovo.com) $$

La Mora (Piemonte)
La Cascina del Monastero This huge old farm building with cozy, beam-ceilinged rooms makes a great base for exploring the Langhe wine country. The farm bottles its own vintage and serves its own produce and cheeses at a sumptuous breakfast. (La Mora, Piemonte; ☎ **0173-509245**; www.cascinadelmonastero.it) $$

Ravenna (Emilia-Romagna)
Albergo Cappello Beamed, frescoed ceilings adorn the spacious guest rooms and suites of this 14th-century palazzo near the dazzling mosaics of San Vitale. (Ravenna, Emilia-Romagna; ☎ **0544-219813**; www.albergocappello.it) $$$

Rome
Hotel Navona The location alone, steps from Rome's most beautiful piazza, makes these centuries-old premises a bargain. Add tasteful surroundings and friendly service, and it's hard to imagine wanting to stay anywhere else in Rome. (**Rome;** ☎ **06-6864203**; www.hotelnavona.com) $$$

Siena
Palazzo Ravizza This Renaissance palazzo in the heart of Italy's most beautiful city shelters guests in distinctive, frescoed rooms filled with antiques. A rear garden overlooks the Tuscan hills. (Siena; [tel] **0577-280462**; www.palazzoravizza.it) $$$

LODGING

CHAPTER FOUR

DINING

This chapter includes a menu reader and the language you need to communicate in a range of dining establishments and food markets.

FINDING A RESTAURANT

Would you recommend a good ____ restaurant?	**Può consigliarmi un buon ristorante ____** *PWOH kohn-seel-LYAHR-mee oon bwon ree-stoh-RAHN-teh*
local	**locale?** *loh-KAH-leh*
French	**francese?** *frahn-CHEH-zeh*
German	**tedesco?** *teh-DEHS-koh*
Chinese	**cinese?** *chee-NEH-zeh*
Japanese	**giapponese?** *jahp-poh-NEH-zeh*
Asian	**asiatico?** *ah-ZYAH-tee-koh*
Greek	**greco?** *GREH-koh*
steakhouse	**con specialità di carne?** *kohn speh-chah-lee-TAH dee KAHR-neh*

seafood	**con specialità di pesce?**
	kohn speh-chah-lee-TAH dee PEH-sheh
vegetarian	**vegetariano?**
	veh-jeh-tah-RYAH-noh
buffet-style	**stile buffet?**
	STEE-leh boof-FEH
budget	**economico?**
	eh-koh-NOH-mee-koh
Would you recommend a good pizza restaurant?	**Può consigliarmi una buona pizzeria?**
	PWOH kohn-seel-LYAHR-mee OO-nah bwon-nah peet-tseh REE-ah
Which is the best restaurant in town?	**Qual è il miglior ristorante in città?**
	kwah-LEH eel meel-LYOHR ree-stoh-RAHN-teh een cheet-TAH
Is there a late-night restaurant nearby?	**C'è un ristorante qui vicino aperto fino a tardi?**
	ch-EH oon ree-stoh-RAHN-teh kwee vee-CHEE-noh
Is there a restaurant that serves breakfast nearby?	**C'è un ristorante qui vicino che serve la colazione?**
	ch-EH oon ree-stoh-RAHN-teh kwee vee-CHEE- noh keh SEHR-veh lah koh-lah-TSYOH-neh
Is it very expensive?	**È molto caro?**
	EH MOHL-toh KAH-roh
Do I need a reservation?	**Bisogna prenotare?**
	bee-ZOHN-nyah preh-noh-TAH-reh
Do I have to dress up?	**Bisogna vestirsi bene?**
	bee-ZOHN-nyah vehs-TEER-see BEH-neh

Do they serve lunch?	**Servono il pranzo?**
	SEHR-voh-noh eel PRAHN-tsoh
What time do they open for dinner?	**A che ora aprono per la cena?**
	ah keh OH-rah AH-proh-noh pehr lah CHEH-nah
For lunch?	**Per il pranzo?**
	pehr eel PRAHN-tsoh
What time do they close?	**A che ora chiudono?**
	ah keh OH-rah KYOO-doh-noh
Do you have a take out menu?	**C'è un menu da asporto?**
	ch-EH oon meh-NOO dah ahs-POHR-toh
Do you have a bar?	**C'è un bar?**
	ch-EH oon bar
Is there a café nearby?	**C'è un caffè qui vicino?**
	ch-EH oon kahf-FEH kwee vee-CHEE-noh

GETTING SEATED

Are you still serving?	**Siete ancora aperti?**
	SYEH-teh ahn-KOH-rah ah-PEHR-tee
How long is the wait?	**Quanto c'è da aspettare?**
	KWAHN-toh ch-EH dah ahs-peht-TAH-reh
Do you have a nonsmoking section?	**C'è una sezione per non fumatori?**
	ch-EH OO-nah seh-TSYOH-neh pehr nohn foo-mah-TOH-ree
A table for ____, please.	**Un tavolo per ____, per favore.**
	oon TAH-voh-loh pehr ____ pehr fah-VOH-reh

For a full list of numbers, see p7.

Do you have a quiet table?	**C'è un tavolo tranquillo?**
	ch-EH oon TAH-voh-loh trahn-KWIL-loh

Listen Up: Restaurant Lingo

Sezione fumatori o non fumatori? *seh-TSYOH-neh foo-mah-TOH-ree oh nohn foo-mah-TOH-ree*	Smoking or nonsmoking?
È necessaria la giacca. *EH neh-chehs-SAH-ryah lah JAHK-kah*	You'll need a jacket.
Mi dispiace, non sono permessi i pantaloni corti. *mee dee-SPYAH-cheh nohn SOH-noh pehr-MEHS-see ee pahn-tah-loh-nee KOHR-tee*	I'm sorry, no shorts are allowed.
Posso portarle qualcosa da bere? *POHS-soh pohr-TAHR-leh kwahl-KOH-zah dah BEH-reh*	May I bring you something to drink?
Gradisce la carta dei vini? *grah-DEESH-eh lah KAHR-tah day VEE-nee*	Would you like to see a wine list?
Vuol sentire le nostre specialità? *vwol sehn-TEE-reh leh NOHS-treh speh-chah-lee-TAH*	Would you like to hear our specials?
È pronto -a per ordinare? *EH PROHN-toh -ah pehr ohr-dee-NAH-reh*	Are you ready to order?
Mi dispiace signore / signora, ma la suacarta di credito è stata rifiutata. *mee dee-SPYAH-cheh seen-NYOH-reh / seen-NYOH-rah mah lah SOO-ah KAHR-tah dee KREH-dee-toh EH STAH-tah ree-few-TAH-tah*	I'm sorry sir / madame, your credit card was declined.

May we sit outside / inside please?	**Possiamo sederci fuori / dentro, per favore?**
	pohs-SYAH-moh seh-DEHR-chee FWO-ree / DEHN-troh pehr fah-VOH-reh
May we sit at the counter?	**Possiamo sederci al banco?**
	pohs-SYAH-moh seh-DEHR-chee ahl BAHN-koh
A menu please?	**Un menu per favore?**
	oon meh-NOO pehr fah-VOH-reh

ORDERING

Do you have a special tonight?	**Qual è la specialità di questa sera?**
	kwah-LEH lah speh-chah-lee-TAH dee KWEHS-tah SEH-rah
What do you recommend?	**Cosa consiglia?**
	KOH-sah kohn-SEEL-lyah
May I see a wine list?	**Posso vedere la carta dei vini?**
	POHS-soh veh-DEH-reh lah KAHR-tah day VEE-nee
Do you serve wine by the glass?	**Servite il vino a bicchiere?**
	sehr-VEE-teh eel VEE-noh ah beek-KYEH-reh
May I see a drink list?	**Posso vedere la lista delle bevande?**
	POHS-soh veh-DEH-reh lah LEES-tah DEHL-leh beh-VAHN-de
I would like it cooked ____	**Lo / La vorrei ____**
	loh / lah vohr-RAY
rare.	**cotto -a al sangue.**
	KOHT-toh -ah ahl SAHN-gweh
medium rare.	**cotto -a quasi al sangue.**
	KOHT-toh -ah KWAH-zee ahl SAHN-gweh
medium.	**cotto -a mediamente.**
	KOHT-toh -ah meh-dyah-MEHN-teh

medium well.	**cotto -a abbastanza bene.**
	KOHT-toh -ah ahb-bah-STAHN-tsah BEH-ne
well.	**ben cotto -a.**
	behn KOHT-toh -ah
charred.	**rosolato -a.**
	roh-zoh-LAH-toh -ah
Do you have a ____ menu?	**Avete un menu____**
	ah-VEH-teh oon meh-NOO
children's	**per i bambini?**
	pehr ee bahm-BEE-nee
diabetic	**per diabetici?**
	pehr dyah-BEH-tee-chee
kosher	**kasher?**
	KAH-sher
vegetarian	**vegetariano?**
	veh-jeh-tah-RYAH-noh
What is in this dish?	**Cosa c'è in questo piatto?**
	KOH-sah ch-EH een KWEHS-toh PYAHT-toh
How is it prepared?	**Come viene preparato?**
	KOH-meh VYEH-neh preh-pah-RAH-toh
What kind of oil is that cooked in?	**In che tipo di olio viene cotto?**
	een keh TEE-poh dee OH-lyoh VYEH-ne KOHT-toh
Do you have any low-salt dishes?	**Avete dei piatti poco salati?**
	ah-VEH-teh day PYAHT-tee POH-koh sah-LAH-tee
On the side, please.	**A parte, per favore.**
	ah PAHR-teh pehr fah-VOH-reh
May I make a substitution?	**Posso sostituire una cosa?**
	POHS-soh soh-stee-too-EE-reh OO-nah KOH-sah

DINING

I'd like to try that.	**Vorrei provare quello.**
	vohr-RAY proh-VAH-reh
	KWEHL-loh
Is that fresh?	**È fresco -a?**
	EH FREHS-koh -ah
Waiter!	**Cameriere -a!**
	kah-meh-RYEH-reh -ah
Extra butter, please.	**Mi porta altro burro, per favore.**
	mee POHR-tah AHL-troh BOOR-
	roh pehr fah-VOH-reh
No butter, thanks.	**Niente burro, grazie.**
	NYEHN-teh BOOR-roh GRAH-tsyeh
No cream, thanks.	**Niente panna, grazie.**
	NYEHN-teh PAHN-nah GRAH-tsyeh
No salt, please.	**Niente sale, per favore.**
	NYEHN-teh SAH-leh pehr-fah-
	VOH-reh
May I have some oil, please?	**Mi porta un po' di olio, per favore?**
	mee POHR-tah oon POH dee oh-
	LYOH pehr fah-VOH-reh
More bread, please.	**Altro pane, per favore.**
	AHL-troh PAH-neh pehr fah-
	VOH-reh
I am lactose intolerant.	**Ho intolleranza al lattosio.**
	OH een-tohl-leh-RAHN-tsah ahl
	laht-TOH-zyoh
Would you recommend something without milk?	**Mi consiglia qualcosa senza latte?**
	mee kohn-SEEL-lyah kwahl-KOH-
	zah SEHN-tsah LAHT-teh
I am allergic to_____	**Sono allergico -a _____**
	SOH-noh ahl-LEHR-jee-koh -kah
nuts.	**a noci e nocciole.**
	ah NOH-chee eh noht-CHOH-leh
peanuts.	**alle arachidi.**
	AHL-leh ah-RAH-kee-dee

seafood.	**ai frutti di mare.**
	eye FROOT-tee dee MAH-reh
shellfish.	**a molluschi e crostacei.**
	ah mohl-LOOS-kee eh krohs-TAH-cheh-ee
Water, please?	**Acqua, per favore?**
	AHK-wah pehr fah-VOH-reh
with ice	**con ghiaccio**
	kohn GYAT-choh
without ice	**senza ghiaccio**
	SEHN-tsah GYAT-choh
I'm sorry, I don't think this is what I ordered.	**Scusi, ma non credo di aver ordinato questo.**
	SKOO-zee mah nohn KREH-doh dee ah-VEHR ohr-dee-NAH-toh KWEHS-toh
My meat is a little over / under cooked.	**La carne è un po' troppo cotta / troppo poco cotta.**
	lah KAHR-neh EH oon POH TROHP-poh KOHT-tah /TROHP-poh POH-koh KOHT-tah
My vegetables are a little over / under cooked.	**Le verdure sono un po' troppo cotte / troppo poco cotte.**
	leh vehr-DOO-reh SOH-noh oon POH TROHP-poh KOHT-teh / TROHP-poh POH-koh KOHT-teh
There's a bug in my food!	**C'è un insetto nel mio cibo!**
	ch-EH oon een-SEHT-toh nehl MEE-oh CHEE-boh
May I have a refill?	**Me ne porta un altro?**
	meh neh POHR-tah oon AHL-troh
A dessert menu, please.	**Il menu dei dolci, per favore.**
	eel MEH-noo day DOHL-chee pehr fah-VOH-reh

DRINKS

Carafes of **vino della casa** (house wine) are usually three sizes: **litro** *LEE-troh* (liter), **mezzo litro** (half liter) and **un quarto** (quarter), akin to two generous glasses. Remember that standard wine bottles hold 750ml; it's easy to underestimate the 25% extra wallop of a liter (and Italians frown on public drunkenness, even while encouraging **un po' di vino**—a little wine—with midday and evening meals).

alcoholic	**alcooliche**
	ahl-KOH-lee-keh
neat / straight	**liscio -a**
	LEE-shoh -ah
on the rocks	**con ghiaccio**
	kohn GYAT-choh
with (seltzer or soda)	**con selz / acqua frizzante**
water	*kohn seltz / AHK-wah freet-TSAHN-teh*
beer	**birra**
	BEER-rah
brandy	**brandy**
	brandy
coffee	**caffè**
	kahf-FEH
cappuccino	**cappuccino**
	kahp-pooch-CHEE-noh
concentrated	**ristretto**
	rees-TREHT-toh
espresso	**caffè**
	kahf-FEH
iced coffee	**caffè freddo**
	kahf-FEH FREHD-doh
with a drop of alcohol	**corretto**
	kohr-REHT-toh
with a drop of milk	**macchiato**
	mahk-KYAH-toh

How Do You Take It?

Prendere generally means to take. But if a bartender asks, **Prende qualcosa?**, he's not inviting you to steal his fancy corkscrew. He's asking what you'd like to drink.

cognac	**cognac**
	cognac
fruit juice	**succo di frutta**
	SOOK-koh dee FROOT-tah

For a full list of fruits, see p116.

gin	**gin**
	gin
hot chocolate	**cioccolata calda**
	chohk-koh-LAH-tah KAHL-dah
lemonade	**limonata**
	lee-moh-NAH-tah
liqueur	**liquore**
	lee-KWOH-reh
milk	**latte**
	LAHT-teh
milk shake	**frappè**
	frahp-PEH
non-alcoholic	**analcolici**
	ah-nahl-KOH-lee-chee
rum	**rum**
	room
tea	**tè**
	teh
vodka	**vodka**
	vodka

DINING

wine	**vino**
	VEE-noh
dry white wine	**vino bianco secco**
	VEE-noh BYAHN-koh
	SEHK-koh
full-bodied wine	**vino corposo**
	VEE-noh kohr-POH-zoh
house wine	**vino della casa**
	VEE-noh DEHL-lah KAH-zah
light-bodied wine	**vino leggero**
	VEE-noh lehd-JEH-roh
red wine	**vino rosso**
	VEE-noh ROHS-soh
rosé	**rosato**
	roh-ZAH-toh
sparkling sweet wine	**spumante**
	spoo-MAHN-teh
sweet wine	**vino dolce**
	VEE-noh DOHL-cheh

SETTLING UP

Check please.	**Il conto per favore.**
	eel KOHN-toh pehr fah-VOH-reh
I'm full!	**Sono sazio -a!**
	SOH-noh SAH-tsyoh -tsyah
The meal was excellent.	**Il cibo era squisito.**
	eel CHEE-boh EH-rah skwee-ZEE-toh
There's a problem with my bill.	**C'è un problema con il conto.**
	ch-EH oon proh-BLEH-mah kohn eel KOHN-toh
Is the tip included?	**La mancia è inclusa?**
	lah MAHN-chah EH een-KLOO-zah
My compliments to the chef!	**I miei complimenti al cuoco!**
	ee MEE-eh-ee kohm-plee-MEHN-tee ahl KWO-koh

MENU READER

Italian cuisine varies broadly from region to region, but we've tried to make our list of classic dishes as encompassing as possible.

APPETIZERS (ANTIPASTI)

affettati misti: mixed cold cuts and vegetables (often buffet)
ahf-feht-TAH-tee MEES-tee

bruschetta: toasted bread slices with various toppings
broos-KEHT-tah

crocchette: croquettes
krohk-KEHT-teh

crostini: little toasts topped with a variety of ingredients
krohs-TEE-nee

insalata di frutti di mare: seafood salad
een-sah-LAH-tah dee FROOT-tee dee MAH-reh

insalata di nervetti: calf's foot and veal shank salad
een-sah-LAH-tah dee nehr-VEHT-tee

mozzarella con pomodori: mozzarella and tomatoes
moht-tsah-REHL-lah kohn poh-moh-DOH-ree

olive: olives
oh-LEE-veh

peperonata: mixed sweet peppers stewed with tomatoes
peh-peh-roh-NAH-tah

prosciutto: ham
proh-SHOOT-toh

  prosciutto cotto: cooked ham
  proh-SHOOT-toh KOHT-toh

  prosciutto crudo: air cured ham
  proh-SHOOT-toh KROO-doh

SALADS (INSALATI)

insalata caprese: tomato and mozzarella salad
een-sah-LAH-tah kah-PREH-zeh

insalata di crescione: watercress salad
een-sah-LAH-tah dee kreh-SHOH-neh

insalata di lattuga romana: romaine salad
een-sah-LAH-tah dee laht-TOO-gah roh-MAH-nah

insalata mista: mixed salad
een-sah-LAH-tah MEES-tah

insalata di pomodori: tomato salad
een-sah-LAH-tah dee poh-moh-DOH-ree

insalata di rucola: arugula / rocket salad
een-sah-LAH-tah dee ROO-koh-lah

insalata di spinaci: spinach salad
een-sah-LAH-tah dee spee-NAH-chee

insalata verde: green salad
een-sah-LAH-tah VEHR-deh

PIZZA TYPES

bianca: white, without tomato sauce
BYAHN-kah

capricciosa: with a mixture of toppings (artichoke hearts, ham, olives, pickled mushrooms, capers, sometimes egg)
kah-preet-CHOH-zah

con funghi: with mushrooms
kohn FOON-gy

margherita: with tomato sauce, basil, and mozzarella
mahr-ghe-REE-tah

marinara: with tomato sauce, garlic, capers, oregano, and sometimes anchovies
mah-ree-NAH-rah

napoletana: with fresh tomatoes, garlic, oregano, anchovies, and mozzarella; toppings may vary
nah-poh-leh-TAH-nah

quattro stagioni: (four seasons) same toppings as capricciosa
KWAHT-troh stah-JOH-nee

siciliana: usually with capers, onions, and anchovies
see-chee-LYAH-nah

SAUCES (SALSA)

bagna cauda: hot anchovy, garlic, and oil dip
BAHN-nyah KOW-dah

pesto: basil, pine nuts, and garlic sauce
PEHS-toh

pizzaiola: tomato sauce with onion and garlic
PEET-sah-YOH-lah

salsa verde: green sauce with parsley, anchovies, capers, and
garlic
SAHL-sah VERH-deh

SOUPS (ZUPPA)

acquacotta: Tuscan vegetable soup with poached egg
AHK-wah KOHT-tah

fagioli e farro: beans and spelt
fah-JOH-lee eh FAHR-roh

minestrone: mixed vegetable soup
mee-nehs-TROH-neh

di pane: bread (recipes vary greatly)
dee PAH-neh

pavese: bread and egg, Pavia style
pah-VEH-zeh

porri e patate: leek and potato
POHR-ree eh pah-TAH-teh

ribollita: Tuscan bean and bread vegetable soup
ree-bohl-LEE-tah

zuppa: soup
DZOOP-pah

PASTA DISHES

agnolotti: meat-stuffed pasta
ahn-nyoh-LOHT-tee

bucatini: hollow thick spaghetti, usually all'amatriciana (with
a bacon and tomato sauce)
boo-kah-TEE-nee

cannelloni: stuffed pasta tubes, topped with a sauce and
　baked
kahn-nehl-LOH-nee
cappellacci alla ferrarese: pumpkin-stuffed pasta, Ferrara style
kahp-pehl-LAHT-chee AHL-lah fehr-rah-REH-zeh
cappelletti: meat-stuffed pasta usually served in broth
kahp-pehl-LEHT-tee
fusilli: spiral-shaped pasta
foo-ZEEL-lee
gnocchi: potato dumplings
NYOHK-kee
pansotti: swiss chard- and herbs-stuffed pasta, usually
　served with walnut sauce, a Ligurian specialty
pahn-SOHT-tee
pappardelle alla lepre: wide pasta ribbons with hare sauce
pahp-pahr-DEHL-leh AHL-lah LEH-preh
penne strascicate: pasta quills sauteed with meat sauce
PEHN-neh strah-shee-KAH-teh

PASTA SAUCES (SUGI)

alfredo: butter and parmesan cheese
ahl-FREH-doh
amatriciana: bacon and tomato
ah-mah-tree-CHAH-nah
arrabbiata: tomato and hot pepper
ahr-rahb-BYAH-tah
bolognese: ground meat and tomato
boh-lohn-NYEH-zeh
carbonara: bacon and egg
kahr-boh-NAH-rah
panna: cream
PAHN-nah
pesto alla genovese: basil, pine nuts, and garlic
PEHS-toh AHL-lah jeh-noh-VEH-zeh
pomodoro: tomato
poh-moh-DOH-roh

puttanesca: tomato, anchovy, garlic, and capers
poot-tah-NEHS-kah

quattro formaggi: four cheeses
KWAHT-troh fohr-MAHD-jee

ragù: ground meat and tomato
rah-GOO

vongole: clams and tomato
VOHN-goh-leh

RISOTTO (RISOTTO)

risotto ai frutti di mare: with seafood
ree-ZOHT-toh eye FROOT-tee dee MAH-reh

risotto ai funghi: with parmesan and porcine mushrooms
ree-ZOHT-toh eye FOON-gy

risotto alla milanese: with saffron and parmesan cheese,
  Milanese style
ree-ZOHT-toh AHL-lah mee-lah-NEH-zeh

MEAT (CARNE)

For more meats, see p113.

abbacchio alla romana: roasted spring lamb, Roman style
ahb-BAHK-kyoh AHL-lah roh-MAH-nah

bollito misto: boiled cuts of beef and veal served with a
  sauce
bohl-LEE-toh MEES-toh

carpaccio: thin slices of raw meat—beef, horse, or swordfish—dressed with olive oil and lemon juice
kahr-PAHT-choh

cinghiale: wild boar, usually braised or roasted
cheen-GYAH-leh

involtini: thin slices of meat filled and rolled
een-vohl-TEE-nee

spezzatino: meat stew
speht-sah-TEE-noh

spiedini: skewered chunks of meat (also available with
  seafood)
spyeh-DEE-nee

BEEF (MANZO)

bistecca alla fiorentina: grilled T-bone steak, Florentine style
bees-TEHK-kah AHL-lah fyoh-rehn-TEE-nah

bresaola: air-dried beef, served in thin slices
breh-ZAH-oh-lah

osso buco: braised veal shank
OHS-soh BOO-koh

peposo: peppery stew
peh-POH-zoh

stracotto: beef stew with vegetables
strah-KOHT-toh

stufato: stew
stoo-FAH-toh

ORGAN MEATS (ORGANI)

busecca alla milanese: milanese tripe (beef stomach) soup
boo-SEHK-kah AHL-lah mee-lah-NEH-zeh

cervello al burro nero: brains in black-butter sauce
chehr-VEHL-loh ahl BOOR-roh NEH-roh

fegato alla veneziana: calf's liver fried with onions, Venetian
style
FEH-gah-toh AHL-lah veh-neh-TSYAH-nah

VEAL (VITELLO)

bocconcini: stewed or braised chunks
bohk-kohn-CHEE-nee

cima alla genovese: flank steak Genoese style, filled with
egg, and vegetables
CHEE-mah AHL-lah jeh-noh-VEH-zeh

costoletta alla milanese: breaded cutlet, Milanese style
kohs-toh-LEHT-tah AHL-lah mee-lah-NEH-zeh

lombata di vitello: loin (recipes vary)
lohm-BAH-tah dee vee-TEHL-loh

piccata al Marsala: thin cutlets cooked in Marsala (sweet
wine) sauce
peek-KAH-tah ahl mahr-SAH-lah

saltimbocca: veal and ham rolls
sahl-teem-BOHK-kah

scaloppina alla: cutlet filled with cheese and Valdostana: ham, Valdostana (alpine) style, typically with gruyère or fontina cheese
skah-lohp-PEE-nah AHL-lah vahl-dohs-TAH-nah

vitello tonnato: cold slices of boiled veal served with tuna-mayonnaise sauce
vee-TEHL-loh tohn-NAH-toh

PORK (MAIALE)

arista di maiale: roast loin
ah-REES-tah dee mah-YA-leh

braciola: grilled chop
brah-CHOH-lah

zampone: sausage stuffed pig's trotter
dzahm-POH-neh

POULTRY (POLLAME)

pollo alla cacciatora: chicken braised with mushrooms in tomato sauce, hunter's style
POHL-loh AHL-lah kaht-chah-TOH-rah

pollo alla diavola: chicken chargrilled with lemon and pepper
POHL-loh AHL-lah DYAH-voh-lah

pollo al mattone: chicken grilled with herbs under a brick
POHL-loh ahl maht-TOH-neh

FISH AND SEAFOOD (PESCE E FRUTTI DI MARE)

For more fish and seafood, see p114.

anguilla alla veneziana: eel cooked in tomato sauce, Venetian style
ahn-GWEEL-lah AHL-lah veh-neh-TSYAH-nah

aragosta: lobster
ah-rah-GOHS-tah

baccalà: stockfish
bahk-kah-LAH

cacciucco alla livornese: tomato seafood chowder, Leghorn style
kaht-CHOOK-koh AHL-lah lee-vohr-NEH-zeh

cozze ripiene: stuffed mussels
KOHT-seh ree-PYEH-neh

fritto misto: mixed fried fish
FREET-toh MEES-toh
gamberi grigliati: grilled shrimp with garlic
GAHM-beh-ree greel-LYAH-tee
nero di seppie e polenta: baby squid in ink squid sauce
  served with polenta (corn meal)
NEH-roh dee SEHP-pyeh eh poh-LEHN-tah
pesci al cartoccio: fish baked in parchment paper
PEH-shee ahl kahr-TOHT-choh

SIDE DISHES (CONTORNI)

frittata: omelette
freet-TAH-tah
piselli al prosciutto: peas with ham
pee-ZEHL-lee ahl proh-SHOOT-toh

SWEET BREADS / DESSERTS / SWEETS (DOLCI)

amaretti: almond macaroons
ah-mah-REHT-tee
biscotti: cookies
bees-KOHT-tee
cannoli: crispy pastry rolls filled with sweetened ricotta and
  candied fruit
kahn-NOH-lee
cassata alla siciliana: traditional Sicilian cake with ricotta,
  chocolate, and candied fruit
kahs-SAH-tah AHL-lah see-chee-LYAH-nah
formaggi: cheeses
fohr-MAHD-jee
  asiago: nutty-flavored hard cheese
  ah-ZYAH-goh
  fontina: semi-soft, melting cheese
  fohn-TEE-nah
  formaggio al latte di capra: goat's milk cheese
  fohr-MAHD-joh ahl LAHT-teh dee KAH-prah
  formaggio al latte di pecora: ewe's milk cheese
  fohr-MAHD-joh ahl LAHT-teh dee PEH-koh-rah

gorgonzola: pungent blue cheese
gohr-gohn-DZOH-lah

mascarpone: rich, dessert cream cheese
mahs-kahr-POH-neh

mozzarella: fresh, soft cow's milk cheese
moht-tsah-REHL-lah

mozzarella di bufala: buffalo mozzarella
moht-tsah-REHL-lah dee BOO-fah-lah

frutta: fruit
FROOT-tah
For a full listing of fruit, see p116.

gelato: Italian ice cream
jeh-LAH-toh

granita: frozen fruit-juice slush
grah-NEE-tah

panettone: Christmas sweet bread with raisins and candied
  citrus peel
pah-neht-TOH-neh

panforte: almond, candied citrus, spices, and honey cake
pahn-FOHR-teh

panna cotta: molded chilled cream pudding
PAHN-nah KOHT-ta

semifreddo: soft and airy, partially frozen ice cream
seh-mee-FREHD-doh

tartufo: chocolate ice cream dessert
tahr-TOO-foh

tiramisù: mascarpone, ladyfingers, and coffee dessert
tee-rah-mee-SOO

torta: cake
TOHR-tah
  alle fragole: with fresh strawberries
  AHL-leh FRAH-goh-leh
  ai frutti di bosco: with mixed berries
  eye FROOT-tee dee BOHS-koh
  al limone: with lemon curd
  ahl lee-MOH-neh

alle mele: with apples
AHL-leh MEH-le
della nonna: custard shortcrust with pine nuts
DEHL-lah NOHN-na
zabaglione: warm custard with Marsala wine
dzah-bahl-LYOH-neh
zuccotto: spongecake filled with fresh cream, chocolate,
candied fruit, and liqueur
dzook-KOHT-toh
zuppa inglese: a type of English trifle (spongecake layered
with cream and fruit)
DZOOP-pah een-GLEH-zeh
parmigiano: Parmesan
pahr-mee-JAH-noh
provolone: cow's milk cheese, sweet to spicy
proh-voh-LOH-neh
ricotta: fresh, soft and mild cheese
ree-KOHT-tah
taleggio: mild dessert cheese
tah-LEHD-joh

BUYING GROCERIES

Most Italians shop at **mercati** (open-air markets) or neighborhood
specialty stores. Because fresh ingredients are so essential to their
cuisine, they often purchase just a day or two's worth of groceries.

AT THE SUPERMARKET

Which aisle has ____	**In quale corsia è / sono ____**
	een KWAH-leh kohr-SEE-ah EH / SOH-noh
baby food?	**il cibo per neonati?**
	eel CHEE-boh pehr neh-oh-NAH-tee
bread?	**il pane?**
	eel PAH-neh
canned goods?	**i cibi in scatola?**
	ee CHEE-bee een SKAH-toh-lah

cheese?	**i formaggi?**
	ee fohr-MAHD-jee
cookies?	**i biscotti?**
	ee bees-KOHT-tee
fruit?	**la frutta?**
	lah FROOT-tah
juice?	**il succo?**
	eel SOOK-koh
paper plates and	**i piatti e tovaglioli di carta?**
napkins?	*ee PYAHT-tee eh toh-vahl-LYOH-*
	lee dee KAHR-tah
snack food?	**gli spuntini?**
	lyee spoon-TEE-nee
spices?	**le spezie?**
	leh SPEH-tsyeh
toiletries?	**gli articoli di igiene personale?**
	lyee ahr-TEE-koh-lee dee ee-JEH-
	neh pehr-soh-NAH-leh
water?	**l'acqua?**
	LAHK-wah

AT THE BUTCHER SHOP

Is the meat fresh?	**È fresca la carne?**
	EH FREHS-kah lah KAHR-neh
Do you sell ____	**Ha ____**
	AH
fresh beef?	**del manzo fresco?**
	dehl MAHN-tsoh FREHS-koh
fresh lamb?	**dell'agnello fresco?**
	dehl-ahn-NYEHL-loh FREHS-koh
fresh pork?	**del maiale fresco?**
	dehl mah-YA-leh FREHS-koh

I would like a cut of ___	**Vorrei un taglio di ___**
	vohr-RAY oon TAHL-lyoh dee
brisket.	**punta di petto.**
	POON-tah dee PEHT-toh
chops.	**braciole.**
	brah-CHOH-leh
filet.	**filetto.**
	fee-LEHT-toh
T-bone.	**fiorentina.**
	fyoh-rehn-TEE-nah
tenderloin.	**filetto.**
	fee-LEHT-toh
rump.	**girello.**
	jee-REHL-loh
rump roast.	**scamone.**
	skah-MOH-neh
Thick / Thin cuts, please.	**Tagli spessi / sottili, per favore.**
	TAHL-lyee SPEHS-see pehr fah-VOH-reh
Please trim the fat.	**Tolga il grasso, per favore.**
	TOHL-gah eel GRAHS-soh pehr fah-VOH-reh
Do you have any sausage?	**Ha della salsiccia?**
	AH DEHL-lah sahl-SEET-chah
Is the ___ fresh?	**È fresco ___?**
	EH FREHS-koh
clams	**Sono fresche le vongole?**
	SOH-noh FREHS-kee leh VOHN-goh-leh
fish	**È fresco il pesce?**
	EH FREHS-koh eel PEH-sheh
flounder	**È fresca la passera?**
	EH FREHS-kah lah PAHS-seh-rah

octopus	**È fresco il polpo?** *EH FREHS-koh eel POHL-poh*
oysters	**Sono fresche le ostriche?** *SOH-noh FREHS-kee leh OHS-tree-keh*
sea bass	**È fresco il branzino?** *EH FREHS-koh eel BRAHN-dzee-noh*
seafood	**Sono freschi i frutti di mare?** *SOH-noh FREHS-kee ee FROOT-tee dee MAH-reh*
shark	**È fresco il palombo?** *EH FREHS-koh eel pah-LOHM-boh*
shrimp	**Sono freschi i gamberi?** *SOH-noh FREHS-kee ee GAHM-beh-ree*
squid	**Sono freschi i calamari?** *SOH-noh FREHS-kee ee kah-lah-MAH-ree*
May I smell it?	**Posso sentire l'odore?** *POHS-soh sehn-TEE-reh loh-DOH-reh*
Would you please ____	**Me lo può ____ per favore?** *meh loh PWOH ____ pehr fah-VOH-reh*
clean it?	**pulire?** *poo-LEE-reh*
filet it?	**sfilettare?** *sfee-leht-TAH-reh*
debone it?	**togliere le lische?** *TOHL-lyeh-reh leh LEES-keh*
remove the head and tail?	**togliere testa e coda?** *TOHL-lyeh-reh TEHS-tah eh KOH-dah*

AT THE PRODUCE STAND / MARKET
Fruits

apple	**mela** *MEH-lah*
apricot	**albicocca** *ahl-bee-KOHK-kah*
banana	**banana** *bah-NAH-nah*
blackberries	**more** *MOH-reh*
blood orange	**arancia sanguinella** *ah-RAHN-chah sahn-gwee-NEHL-lah*
blueberry (European)	**mirtillo** *meer-TEEL-loh*
cantaloupe	**melone** *meh-LOH-neh*
cherry	**ciliegia** *chee-LYEH-jah*
citron	**cedro** *CHEH-droh*
coconut	**cocco** *KOHK-koh*
fig	**fico** *FEE-koh*
grapes (green, red)	**uva (bianca, nera)** *OO-vah BYAHN-kah NEH-rah*
grapefruit	**pompelmo** *pohm-PEHL-moh*
gooseberry	**uvaspina** *oo-vah-SPEE-nah*
guava	**guava** *GWAH-vah*
honeydew	**melone verde** *meh-LOH-neh VERH-deh*

kiwi	**kiwi**
	kiwi
lemon	**limone**
	lee-MOH-neh
lime	**limetta**
	lee-MEHT-tah
mango	**mango**
	MAHN-goh
melon	**melone**
	meh-LOH-neh
orange	**arancia (pl. arance)**
	ah-RAHN-chah
papaya	**papaia**
	pah-PAH-yah
peach	**pesca**
	PEHS-kah
pear	**pera**
	PEH-rah
pineapple	**ananas**
	AH-nah-nahs
plum	**prugna**
	PROON-nyah
yellow plum	**prugna gialla**
	PROON-nyah JAHL-lah
prune	**prugna secca**
	PROON-nyah SEHK-kah
raspberry	**lampone**
	lahm-POH-neh
strawberry	**fragola**
	FRAH-goh-lah
wild strawberry	**fragolina di bosco**
	frah-goh-LEE-nah dee BOHS-koh
tangerine	**mandarino**
	mahn-dah-REE-noh
watermelon	**anguria**
	ahn-GOO-ryah

Vegetables

artichoke	**carciofo**
	kahr-CHOH-foh
asparagus	**asparago**
	ahs-PAH-rah-goh
green asparagus	**asparago verde**
	ahs-PAH-rah-goh VERH-deh
white asparagus	**asparago bianco**
	ahs-PAH-rah-goh BYAHN-koh
avocado	**avocado**
	ah-voh-KAH-doh
bamboo shoots	**germogli di bamboo**
	jehr-MOHL-lyee dee bahm-BOO
beans	**fagioli**
	fah-JOH-lee
green beans	**fagiolino verde**
	fah-joh-LEE-noh VERH-deh
bean sprouts	**germoglio di soia**
	jehr-MOHL-lyoh dee SOH-yah
broccoli	**broccoli**
	BROHK-koh-lee
cabbage	**cavolo**
	KAH-voh-loh
carrot	**carota**
	kah-ROH-tah
cauliflower	**cavolfiore**
	kah-vohl-FYOH-reh
celery	**sedano**
	SEH-dah-noh
corn	**mais**
	mice
cucumber	**cetriolo**
	cheh-tree-OH-loh
eggplant / aubergine	**melanzana**
	meh-lahn-TSAH-nah

fennel	**finocchio**
	fee-NOHK-kyoh
garlic	**aglio**
	AHL-lyoh
lettuce	**lattuga**
	laht-TOO-gah
arugula	**rucola**
	ROO-koh-lah
radicchio	**radicchio**
	rah-DEEK-kyoh
mushrooms	**funghi / porcini**
	FOON-gy / pohr-CHEE-nee
white truffles	**tartufi bianchi**
	tahr-TOO-fee BYAHN-kee
black truffles	**tartufi neri**
	tahr-TOO-fee NEH-ree
nettles	**ortiche**
	ohr-TEE-keh
olives (green / black)	**olive (verde / nere)**
	oh-LEE-veh (VEHR-dee / NEH-reh)
onion	**cipolla**
	chee-POHL-lah
peas	**piselli**
	pee-ZEHL-lee
peppers	**peperoni**
	peh-peh-ROH-nee
green	**verdi**
	VERH-dee
hot	**peperoncino**
	peh-peh-rohn-CHEE-noh
red	**rossi**
	ROHS-see
yellow	**gialli**
	JAHL-lee
potato	**patata**
	pah-TAH-tah

pumpkin	**zucca**
	DZOOK-kah
sorrel	**acetosella**
	ah-cheh-toh-ZEHL-lah
spinach	**spinaci**
	spee-NAH-chee
squash	**zucca**
	DZOOK-kah
tomato	**pomodoro**
	poh-moh-DOH-roh
yam	**patata dolce**
	pah-TAH-tah DOHL-cheh
zucchini	**zucchini**
	dzook-KEE-nee

Fresh herbs and spices

anise	**anice**
	AH-nee-cheh
basil	**basilico**
	bah-ZEE-lee-koh
bay leaf	**alloro**
	ahl-LOH-roh
black pepper	**pepe nero**
	PEH-peh NEH-roh
clove	**chiodo di garofano**
	KYOH-doh dee gah-ROH-fah-noh
dill	**aneto**
	ah-NEH-toh
garlic	**aglio**
	AHL-lyoh
marjoram	**maggiorana**
	mahd-joh-RAH-nah
oregano	**origano**
	oh-REE-gah-noh
paprika	**paprica**
	PAH-pree-kah

parsley	**prezzemolo**
	preht-TSEH-moh-loh
rosemary	**rosmarino**
	rohz-mah-REE-noh
saffron	**zafferano**
	dzahf-feh-RAH-noh
sage	**salvia**
	SAHL-vyah
salt	**sale**
	SAH-leh
sugar	**zucchero**
	DZOOK-keh-roh
thyme	**timo**
	TEE-moh

AT THE DELI

What kind of salad is that?	**Che tipo di insalata è quella?**
	keh TEE-poh dee een-sah-LAH-tah EH KWEHL-lah
What type of cheese is that?	**Che tipo di formaggio è quello?**
	keh TEE-poh dee fohr-MAHD-joh EH KWEHL-loh
What type of bread is that?	**Che tipo di pane è quello?**
	keh TEE-poh dee PAH-neh EH KWEHL-loh
May I have some of that please?	**Posso avere un po' di quello, per favore?**
	POHS-soh ah-VEH-reh oon POH dee KWEHL-loh pehr fah-VOH-reh
Is the salad fresh?	**Questa insalata è fresca?**
	KWEHS-tah een-sah-LAH-tah EH FREHS-kah
I'd like ____, please.	**Vorrei ____ , per favore.**
	vohr-RAY ____ pehr fah-VOH-reh
chicken salad	**un'insalata di pollo**
	oon-een-sah-LAH-tah dee POHL-loh

DINING

ham	**del prosciutto**
	dehl proh-SHOOT-toh
mayonnaise	**della maionese**
	DEHL-lah mah-yoh-NEH-zeh
mustard	**della senape**
	DEHL-lah SEH-nah-peh
a pickle	**un cetriolo sott'aceto**
	oon cheh-tree-OH-loh soht-tah-CHEH-toh
roast beef	**rosbif**
	ROHZ-beef
a salad	**un'insalata**
	oon-een-sah-LAH-tah
a sandwich	**un panino**
	oon pah-NEE-noh
shrimp cocktail	**cocktail di gamberetti**
	KOHK-tehl dee gahm-beh-REHT-tee
a package of tofu	**un pacchetto di tofu**
	oon pahk-KEHT-toh dee TOH-foo
tuna salad	**un'insalata di tonno**
	oon-een-sah-LAH-tah dee TOHN-noh
I'd like that cheese.	**Mi piace quel formaggio.**
	mee PYAH-cheh kwehl fohr-MAHD-joh
Is that smoked?	**È affumicato -a?**
	EH ahf-FOO-mee-kah-toh -tah
pound (in kgs)	**mezzo chilo**
	MEHD-zoh KEE-loh
a quarter-pound (in kgs)	**un etto**
	oon EHT-toh
a half-pound (in kgs)	**due etti**
	DOO-eh EHT-tee

FOOD & WINE BY REGION

Apulia

What to Eat *Orecchiette* (pasta shaped like little ears, often served with *cima di rape* or turnip greens); *braciola* (veal roll stewed in tomato sauce).

What to Drink *Salice Salentino* (a hearty red).

Campagnia

What to Eat Pizza; *insalata Caprese* (salads of mozzarella, tomatoes, and basil); *spaghetti alle vongole veraci* (with clams); *spaghetti alle cozze* (with mussels); *mozzarella di bufala* (cheese made from the milk of bison).

What to Drink *Lacryma Christi* ("Tears of Christ," a white that grows in volcanic soil); *Taurasi* (a potent red).

Emilia-Romagna

What to Eat *Prosciutto di Parma* (the region's justly famous ham); *tortellini* (pasta stuffed with meat or cheese and often topped with a creamy, buttery sauce); any pasta served *alla bolognese* (with meat and tomato sauce); *bollito misto* (mixed meats, boiled); *Parmigiano-Reggiano* (Parmesan cheese).

What to Drink *Lambrusco* (sparkling red); *Sangiovese di Romagna* (dry red).

Lazio

What to Eat *Bucatini all'amatriciana* (thick hollow spaghetti in a sauce of tomatoes, onions, hot peppers, and pancetta); *spaghetti alla carbonara* (with egg and pancetta); *saltimbocca* (thin slices of veal sautéed in white wine with prosciutto); *gnocchi* (potato dumplings); *carciofi alla romana* (tender artichokes fried in oil).

What to Drink *Est! Est!! Est!!!* (fruity white); *Frascati* (young, refreshing white from the hills above Rome).

Liguria

What to Eat　*Farinata* (chick-pea-flour crepe); *zuppa di datteri* (seafood soup); *pesto* (sauce of ground basil, pine nuts, and olive oil, served over pasta, with meat, in soup); *focaccia* (flat bread often topped with herbs).

What to Drink　*Dolceacqua* (full-bodied red from town of same name); *Pigato* (light white); *Bianco delle Cinqueterre* (dry white from the seaside region).

Lombardy

What to Eat　*Minestrone alla Milanese* (vegetable soup with rice and bacon); *osso buco* (sliced veal sautéed with the bone and marrow); *cotoletta alla Milanese* (breaded veal scallop); *risotto* (the region's arborio rice cooked with broth and various ingredients); *Gorgonzola* (creamy cheese laced with bluish mold).

What to Drink　*Barbera* (smooth red); *Trebbiano* (light white).

Piemonte

What to Eat　*Polenta* (corn meal mush, Italian style); *tartufi* (truffles); *fonduta* (a fonduelike mixture of fontina cheese with milk and eggs); *bagna cauda* (raw vegetables dipped in steaming sauce of olive oil, garlic, anchovies); *agnoloti* (thick pasta stuffed with cheese and meat); *amaretti* (almond cookies).

What to Drink　*Barbarsesco, Barolo, Barbera, Dolcetto, Nebbiolo* (all smooth reds).

Sicily

What to Eat　*Rancini* (rice balls); *pesce spada* (swordfish); *pasta alla Norma*, with *melanzana* (eggplant, tomatoes, and ricotta); *cassata* (sponge cake with ricotta, chocolate cream, and candied fruits).

What to Drink　*Marsala* (sweet dessert wine); *Nero d'Avola* (a rich red wine).

Tuscany

What to Eat   *Ribollita* (vegetable soup); *cacciucco* (fish stew); *bistecca alla fiorentina* (thick T-bone, usually cooked on a wood grill); *pollo alla diavola* (chicken sprinkled with hot pepper); *panzanella* (salad of tomatoes, basil, cucumber, onion, and bread); *pecorino* (sheep's milk cheese, raw or aged); *fagioli all'olio* (white beans served with olive oil).

What to Drink   *Chianti* (Vino Nobile di Montepulciano, Brunello di Montalcino, both rich reds); *Vernaccia di San Gimignano* (crisp white).

Umbria

What to Eat   *Porchetta* (roast suckling pig); *piccione* (squab); *cinghiale* (wild boar); *tartufi nero* (black truffles); *caciotta* (part sheep's milk, part goat's milk cheese); *Perugina* (chocolates)

What to Drink   *Orvieto* (white, often quite dry); *Torgiano* (especially Torre di Giano, fruity red).

Veneto

What to Eat   *Gamberetti* (small shrimp, sautéed); *fegato alla veneziana* (liver and onions); *risotto nero* (rice cooked with cuttlefish in black ink); *risi e bisi* (rice and peas); *asiago* (hard cheese made with cow's milk); *pecorino* (sheep's milk cheese).

What to Drink   *Prosecco* (sparking white); *Soave* (delicate, dry white); *Valpolicella* (dry red).

ITALIAN CAFFÈ

Caffè Americano: American-style, watered-down coffee; expect a sneer from the bar man when you order
Caffè coretto: espresso "corrected" with a shot of liquor
Caffè hag: decaf
Caffè macchiato: espresso with a wee drop of steamed milk
Cappuccino: espresso with a top layer of foamed milk, sipped for breakfast but never after dinner.

DINING

Demitasse caffè: straight espresso, downed in one gulp
Latte macchiato: glass of hot milk with a shot of espresso

OUR FAVORITE COFFEE STOPS

Florence
Caffè Rivoire   Old-world ambience with views of a stunning square and a replica of Michelangelo's *David*. (Piazza della Signoria, Florence; ✆ 055-214412)

Genoa
Antica Pasticceria Gelateria Klainguti   At this colorful port city's best and oldest cafe, enjoy your coffee with an astonishing array of pastries. (Piazza Soziglia, Genoa; ✆ 010-2474552)

Naples
Gran Caffè Gambrinus   Belle Epoque elegance in the middle of Italy's rowdiest city. (Piazza Trieste e Trento, Naples; ✆ 081-417582)

Rome
Caffè del Grecco   Casanova, Goethe, and legions of others have stopped in for a cuppa over the past 250 years. (Via Condotti 96, Rome; ✆ 06-6791700)

Sant'Eustachio   Reputed to serve the best coffee in Rome, with the crowds to prove it. (Piazza Sant'Eustachio 82, Rome; ✆ 06-6861309)

Venice
Caffè Florian   A seat on the terrace at one of the world's most venerable cafes often comes with an orchestral serenade as well as the spectacle of San Marco's ornate facade. (Piazza San Marco, Venice; ✆ 041-5205641)

CHAPTER FIVE

SOCIALIZING

Italians are a gregarious and curious people. They often initiate conversations with foreigners (some of which can seem quite personal). In this family-oriented country, a solo traveler is often viewed with sympathy; don't assume that every invitation is a scam or flirtation. Here you'll find the language to make new friends.

GREETINGS

Hello.	**Salve.**
	SAHL-veh
Good morning.	**Buon giorno.**
	bwon JOHR-noh
Good afternoon.	**Buon pomeriggio.**
	bwon poh-meh-REED-joh
Good evening.	**Buona sera.**
	BWOH-nah SEH-rah
Good night.	**Buona notte.**
	BWOH-nah NOHT-teh
How are you?	**Come va?**
	KOH-meh vah
Finc, thanks.	**Bene, grazie.**
	BEH-neh GRAH-tsyeh
And you?	**E tu / lei / voi?**
	eh too / lay / voy
I'm exhausted.	**Sono esausto -a.**
	SOH-noh eh-ZOWS-toh -tah
I have a headache.	**Ho il mal di testa.**
	OH eel mahl dee TEHS-tah
I'm terrible.	**Sto male.**
	stoh MAH-leh
I have a cold.	**Ho il raffreddore.**
	OH eel rahf-frehd-DOH-reh

Listen Up: Common Greetings

Ciao. *CHAH-oh*	Hi / Bye.
Salve. *SAHL-veh*	Hello.
È un piacere. *EH oon pyah-CHEH-reh*	It's a pleasure.
Piacere. *pyah-CHEH-reh*	How do you do / nice to meet you.
Molto piacere. *MOHL-toh pyah-CHEH-reh*	Delighted.
Come va? *KOH-meh vah*	How's it going?
Addio. *ahd-DEE-oh*	Goodbye.
Arrivederci. *ahr-ree-veh-DEHR-chee*	See you later.
Ci vediamo. *chee veh-DYAH-moh*	See you later.

THE LANGUAGE BARRIER

I don't understand.	**Non capisco.** *nohn kah-PEES-koh*
Please speak more slowly.	**Parli più lentamente, per favore.** *PAHR-lee PYOO lehn-tah-MEHN-teh pehr fah-VOH-reh*
Please speak louder.	**Parli più a voce alta, per favore.** *PAHR-lee PYOO ah VOH-cheh AHL-tah pehr fah-VOH-reh*
Do you speak English?	**Parla inglese?** *PAHR-lah een-GLEH-seh*
I speak ____ better than Italian.	**Parlo ____ meglio dell'italiano.** *PAHR-loh ____ MEHL-lyoh DEHL-lee-tah-LYAH-noh*

Please spell that.	**Come si scrive, per favore?** *KOH-meh see SKREE-veh pehr fah-VOH-reh*
Please repeat that?	**Me lo ripete, per favore?** *meh loh ree-PEH-teh pehr fah-VOH-reh*
How do you say ____?	**Come si dice ____?** *KOH-meh see DEE-cheh*
Would you show me that in this dictionary?	**Me lo mostra in questo dizionario?** *meh loh MOHS-trah een KWEHS-toh dee-tsyoh-NAH-ryoh*

Curse Words

Here are some common curse words.

merda *MEHR-dah*	shit
figlio di puttana *FEEL-lyoh dee poot-TAH-nah*	son of a bitch (literally "son ofa whore")
stronzo *STROHN-tsoh*	jerk (literally "turd", quite common)
Cazzo! *KAHT-soh*	Damn! (literally "dick," stronger than "damn," very frequently used)
Che cazzo vuoi? *keh KAHT-soh VWOH-ee*	What the hell do you want?
culo *KOO-loh*	ass (meaning the behind)
incasinato *een-kah-zee-NAH-toh*	screwed up
Vaffanculo! *vahf-fahn-KOO-loh*	Fuck off!

GETTING PERSONAL

Italians are generally friendly, yet more formal than Americans.
Remember to use the formal **lei** (third-person singular) until
given permission to employ the more familiar **tu**.

INTRODUCTIONS

What is your name?	**Come si chiama?**
	KOH-meh see KYAH-mah
My name is ____.	**Mi chiamo ____.**
	mee KYAH-moh
I'm pleased to meet you.	**Piacere di conoscerla.**
	pyah-CHEH-reh dee koh-NOSH-ehr-lah
May I introduce my ____	**Posso presentarle mio -a ____**
	POHS-soh preh-zehn-TAHR-leh MEE-oh -ah
boyfriend / girlfriend?	**il / la mio -a ragazzo -a?**
	eel / lah MEE-oh -ah rah-GAHT-soh -sah
friend?	**il / la mio -a amico -a?**
	eel / lah MEE-oh -ah ah-MEE-koh -kah
husband?	**marito?**
	mah-REE-toh
son / daughter?	**figlio -a**
	FEEL-lyoh -lyah
wife?	**moglie?**
	MOHL-lyeh
How is your ____	**Come sta -anno il / la suo -a ____**
	KOH-meh stah -STAHN-noh eel / lah SOO-oh -ah
aunt / uncle?	**zio -a?**
	DZEE-oh -ah
boss?	**capo?**
	KAH-poh

brother / sister?	**fratello / sorella?**
	frah-TEHL-loh / soh-REHL-lah
cousin?	**cugino -a?**
	koo-JEE-noh -nah
family?	**famiglia?**
	fah-MEEL-lyah
father?	**padre?**
	PAH-dreh
fiancée / fiancé?	**fidanzato -a?**
	fee-dahn-TSAH-toh -tah
mother?	**madre?**
	MAH-dreh
neighbor?	**vicino -a?**
	vee-CHEE-noh -nah
niece / nephew / grandchild?	**nipote?**
	nee-POH-teh
partner?	**partner?**
	partner
How are your ___	**Come sta -anno i suoi ___**
	KOH-meh stah -STAHN-noh ee soo-OH-ee
children?	**bambini / figli (if older than teens)**
	bahm-BEE-nee / FEEL-lyee
grandparents?	**nonni?**
	NOHN-nee
parents?	**genitori?**
	jeh-nee-TOH-ree

Dos and Don'ts.

Don't refer to your parents as **i parenti** (*ee pah-REHN-tee*), which means relatives. Do call them **i genitori** (*ee jeh-nee-TOH-ree*).

Are you married?	**È sposato -a?**
	EH spoh-ZAH-toh -tah
I'm married.	**Sono sposato -a.**
	SOH-noh spoh-ZAH-toh -tah
I'm single.	**Non sono sposato -a.**
	nohn SOH-noh spoh-ZAH-toh -tah
I'm divorced.	**Sono divorziato -a.**
	SOH-noh dee-vohr-TZYAH-toh -tah
I'm a widow / widower.	**Sono vedovo -a.**
	SOH-noh VEH-doh-voh -vah
We're separated.	**Siamo separati.**
	SYAH-moh seh-pah-RAH-tee
I live with my boyfriend / girlfriend.	**Vivo con il mio / la mia ragazzo -a.**
	VEE-voh kohn eel MEE-oh / lah MEE-ah rah-GAHT-soh -sah
How old are you?	**Quanti anni ha?**
	KWAHN-tee AHN-nee AH
How old are your children?	**Quanti anni hanno i suoi bambini?**
	KWAHN-tee AHN-nee AHN-noh ee soo-OH-ee bahm-BEE-nee
Wow, that's very young.	**Ah, è molto giovane.**
	AH EH MOHL-toh JOH-vah-neh
No, you're not! You're much younger.	**No, davvero! Lei è molto più giovane.**
	noh dahv-VEH-roh lay EH MOHL-toh PYOO JOH-vah-neh
Your wife / daughter is beautiful.	**Sua moglie / figlia è bellissima.**
	SOO-ah MOHL-lyeh / FEEL-lyah EH behl-LEES-see-mah
Your husband / son is handsome.	**Suo marito / figlio è molto bello.**
	SOO-oh mah-REE-toh / FEEL-lyoh EH MOHL-toh BEHL-loh
What a beautiful baby!	**Che bel -la bambino -a!**
	keh behl -lah bahm-BEE-noh -nah

Are you here on business?	**È qui per affari?** *EH kwee pehr ahf-FAH-ree*
I am vacationing.	**Sono in vacanza.** *SOH-noh een vah-KAHN-tsah*
I'm attending a conference.	**Sto partecipando ad una conferenza.** *stoh pahr-teh-chee-PAHN-doh ah-DOO-nah kohn-feh-REHN-tsah*
How long are you staying?	**Quanto tempo si ferma?** *KWAHN-toh TEHM-poh see FEHR-mah*
I'm a student.	**Sono studente / studentessa.** *SOH-noh stoo-DEHN-teh / stoo-DEHN-tehs-sah*
What are you studying?	**Cosa studia?** *KOH-zah STOO-dyah*
Where are you from?	**Di dov'è?** *Dee dohv-EH*

PERSONAL DESCRIPTIONS

African-American	**afroamericano -a** *AH-froh-ah-meh-ree-KAH-noh -nah*
afro	**capigliatura africana** *kah-peel-lyah-TOO-rah ah-free-KAH-nah*
Asian	**asiatico -a** *ah-ZYAH-tee-koh -kah*
biracial	**meticcio -a** *meh-TEET-choh -chah*
black	**nero -a** *NEH-roh -rah*
blonde	**biondo -a** *BYOHN-doh -dah*
blue eyes	**occhi azzurri** *OHK-kee ahd-DZOOR-ree*

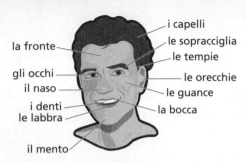

i capelli
le sopracciglia
la fronte
le tempie
gli occhi
il naso
i denti
le labbra
le orecchie
le guance
la bocca
il mento

brown eyes	**occhi castani**	
	OHK-kee kahs-TAH-nee	
brunette	**castano -a**	
	KAHS-tah-noh -nah	
caucasian	**caucasico -a**	
	kow-KAH-zee-koh -kah	
curly hair	**capelli ricci**	
	kah-PEHL-lee REET-chee	
eyebrows	**sopracciglia**	
	soh-praht-CHEEL-lyah	
eyelashes	**ciglia**	
	CHEEL-lyah	
face	**viso**	
	VEE-zoh	
fat	**grasso -a**	
	GRAHS-soh -sah	
freckles	**lentiggini**	
	lehn-TEED-jee-nee	
green eyes	**occhi verdi**	
	OHK-kee VERH-dee	

hazel eyes	**occhi nocciola**
	OHK-kee noht-CHOH-lah
kinky hair	**capelli crespi**
	kah-PEHL-lee KREHS-pee
long hair	**capelli lunghi**
	kah-PEHL-lee LOON-gy
mocha-skinned	**dalla pelle color caffè**
	DAHL-lah PEHL-leh koh-LOHR kahf-FEH
moles	**nei**
	nay
olive-skinned	**con la pelle olivastra**
	kohn lah PEHL-leh oh-lee-VAHS-trah
pale	**pallido -a**
	PAHL-lee-doh -dah
redhead	**rosso -a**
	ROHS-soh -sah
short	**basso -a**
	BAHS-soh -sah
short hair	**capelli corti**
	kah-PEHL-lee KOHR-tee
straight hair	**capelli dritti**
	kah-PEHL-lee DREET-tee
tall	**alto -a**
	AHL-toh -tah
tanned	**abbronzato -a**
	ahb-brohn-DZAH-toh -tah
thin	**magro -a**
	MAH-groh -grah
white	**bianco -a**
	BYAHN-koh -kah

Listen Up: Nationalities

Sono _____	I'm _____
SOH-noh	
brasiliano -a.	Brazilian.
brah-zee-LYAH-noh -nah	
francese.	French.
frahn-CHEH-zeh	
greco -a.	Greek.
GREH-koh -kah	
portoghese.	Portuguese.
pohr-toh-GHEH-zeh	
rumeno -a.	Romanian.
roo-MEH-noh -nah	
russo -a.	Russian.
ROOS-soh -sah	
spagnolo -a.	Spanish.
spahn-NYOH-loh -lah	
svizzero -a.	Swiss.
ZVEET-seh-roh -rah	
tedesco -a.	German.
teh-DEHS-koh -kah	
ungherese.	Hungarian.
oon-gheh-REH-zeh	

For more nationalities, see p232 and English / Italian dictionary.

DISPOSITIONS AND MOODS

angry	**arrabbiato -a**
	ahr-rahb-BYAH-toh -tah
anxious	**ansioso -a**
	ahn-SYOH-zoh -zah
confused	**confuso -a**
	kohn-FOO-zoh -zah
depressed	**depresso -a**
	deh-PREHS-soh -sah
enthusiastic	**entusiasta**
	ehn-too-ZYAHS-tah

happy	**felice**
	feh-LEE-cheh
sad	**triste**
	TREES-teh
stressed	**stressato -a**
	strehs-SAH-toh -tah
tired	**stanco -a**
	STAHN-koh -kah

SOCIALIZING

PROFESSIONS

What do you do for a living?	**Che lavoro fa?**
	keh lah-VOH-roh fah
Here is my business card.	**Ecco il mio biglietto da visita.**
	EHK-koh eel MEE-oh beel-LYEHT-toh dah VEE-zee-tah
I am ____	**Sono ____**
	SOH-noh
an accountant.	**contabile.**
	kohn-TAH-bee-leh
an artist.	**artista.**
	ahr-TEES-tah
a craftsperson.	**artigiano -a.**
	ahr-tee-JAH-noh -nah
a designer.	**stilista.**
	stee-LEES-tah
a doctor.	**medico.**
	MEH-dee-koh
an editor.	**redattore / redattrice.**
	reh-daht-TOH-reh / reh-daht-TREE-che
an educator.	**educatore / educatrice.**
	eh-doo-kah-TOH-reh / eh-doo-kah-TREE-cheh
an engineer.	**ingegnere.**
	een-jehn-NYEH-reh

a government employee.	**impiegato -a statale.** *eem-pyeh-GAH-toh -tah stah-TAH-leh*
a homemaker.	**casalinga.** *kah-zah-LEEN-gah*
a lawyer.	**avvocato / avvocassa.** *ahv-voh-KAH-toh / ahv-voh-KAHS-sah*
a military professional.	**un militare.** *oon mee-lee-TAH-reh*
a musician.	**musicista.** *moo-zee-CHEES-tah*
a nurse.	**infermiere -a.** *een-fehr-MYEH-reh -rah*
a salesperson.	**commesso -a.** *kohm-MEHS-soh -sah*
a writer.	**scrittore / scrittrice.** *skreet-TOH-reh / skreet-TREE-cheh*

DOING BUSINESS

I'd like an appointment.	**Vorrei un appuntamento.** *vohr-RAY oon ahp-poon-tah-MEHN-toh*
I'm here to see ____.	**Sono qui per vedere ____.** *SOH-noh kwee pehr veh-DEH-reh*
May I photocopy this?	**Posso fotocopiare questo?** *POHS-soh foh-toh-koh-PYAH-reh KWEHS-toh*
May I use a computer here?	**Posso usare il computer qui?** *POHS-soh oo-ZAH-reh eel computer kwee*
What's the password?	**Qual è la password?** *kwah-LEH lah password*
May I access the Internet?	**Posso accedere a Internet?** *POHS-soh aht-CHEH-deh-reh ah internet*

May I send a fax?

Posso inviare un fax?
POHS-soh een-VYAH-reh oon fax

May I use the phone?

Posso usare il telefono?
POHS-soh oo-ZAH-reh eel teh-LEH-foh-noh

PARTING WAYS

Keep in touch.

Teniamoci in contatto.
teh-NYAH-moh-chee een kohn-TAHT-toh

Please write or email.

Scriva o invii un e-mail.
SKREE-vah oh een-VEE-ee oon e-mail

Here's my phone number. Call me.

Ecco il mio numero di telefono. Mi chiami.
EHK-koh eel MEE-oh NOO-meh-roh dee teh-LEH-foh-noh mee KYAH-mee.

May I have your phone number / email, please?

Posso avere il suo numero di telefono / indirizzo e-mail, per favore?
POHS-soh ah-VEH-reh eel SOO-oh NOO-meh-roh dee teh-LEH-foh-noh / een-dee-REET-soh e-mail pehr fah-VOH-reh

May I have your card?

Posso avere il suo biglietto da visita?
POHS-soh ah-VEH-reh eel SOO-oh beel-LYEHT-toh dah VEE-zee-tah

Give me your address and I'll write.

Mi dia il suo indirizzo e le scriverò.
mee DEE-ah eel SOO-oh een-dee-REET-soh eh leh skree-veh-ROH

TOPICS OF CONVERSATION

As in the United States, Europe, or anywhere in the world, the weather and current affairs are common conversation topics.

THE WEATHER

It's ___	**È ___**
	EH
Is it always so ___	**È sempre così ___**
	EH SEHM-preh koh-ZEE
cloudy?	**nuvoloso?**
	noo-voh-LOH-zoh
humid?	**umido?**
	OO-mee-doh
warm?	**caldo?**
	KAHL-doh
cool?	**fresco?**
	FREHS-koh
rainy?	**piovoso?**
	pyoh-VOH-zoh
windy?	**C'è sempre così tanto vento?**
	ch-EH SEHM-preh koh-ZEE TAHN-toh VEHN-toh
sunny?	**sole?**
	SOH-leh
Do you know the weather forecast for tomorrow?	**Conosce le previsioni del tempo per domani?**
	koh-NOH-sheh leh preh-vee-ZYOH-nee dehl TEHM-poh pehr doh-MAH-nee

THE ISSUES

What do you think about _____
Che ne pensa _____
keh neh PEHN-sah

American Republicans?
dei repubblicani americani?
day reh-poob-blee-KAH-nee ah-meh-ree-KAH-nee

American Democrats?
dei democratici americani?
day deh-moh-KRAH-tee-chee ah-meh-ree-KAH-nee

democracy?
della democrazia?
DEHL-lah deh-moh-krah-TSEE-ah

socialism?
del socialismo?
dehl soh-chah-LEEZ-moh

the environment?
dell'ambiente?
DEHL-lahm-BYEHN-teh

women's rights?
dei diritti delle donne?
day dee-REET-tee DEHL-leh DOHN-neh

gay rights?
dei diritti degli omosessuali?
day dee-REET-tee DEHL-lyee oh-moh-sehs-SWAH-lee

the economy?
dell'economia?
dehl-leh-koh-noh-MEE-ah

What political party do you belong to?
A quale partito politico appartiene?
ah KWAH-leh pahr-TEE-toh poh-LEE-tee-koh ahp-pahr-TYEH-neh

What did you think of the election?
Come le sono sembrate le elezioni?
KOH-meh leh SOH-noh sehm-BRAH-teh leh eh-leh-TSYOH-nee

What do you think of the war in _____.
Cosa pensa della guerra in _____.
KOH-zah PEHN-sah DEHL-lah GWEHR-rah een

RELIGION

Do you go to church / temple / mosque?	**Lei frequenta una chiesa / un tempio / una moschea?**
	lay freh-KWEHN-tah OO-nah KYEH-zah / oon TEHM-pyoh / OO-nah mohs-KEH-ah
Are you religious?	**Lei è osservante?**
	lay EH ohs-sehr-VAHN-teh
I'm ____ / I was raised ____	**Sono ____ / Sono cresciuto -a ____**
	SOH-noh ____ / SOH-noh kreh-SHOO-toh -tah
agnostic.	**agnostico -a.**
	ahn-NYOHS-tee-koh -kah
atheist.	**ateo -a.**
	AH-teh-oh -ah
Buddhist.	**buddista.**
	bood-DEES-tah
Catholic.	**cattolico -a.**
	kaht-TOH-lee-koh -kah
Greek Orthodox.	**greco ortodosso -a.**
	GREH-koh ohr-toh-DOHS-soh -sah
Hindu.	**hindu.**
	hindu
Jewish.	**ebreo -a.**
	eh-BREH-oh -ah
Muslim.	**mussulmano -a.**
	moos-sool-MAH-noh -nah
Protestant.	**protestante.**
	proh-tehs-TAHN-teh
I'm spiritual but I don't attend services.	**Sono spirituale ma non osservante.**
	SOH-noh spee-ree-TWAH-leh mah nohn ohs-sehr-VAHN-teh

I don't believe in that.	**Non ci credo.**
	nohn chee KREH-doh
That's against my beliefs.	**È contrario alle mie convinzioni.**
	EH kohn-TRAH-ryoh AHL-leh MEE-
	eh kohn-veen-TSYOH-nee
I'd rather not talk	**Preferisco non parlarne.**
about it.	*preh-feh-REES-koh nohn pahr-*
	LAHR-neh

GETTING TO KNOW SOMEONE

Following are some conversation starters.

MUSICAL TASTES

What kind of music do you like?	**Che tipo di musica le piace?**
	keh TEE-poh dee MOO-zee-kah leh
	PYAH-cheh
I like _____	**Mi piace _____**
	mee PYAH-cheh
calypso.	**la calypso.**
	lah calypso
country and western.	**la musica country e western.**
	lah MOO-zee-kah country eh
	western.
classical.	**la classica.**
	lah KLAHS-see-kah
disco.	**La musica de discoteca.**
	lah MOO-zee-kah dah dees-koh
	TEH-kah
hip hop.	**la hip hop.**
	lah hip hop
jazz.	**il jazz.**
	eel jazz
New Age.	**la New Age.**
	lah new age

opera.	**l'opera.**
	LOH-peh-rah
pop.	**la pop.**
	lah pop
reggae.	**il reggae.**
	eel reggae
rock 'n' roll.	**il rock 'n' roll.**
	eel rock 'n' roll
show-tunes / musicals.	**le canzoni da musical.**
	leh kahn-TSOH-nee dah musical
techno.	**la techno.**
	lah techno

HOBBIES?

What do you like to do in your spare time?	**Cosa le piace fare nel tempo libero?**
	KOH-zah leh PYAH-cheh FAH-reh nehl TEHM-poh LEE-beh-roh
I like ____	**Mi piace ____**
	mee PYAH-cheh
camping.	**andare in campeggio.**
	anh-DAH-reh een kahm-PEHD-joh
cooking.	**cucinare.**
	koo-chee-NAH-reh
dancing.	**andare a ballare.**
	anh-DAH-reh ah bahl-LAH-reh
drawing.	**disegnare.**
	dee-zehn-NYAH-reh
eating out.	**mangiare fuori.**
	mahn-JAH-reh FWOH-ree
going to the movies.	**andare al cinema.**
	anh-DAH-reh ahl CHEE-neh-mah
hanging out.	**ritrovarmi con gli amici.**
	ree-troh-VAHR-mee kohn lyee ah-MEE-chee

hiking.	**fare camminate.**
	FAH-reh kahm-mee-NAH-teh
playing guitar.	**suonare la chitarra.**
	swoh-NAH-reh lah kee-
	TAHR-rah
piano.	**il pianoforte.**
	eel pyah-noh-FOHR-teh

For other instruments, see the English / Italian dictionary.

painting.	**dipingere.**
	dee-PEEN-jeh-reh
reading.	**leggere.**
	LEHD-jeh-reh
sewing.	**cucire.**
	koo-CHEE-reh
shopping.	**fare shopping.**
	FAH-reh shopping
sports.	**fare sport.**
	FAH-reh sport
traveling.	**viaggiare.**
	vyahd-JAH-reh
watching TV.	**guardare la TV.**
	ghwar-DAH-reh lah tee-VOO
Do you like to dance?	**Vuole ballare?**
	VWOH-leh bahl-LAH-reh
Would you like to go out?	**Vuole uscire?**
	VWOH-leh oo-SHEE-reh
May I buy you dinner sometime?	**Posso ti fuori a cena qualche volta?**
	POHS-soh tee FWOH-ree ah CHEH-nah KWAHL-keh VOHL-tah
What kind of food do you like?	**Che tipo di cibo le piace?**
	keh TEE-poh dee CHEE-boh leh PYAH-cheh

For a full list of food types, see Dining in Chapter 4.

Would you like to go _____	**Le piacerebbe andare _____** *leh pyah-CHEH-rehb-beh ahn-DAH-reh*
to the beach?	**alla spiaggia?** *AHL-lah SPYAHD-jah*
to a concert?	**ad un concerto?** *ah-DOON kohn-CHEHR-toh*
dancing?	**a ballare?** *ah bahl-LAH-reh*
to a movie?	**al cinema?** *ahl CHEE-neh-mah*
to a museum?	**al museo?** *ahl moo-ZEH-oh*
for a walk in the park?	**a passeggiare nel parco?** *ah pahs-sehd-JAH-reh nehl PAHR-koh*
to the zoo?	**allo zoo?** *AHL-loh DZOH-oh*
Would you like to get _____	**Andiamo _____** *ahn-DYAH-moh*
coffee?	**a prendere un caffè?** *ah PREHN-deh-reh oon kahf-FEH*
dinner?	**a cena?** *ah CHEH-nah*
lunch?	**a pranzo?** *ah PRAHN-tsoh*
What kind of books do you like to read?	**Che tipo di libri le piace leggere?** *keh TEE-poh dee LEE-bree leh PYAH-cheh LEHD-jeh-reh*
I like _____	**Mi piacciono _____** *mee PYAHT-choh-noh*
auto-biographies.	**le autobiografie.** *leh ow-toh-byoh-grah-FEE-eh*

biographies.	**le biografie.**
	leh byoh-grah-FEE-eh
dramas.	**le storie drammatiche.**
	leh STOH-ryeh drahm-MAH-tee-keh
history.	**gli argomenti storici.**
	lyee ahr-goh-MEHN-tee STOH-ree-chee
mysteries.	**i gialli.**
	ee JAHL-lee
novels.	**i romanzi.**
	ee roh- MAHN-dzee
romance.	**i romanzi d'amore.**
	ee roh- MAHN-dzee dah-MOH-reh
Westerns.	**i romanzi western.**
	ee roh- MAHN-dzee western

For dating terms, see Nightlife in Chapter 10.

MEET THE ITALIANS

Servas (an Esperanto word meaning "to serve") supports global goodwill by arranging free home stays of up to 2 nights for travelers. Single-day visits, including a meal and sightseeing, can also be arranged. For details, visit **www.servas.org**. **Friendship Force International** also supports home stays around the world. Travelers pay a fee for a list of hosts for stays of up to a week. Contact them at ✆ **404/522-9490** or www.friendshipforce.org. Check, too, with tourist offices in towns you plan to visit.

LANGUAGE SCHOOLS

Schools and programs offering courses on Italian language usually also provide a good introduction to art history, history, and general Italian culture. Often they'll also arrange housing with Italian families. Expect to pay 400€ for a 2-week course, not including housing.

Some well-reputed schools include **Centro Linguistico Italiano Dante Aligheri,** Florence Piazza della Repubblica 5, **Florence** (✆ **055/ 210808**; www.clidante.com); **Cultura Italiano,** via castiglione 4, **Bologna** (✆ **051/228003**; www.culturaitaliana.it); and **Università per Stranieri di Perugia (University of Perugia for Foreigners),** Piazza Fortebraccio, **Perugia** (✆ **075- 57461**; www.unistrapg.it).

For other language programs located around Italy, contact: **American Institute for Foreign Study** (✆ **800-727-AIFS**; www.aifs.org), and **Language Study Abroad** (✆ **760/416-0314**; www.languagestudy.com).

THE PASSEGGIATA

The Passeggiata This time-honored tradition takes place nightly in every town in Italy. Shortly after 6pm, men and women, young and old alike, stroll before dinner in the town center, usually through the main piazza and surrounding streets. Often members of the same sex link arms or kiss each other in greeting. There's no easier way to feel a part of everyday life in Italy than to make the *passeggiata* part of your evening routine.

ITALIAN FESTIVALS

Italians like to socialize at a year-long roster of fairs, festivals, and other events. Here are some especially colorful happenings.

January

Fair of St. Orso, AOSTA, VALLE D'AOSTA   More than 700 woodcarvers descend from the mountains to follow a thousand-year-old tradition and display hand-crafted items. *January 30–31.*

February

Carnevale, VENICE   The city becomes a stage for 2 event-packed weeks, when *campos*, streets, and even the Grand Canal are jam-packed with costumed and masked figures, concerts enliven every venue in town, and fireworks illuminate the sky. *From two Fridays before Shrove Tuesday to Shrove Tuesday.*

Carnevale, VIAREGGIO   Giant floats topped with effigies of political figures career through the streets of this seaside town. *Four Sundays before Lent.*

April

Easter Festivities, ITALY   In **Florence,** a mechanical dove slides along a wire from the high altar in the Duomo to the piazza outside, where it ignites a cart laden with flowers and fireworks.

On Good Friday, in **Rome,** the Pope leads a procession up Palatine Hill past the Stations of the Cross. On Easter, in **Rome,** the Pope gives his blessing from a balcony overlooking St. Peter's Square. In **Taranto, Apulia,** on Holy Thursday, men wearing white smocks and crowns of thorns walk barefoot from church to church all night behind a statue of Mary, symbolically looking for her son.

In **Trapani, Sicily,** on Holy Thursday, hooded figures carry statues through the town to the accompaniment of bands.

May

Calendimaggio, ASSISI   Houses are bedecked with flowers and citizens parade in medieval costume to celebrate spring. *First Saturday and Sunday after May 1*.

Corso dei Ceri, GUBBIO   Costumed contestants race through town and up the flanks of Monte Ingino carrying *ceri*—20-foot-tall, 900-pound columns topped with statues of St. Ubaldo (patron saint of masons and the town), St. Giorgio (patron saint of traders), and St. Antonio (patron saint of peasants). *May 15*.

Feast of the Crickets, FLORENCE   Florentines compete to find crickets that make the most beautiful music, and carry the contestants through the streets in elaborate cages. *Third Sunday*.

Feast of the Miracle of San Gennaro, NAPLES   Neapolitans pack the Duomo to witness the blood of San Gennaro, the city's patron saint, turn from powder to liquid; if the blood fails to liquify, disaster will befall the city. (Fortunately, it has changed state as anticipated every year since 1456.) *Saturday before the first Saturday in May (and again on September 19)*.

Feast of St. Nicholas, BARI   The town places a statue of its patron saint on a floating altar at sea, and the faithful row out to pay homage. *May 7–8*.

June

Calcio Storico Fiorentino, FLORENCE   In a revival of a medieval football match, teams representing Florence's four parishes parade through town in medieval costume and then square off in dirt-covered Piazza San Croce. *June 24*.

Feast of St. Ranieri, PISA   More than 70,000 candles illuminate houses along the River Arno, where oarsmen in Renaissance costumes compete in a 2-day regatta. The race culminates with the winner scampering up a hemp rope, strung over the water, to claim a colorful banner. *June 16–17.*

July
Festa del Redentore (Feast of the Redeemer), VENICE Venetians walk across the Giudecca Canal on a makeshift bridge in thanks for the lifting of the plague of 1576. Hundreds of boats crowd the canal for firework-illuminated festivities. *Third Saturday and Sunday.*

Palio, SIENA Amid pageantry, feasts, and solemn celebrations, horses race around Siena's Campo, packed with dirt for the occasion. *July 2, August 16.*

September
Giostra di Saracino (Joust of the Saracen), AREZZO Knights in armor joust in the medieval Piazza Grande. *First Sunday.*

Regatta Storico, VENICE A procession of decorated gondolas glide down the Grand Canal. *First Sunday.*

October
Sagra del Tartufo, ALBA The truffle capital of Italy honors the precious fungus with parades, a jousting tournament, and the Palio degli Asini (Race of the Donkeys). *Two weeks, mid-month.*

November
Festa della Salute, VENICE Venetians celebrate deliverance from another plague—the one in 1630 that wiped out a third of the population—with a procession on a pontoon bridge across the mouth of the Grand Canal to the church of La Salute. *November 21.*

December–early January
Christmas and Epiphany celebrations, ITALY **Gubbio** lights up a mountainside with the world's largest Christmas tree. **Rome** hosts a crafts and food fair in the Piazza Navona.

CHAPTER SIX

MONEY & COMMUNICATIONS

This chapter covers money, the mail, phone and Internet service, and other tools you need to connect with the outside world.

MONEY

In 2002, Italy entered the Eurozone, changing its currency from lira to euro. The euro is available in seven different bills (5, 10, 20, 50, 100, 200, and 500) and eight separate coins (1, 2, 5, 10, 20, 50 centesimi, 1 and 2 euro denominations). Bills over 20 euros may be difficult to break.

CURRENCIES

Do you accept _____

Visa / MasterCard / Discover / American Express / Diners' Club?

credit cards?

bills?

coins?

checks?

travelers checks?

money transfer?

Accettate _____
aht-cheht-TAH-teh
Visa / MasterCard / Discover / American Express / Diners' Club?

carte di credito?
KAHR-teh dee KREH-dee-toh

banconote?
bahn-koh-NOH-teh

monete?
moh-NEH-teh

assegni?
ahs-SEHN-nyee

traveller's cheques?
traveller's cheques

un bonifico bancario?
oon boh-NEE-fee-koh bahn-KAH-ree-oh

May I wire transfer funds here?	**Posso effettuare un bonifico bancario qui?** *POHS-soh ehf-feht-TWAH-reh oon boh-NEE-fee-koh bahn-KAH-ree-oh kwee*
Would you please tell me where to find ____	**Potrebbe dirmi dove si trova ____** *poh-TREHB-beh DEER-mee DOH-veh see TROH-vah*
a bank?	**una banca?** *OO-nah BAHN-kah*
a credit bureau?	**un banco di credito?** *oon BAHN-koh dee KREH-dee-toh*
an ATM / cashpoint?	**un bancomat?** *oon BAHN-koh-maht*
a currency exchange?	**un cambio?** *oon kahm-byoh*
A receipt, please.	**Una ricevuta, per favore.** *OO-nah ree-cheh-VOO-tah pehr fah-VOH-reh*
Would you tell me ____	**Può dirmi qual è ____** *PWOH DEER-mee kwah-LEH*
today's interest rate?	**il tasso di interesse oggi?** *eel TAHS-soh dee een-teh-REHS-seh OHD-jee*
the exchange rate for dollars to ____?	**il cambio dal dollaro a ____?** *eel KAHM-byoh dahl DOHL-lah-roh ah*
Is there a service charge?	**C'è una tariffa da pagare?** *ch-EH OO-nah tah-REEF-fah dah pah-GAH-reh*

Listen Up: Bank Lingo

Firmi qui, per favore. *FEER-mee kwee* *pehr fah-VOH-reh*	Please sign here.
Ecco la sua ricevuta. *EHK-koh lah SOO-ah* *ree-che-VOO-tah*	Here is your receipt.
Ha un documento d'identità? *AH oon doh-koo-MEHN-toh* *dee-dehn-tee-TAH*	May I see your ID?
Accettiamo traveller's **cheques.** *aht-cheht-TYAH-moh traveller's* *cheques*	We accept travelers checks.
Solo contanti. *SOH-loh kohn-TAHN-tee*	Cash only.

May I have a cash advance on my credit card?	**Posso avere un anticipo sulla mia carta di credito?** *POHS-soh ah-VEH-reh oon ahn-TEE-chee-poh SOOL-lah MEE-ah KAHR-tah dee KREH-dee-toh kohn-trohl-*
Will you accept a credit card?	**Accettate la carta di credito?** *aht-cheht-TAH-teh lah KAHR-tah dee KREH-dee-toh*
May I have smaller bills, please.	**Banconote più piccole, per favore.** *bahn-koh-NOH-teh PYOO PEEK-koh-leh pehr fah-VOH-reh*
Can you make change?	**Può cambiare?** *PWOH kahm-BYAH-reh*
I only have bills.	**Ho solo banconote.** *OH SOH-loh bahn-koh-NOH-teh*
Some coins, please.	**Degli spiccioli, per favore.** *DEHL-lyee SPEET-choh-lee pehr fah-VOH-reh*

ATM (*Bancomat*)

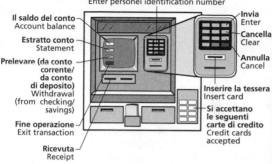

Inserire il numero PIN
Enter personel identification number

Il saldo del conto
Account balance

Estratto conto
Statement

Prelevare (da conto corrente/ da conto di deposito)
Withdrawal (from checking/ savings)

Fine operazione
Exit transaction

Ricevuta
Receipt

Invia
Enter

Cancella
Clear

Annulla
Cancel

Inserire la tessera
Insert card

Si accettano le seguenti carte di credito
Credit cards accepted

PHONE SERVICE

Where can I buy or rent a mobile / cell phone?	**Dove posso comprare o noleggiare un cellulare?** *DOH-veh POHS-soh kohm-PRAH-reh oh noh-lehd-JAH-reh oon chehl-loo-LAH-reh*
What rate plans do you have?	**Che piani rateali avete?** *keh PYAH-nee rah-teh-AH-lee ah-VEH-teh*
Is this good throughout the country?	**Questo funziona in tutto il paese?** *KWEHS-toh foon-TSYOH-nah een TOOT-toh eel pah-EH-zeh*
May I have a pre-paid phone?	**Posso avere un telefono pre-pagato?** *POHS-soh ah-VEH-reh oon teh-LEH-foh-noh preh-pah-GAH-toh*

Where can I buy a phone card?

Dove posso comprare una scheda telefonica?
DOH-veh POHS-soh kohm-PRAH-reh OO-nah SKEH-dah teh-leh-FOH-nee-kah

May I add more minutes to my phone card?

Posso aggiungere altri minuti alla mia scheda telefonica?
POHS-soh ahd-JOON-jeh-reh AHL-tree mee-NOO-tee AHL-lah MEE-ah SKEH-dah teh-leh-FOH-nee-kah

MAKING A CALL

May I dial direct?

Posso chiamare direttamente?
POHS-soh kyah-MAH-reh dee-reht-tah-MEHN-teh

Operator, please.

Il centralista, per favore.
eel chen-trah-lee-NEES-tah pehr fah-VOH-reh

I'd like to make an international call.

Vorrei fare una chiamata internazionale.
vohr-RAY FAH-reh OO-nah kyah-MAH-tah een-tehr-nah-tsyoh-NAH-leh

---

Fuori servizio

Before you stick your coins or bills in a vending machine, watch out for the little sign that says **Fuori Servizio** (Out of Service).

Listen Up: Telephone Lingo

Pronto? / Sì?
PROHN-toh / SEE /

Hello?

Che numero?
keh NOO-meh-roh

What number?

Mi dispiace, la linea è occupata.
mee dee-SPYAH-cheh lah LEE-neh ah EH ohk-koo-PAH-tah

I'm sorry, the line is busy.

Per favore, riagganciare e ricomporre il numero.
pehr fah-VOH-reh ree-ahg-ahg-ghan-CHAH-reh eh ree-kohm-POHR-reh eel NOO-meh-roh

Please, hang up and redial.

Mi dispiace, non risponde nessuno.
mee dee-SPYAH-cheh nohn rees-POHN-deh nehs-SOO-noh

I'm sorry, nobody is answering.

La sua scheda ha ancora dieci minuti a disposizione.
lah SOO-ah SKEH-dah AH ahn-KOH-rah DYEH-chee mee-NOO-tee ah dees-poh-zee-TSYOH-neh

Your card has ten minutes left.

COMMUNICATIONS

I'd like to make a collect call.	**Vorrei fare una chiamata a carico del ricevente.** *vohr-RAY FAH-reh OO-nah kyah-MAH-tah ah KAH-ree-koh dehl ree-cheh-VEHN-teh*
I'd like to use a calling card.	**Vorrei usare la scheda telefonica.** *vohr-RAY oo-ZAH-reh lah SKEH-dah teh-leh-FOH-nee-kah*
Bill my credit card.	**L'addebiti alla mia carta di credito.** *lahd-DEH-bee-tee AHL-lah MEE-ah KAHR-tah dee KREH-dee-toh*
May I bill the charges to my room?	**Posso addebitare i costi alla mia stanza?** *POHS-soh ahd-deh-bee-TAH-reh ee KOHS-tee AHL-lah MEE-ah STAHN-tsah*
May I bill the charges to my home phone?	**Posso addebitare i costi al mio telefono di casa?** *POHS-soh ahd-deh-bee-TAH-reh ee KOHS-tee ahl MEE-oh teh-LEH-foh-noh dee KAH-zah*
Information, please.	**Informazioni, per favore.** *een-fohr-mah-TSYOH-nee pehr fah-VOH-reh*
I'd like the number for ____.	**Vorrei il numero per ____.** *vohr-RAY eel NOO-meh-roh pehr*
I just got disconnected. / I lost the connection.	**È caduta la linea.** *EH kah-DOO-tah lah LEE-neh-ah*
The line is busy.	**La linea è occupata.** *lah LEE-neh-ah EH ohk-koo-PAH-tah*

INTERNET ACCESS

Where is an Internet café?

Dove si trova un punto di accesso a Internet?
DOH-veh see TROH-vah oon POON-toh di aht-CHESS-soh ah internet

Is there a wireless hub nearby?

C'è un collegamento wireless qui vicino?
ch-EH oon kohl-leh-gah-MEHN-toh wireless kwee vee-CHEE-noh

How much do you charge per minute / hour?

Quanto costa al minuto / all'ora?
KWAHN-toh KOHS-tah ahl mee-NOO-toh / ahl-LOH-rah

Can I print here?

Posso stampare qui?
POHS-soh stahm-PAH-reh kwee

Can I burn a CD?

Posso copiare un CD?
POHS-soh koh-PYAH-reh oon chee-DEE

Would you please help me change the language preference to English?

Può aiutarmi a cambiare l'impostazione della lingua all'inglese?
PWOH ah-yoo-TAHR-mee ah kahm-BYAH-reh leem-pohs-tah-TSYOH-neh DEHL-lah LEEN-gwah ahl-leen-GLEH-seh

May I scan something?	**Posso scannerizzare qualcosa?**
	POHS-soh skahn-neh-reed-DZAH-
	reh kwahl-KOH-zah
Can I upload photos?	**Posso caricare foto?**
	POHS-soh kah-ree-KAH-reh
	PHOH-toh
Do you have a USB port so I can download music?	**C'è una presa USB per scaricare musica?**
	ch-EH OO-nah PREH-zah oo-ehsseh-
	bee pehr skah-ree-KAH-reh MOO-
	zee-kah
Do you have a machine compatible with iTunes?	**C'è un apparecchio compatibile con iTunes?**
	ch-EH oon ahp-pah-REHK-kyoh
	kohm-pah-TEE-bee-leh kohn
	iTunes
Do you have a Mac?	**C'è un Mac?**
	ch-EH oon mac
Do you have a PC?	**C'è un PC?**
	ch-EH oon pee-CHEE
Do you have a newer version of this software?	**C'è una versione più recente di questo software?**
	ch-EH OO-nah vehr-SYOH-neh
	PYOO reh-CHEHN-teh dee KWEHS-
	toh software
Do you have broadband?	**C'è il broadband?**
	ch-EH eel broadband
How fast is your connection speed here?	**Che velocità di connessione c'è qui?**
	keh veh-loh-chee-TAH dee kohn-
	nehs-SYOH-neh ch-EH kwee

GETTING MAIL

Where is the post office?	**Dov'è l'ufficio postale?** *doh-VEH loof-FEE-choh pohs-TAH-leh*
May I send an international package?	**Posso inviare un pacco internazionale?** *POHS-soh een-VYAH-reh oon PAHK-koh een-tehr-nah-tsyoh-NAH-leh*
Do I need a customs form?	**Occorre il modulo doganale?** *ohk-KOHR-reh eel MOH-doo-loh doh-gah-NAH-leh*
Do you sell insurance for packages?	**Offrite l'assicurazione per i pacchi?** *ohf-FREE-teh lahs-see-koo-raht-SYOH-neh pehr ee PAHK-kee*
Please, mark it fragile.	**Lo marchi fragile, per favore.** *loh MAHR-kee FRAH-jee-leh pehr fah-VOH-reh*
Please, handle with care.	**Lo maneggi con cura, per favore.** *loh mah-NEHD-jee kohn KOO-rah pehr fah-VOH-reh*
Do you have twine?	**Ha dello spago?** *AH DEHL-loh SPAH-goh*
Do you have a twine clamp? (sometimes required for packages)	**Ha un sigillo?** *AH oon see-GEEL-loh*
Where is a DHL (express) office?	**Dov'è un ufficio DHL?** *doh-VEH oon oof-FEE-choh dee-akka-EHLLEH*

Listen Up: Postal Lingo

Il prossimo! *eel PROHS-see-moh*	Next!
Lo metta qui. *loh MEHT-tah kwee*	Set it here.
Come lo vuole inviare? *KOH-meh loh VWOH-leh een-VYAH-reh*	How would you like to send it?
Che tipo di servizio desidera? *keh TEE-poh dee sehr-VEET-syoh deh-ZEE-deh-rah*	What kind of service would you like?
Come posso aiutarla? *KOH-meh POHS-soh ah-yoo-TAHR-lah*	How can I help you?
Consegne *kohn-SEHN-nyeh*	Dropoff window
Accettazione *aht-cheht-tah-TSYOH-neh*	Pickup window

Do you sell stamps?	**Vende francobolli?** *VEHN-deh frahn-koh-BOHL-lee*
Do you sell postcards?	**Vende cartoline?** *VEHN-deh kahr-toh-LEE-neh*
May I send that first class?	**Posso inviarlo con la posta celere?** *POHS-soh een-VYAHR-loh kohn lah POHS-tah CHEH-leh-reh*
How much to send that express / air mail?	**Quanto costa inviarlo espresso / per posta aerea?** *KWAHN-toh KOHS-tah een-VYAHR-loh ehs-PREHS-soh / pehr POHS-tah ah-EH-reh-ah*

Do you offer overnight delivery?

Offrite la consegna il giorno dopo?
ohf-FREE-teh lah kohn-SEHN-nyah eel JOHR-noh DOH-poh

How long will it take to reach the United States?

Quanto tempo ci vorrà per arrivare negli Stati Uniti?
KWAHN-toh TEHM-poh chee vohr-RAH pehr ahr-ree-VAH-reh NEL-lyee STAH-tee oo-NEE-tee

I'd like to buy an envelope.

Vorrei comprare una busta.
vohr-RAY kohm-PRAH-reh OO-nah BOOS-tah

May I send it airmail?

Posso inviarlo per posta aerea?
POHS-soh een-VYAHR-loh pehr POHS-tah ah-EH-reh-ah

I'd like to send it certified / registered mail.

Vorrei inviarlo per posta raccomandata.
vohr-RAY een-VYAHR-loh pehr POHS-tah rahk-koh-mahn-DAH-tah

MONEY

Getting Cash ATMs are prevalent even in smaller towns. Most are linked to the Cirrus and Plus networks, and chances are good your bank uses one of these. The routine is the same as it is at home: Just pop in your card, punch in your personal identification number (PIN), and the machine will spit out euros drawn directly from your checking account—at a rate that's usually more favorable than what you'd get for traveler's checks or cash. Do keep in mind the following stipulations:

- Your bank will probably charge a fee for using a different bank's ATM, and international fees can be much higher than those at home—often about $5 per ATM withdrawal. Also, some banks have begun tacking on "exchange fees" to convert currency.

- Find out what your daily withdrawal limit is before you leave home. ATM withdrawals in Italy are usually limited to 200€.

- If you use a PIN to withdraw money from your credit card, keep in mind that interest accrues from the day of your withdrawal, even if you pay your monthly bill on time.

- Italian banks take only four-digit PINs. If you have a six-digit PIN, you'll have to change it before you leave home.

Traveler's Checks These are going the way of the dinosaur with the widespread use of ATMs. They are not nearly as convenient to use, and the exchange rate you get at an ATM is likely to be a lot better. On the plus side: If you plan to burn through a lot of cash, traveler's checks could be cheaper to use, given that most ATM withdrawals are limited to a few hundred euros, and banks charge for each withdrawal. If you pay a hotel or other establishment with traveler's checks, you'll get the worst possible exchange rate.

If you decide to purchase traveler's checks, contact **American Express** at © **800/721-9768** in the U.S. and Canada (www.americanexpress.com); **Thomas Cook** at ✆ 800/223-7373 in the U.S. and Canada (www.thomascook.com); **Visa** at ✆ 800/227-6811 in the U.S. and Canada; or **Citicorp** at ✆ 800/645-6556 in the U.S. or Canada (www.citicorp.com).

Credit Cards   Most hotels, restaurants, and shops accept **Visa** and **MasterCard**. Many, but not all, take **American Express** and **Diners Club**. If you lose your card or if it is stolen, call one of these toll-free numbers for use within Italy (do not use the toll-free U.S. number on the back of your card): **Visa** (✆ 800/819-014); **MasterCard** (✆ 800/870-866); **American Express** (✆ 800/872-000 or call collect, **336/393-1111**).

STAYING CONNECTED

Italian **pay phones** come in three varieties: those that take coins only (.10€ for a local call); those that take both coins and phone cards; and those that take phone cards only. You can buy prepaid phone cards (called *carta telefonica* or *scheda telefonica*) in various denominations at *tabacchi* (tobacconists), most newsstands, and some bars. Break off the corner of the card before using it, pick up the receiver, insert the card in the clearly marked slot, wait for the dial tone, and dial the number you wish to reach. On most phones, a digital display will tell you how much money is remaining on the card.

To Dial Direct Internationally from Italy   Dial 00, then the country code, then the area code, then the number. The country code in the United States and Canada is 1.

To Dial One City from Another within Italy   Dial the city code, complete with the initial 0, then the number. Note that numbers in Italy range from four to eight digits.

  Some city codes include: Bari, 080; Bologna, 051; Catania, 095; Florence, 055; Genoa, 010; Milan, 02; Naples, 081; Palermo, 091; Rome, 06; Turin, 011; Venice, 041.

To Place a Local Call   Include the city code, with the 0.

To Use a U.S.-Based Calling Card   For **AT&T,** dial ✆ **171-1011**; for **MCI** ✆ **172-1022**; for **Sprint** ✆ **172-1877**.

Once you're connected, you can either follow recorded prompts or wait for an operator to assist you. If you're using the card from a pay phone, you'll need to insert change or a phone card to reach these carriers.

To Use Other International Calling Cards   International phone cards (*scheda telefonica internazionale*) are available at *tabacchi* (tobacconists), most newsstands, and some bars in various denominations. You don't insert these into the phone; instead, dial the toll-free number listed on the card, then follow instructions and type in the identification number on the card. If you're using the card from a pay phone, you'll need to insert change or a *scheda* to make the connection.

To save some money when making phone calls, try not to use the phone in your room, as hotels often slap huge surcharges onto phone calls. If you're calling home directly, remember that Telecom Italia (the national phone company) charges reduced rates for international calls placed Monday through Saturday, 10pm to 8am and all day Sunday.

Cellphones   If your cellphone is on a **GSM network (Global System for Mobiles),** you can make and receive calls in Italy, provided you've asked your wireless operator to add international roaming to your account. However, you will pay about $1 per minute. You'll get much lower calling rates if you have a cheap, prepaid SIM card (a removable computer memory phone chip) installed in your phone in Italy. SIM cards are available at electronic stores. The hitch is that your phone may be locked, which means you cannot install an SIM card other than the one your cellphone operator supplies.

You can rent a cellphone, but it's best to do so before you leave home, so you can give out your number and make sure the phone works. Besides, many companies abroad rent phones only for use in one country, so you might rent a phone in France that you can't use in Italy.

Rental isn't cheap. You'll pay as much as $50 a week and as much as a $1 a minute. Two wireless companies with good reputations are **InTouch USA** (✆ **800/872-7626**; www.intouchglobal.com) and **RoadPost** (✆ **888/290-1616** or **905/272-5665**; www.roadpost.com).

Internet You'll find Internet cafes and Internet points in most Italian cities and towns; some electronics shops and travel agencies provide travelers with Internet access, as do libraries and youth hostels. Ask your Internet Service Provider (ISP) how to access your e-mail account from Italy; most provide an Interface to use when you're not at your own computer. Or, you may want to open a free web-based e-mail account for your trip at www.yahoo.com or www.hotmail.com.

If you're traveling with your laptop, you'll find it handy to have a Wi-fi (wireless fidelity) connection, which gets you a high-speed connection without cable wire or a phone line. You only need to be within range of a wireless connection network, available in many cafes, hotel lobbies, and other public spaces. The alternative is to plug into a dataport (most business class hotels have these) or go online by plugging into a telephone jack and connecting to the local access number of your ISP. Check your ISP's website or call its toll-free number to learn how to use your account from Italy.

Mail Mail is slow in Italy, so you may get home before your postcards arrive. Postage to the U.S.—for postcards, aerograms, and letters up to 20 grams—is 0.75€. You can buy stamps at post offices and at most *tabacchi* (tobacco shops).

CHAPTER SEVEN

CULTURE

CINEMA

Is there a movie theater nearby?	**C'è un cinema qui vicino?** *ch-EH oon CHEE-neh-mah kwee vee-CHEE-noh*
What's playing tonight?	**Cosa danno stasera?** *KOH-zah DAHN-noh stah-SEH-rah*
Is that in English or Italian?	**È in inglese o in italiano?** *EH een een-GLEH-seh oh een ee-tah-LYAH-noh*
Are there English subtitles?	**Ci sono sottotitoli in inglese?** *chee SOH-noh soht-toh-TEE-toh-lee een een-GLEH-seh*
Is the theater air conditioned?	**La sala è climatizzata?** *lah SAH-lah EH klee-mah-teed-ZAH-tah*
How much is a ticket?	**Quanto costa un biglietto?** *KWAHN-toh KOHS-tah oon beel-LYEHT-toh*
Do you have _____	**Ci sono sconti per _____** *chee SOH-noh SKOHN-tee pehr*
senior discounts?	**anziani?** *ahn-TSYAH-nee*
student discounts?	**studenti?** *stoo-DEHN-tee*
children discounts?	**bambini?** *bahm-BEE-nee*

What time is the movie showing?	**A che ora comincia lo spettacolo?** *ah keh OH-rah koh-MEEN-chah loh speht-TAH-koh-loh*
How long is the movie?	**Quanto dura il film?** *KWAHN-toh DOO-rah eel film*
May I buy tickets in advance?	**Posso comprare i biglietti in anticipo?** *POHS-soh kohm-PRAH-reh ee beel-LYEHT-tee een ahn-TEE-chee-poh*
Is it sold out?	**È tutto esaurito?** *EH TOOT-toh eh-zow-REE-toh*
When does it begin?	**Quando inizia?** *KWAHN-doh ee-NEE-tsyah*

PERFORMANCES

Do you have ballroom dancing?	**C'è il ballo da sala?** *ch-EH eel BAHL-loh dah SAH-lah*
Are there any plays showing right now?	**Ci sono spettacoli teatrali al momento?** *chee SOH-noh speht-TAH-koh-lee tehah-TRAH-lee ahl moh-MEHN-toh*
Where can I buy tickets?	**Dove posso comprare i biglietti?** *DOH-veh POHS-soh kohm-PRAH-reh ee beel-LYEHT-tee*
Are there student discounts?	**Ci sono sconti per studenti?** *chee SOH-noh SKOHN-tee pehr stoo-DEHN-tee*
I need ____ seats.	**Mi servono ____ posti.** *mee SEHR-voh-noh ____ POHS-tee*

For a full list of numbers, see p7.

CULTURE

Listen Up: Box Office Lingo

Cosa le piacerebbe vedere? What would you like to see?
KOH-zah leh pyah-cheh-
REHB-beh veh-DEH-reh

Quanti?   How many?
KWAHN-tee

Per due adulti?   For two adults?
pehr DOO-eh ah-DOOL-tee

Vuole del popcorn?   Would you like
VWOH-leh dehl popcorn   some popcorn?

Vuole altro?   Would you like anything
VWOH-leh AHL-troh   else?

An aisle seat, please.	**Un posto sul corridoio, per favore.** *oon POHS-toh sool kohr-ree-DOH-yoh pehr fah-VOH-reh*
An orchestra seat.	**Un posto in platea.** *oon POHS-toh een plah-TEH-ah*
What time does the play start?	**A che ora inizia lo spettacolo?** *ah keh OH-rah ee-NEE-tsyah loh speht-TAH-koh-loh*
Is there an intermission?	**C'è un intervallo?** *ch-EH oon een-tehr-VAHL-loh*
Do you have an opera house?	**C'è un teatro dell'opera?** *ch-EH oon teh-AH-troh dehl-LOH-peh-rah*

Is there a local symphony?

C'è un'orchestra locale?
ch-EH oon-ohr-KEHS-trah loh-KAH-leh

May I purchase tickets over the phone?

Posso comprare i biglietti per telefono?
POHS-soh kohm-PRAH-reh ee beel-LYEHT-tee pehr teh-LEH-foh-noh

What time is the box office open?

A che ora apre il botteghino?
ah keh OH-rah AH-preh eel boht-teh-GHEE-noh

I need space for a wheelchair, please.

Ho bisogno di spazio per una sedia a rotelle, per favore.
OH bee-ZOHN-nyoh dee SPAH-tsyoh pehr OO-nah SEH-dyah ah roh-TEHL-leh pehr fah-VOH-reh

Do you have private boxes available?

Avete palchi privati disponibili?
ah-VEH-teh PAHL-kee pree-VAH-tee dees-poh-NEE-bee-lee

Is there a church that gives concerts?

C'è una chiesa che dà concerti?
ch-EH OO-nah KYEH-zah keh DAH kohn-CHEHR-tee

A program, please.

Un programma, per favore.
oon proh-GRAHM-mah pehr fah-VOH-reh

Please show us our seats.

Ci mostri i nostri posti, per favore.
chee MOHS-tree ee NOHS-tree POHS-tee pehr fah-VOH-reh

MUSEUMS, GALLERIES & SIGHTS

Do you have a museum guide?	**Ha una guida al museo?** *AH OO-nah GWEE-dah ahl moo-ZEH-oh*
Do you have guided tours?	**Ci sono visite guidate?** *chee SOH-noh VEE-zee-teh gwee-DAH-teh*
What are the museum hours?	**Quali sono gli orari del museo?** **KWAH-lee SOH-noh lyee oh-RAH-ree dehl moo-ZEH-oh**
Do I need an appointment?	**Serve un appuntamento?** *SEHR-veh oon ahp-poon-tah-MEHN-toh*
What is the admission fee?	**Quanto costa l'ingresso?** *KWAHN-toh KOHS-tah leen-GREHS-soh*
Do you have ___	**Ci sono sconti per___** *chee SOH-noh SKOHN-tee pehr*
student discounts?	**studenti?** *stoo-DEHN-tee*
senior discounts?	**anziani?** *ahn-TSYAH-nee*
children discounts?	**bambini?** *bahm-BEE-nee*
Do you have services for the hearing impaired?	**Ci sono servizi per ipoudenti?** *chee SOH-noh sehr-VEET-see pehr ee-poh-oo-DEHN-tee*
Do you have audio tours in English?	**Ci sono guide audiofoniche in inglese?** *chee SOH-noh GWEE-deh ow-dyoh-FOH-nee-keh een een-GLEH-seh*

ITALY'S BEST SMALL TOWNS

Erice (Sicily)   Isolated on the heights of Monte Erice and often lost in the clouds, this hushed medieval town of narrow cobbled streets and lofty promontories has been a favorite with visitors since ancient times.

Gubbio (Umbria)   Proud, austere, and backed by the Apennine mountains, this perfectly preserved remnant of the Middle Ages is so lost in time that it's often referred to as the "City of Silence."

Lucca (Tuscany)   The 19th-century composer Puccini would have no trouble recognizing the hometown he always held close to his music-filled heart. Renaissance walls enclose the old city, where shady squares are lined with old palaces and churches that are exuberant examples of Pisan-Romanesque architecture.

Ravello (Campania)   With steep streets and sculpted gardens clinging to a hillside high above the famed Amalfi Drive, this lush retreat affords breathtaking quiet and a welcome escape from the busy seacoast below.

ITALY'S BEST CATHEDRALS

Florence

Duomo (Cathedral of Santa Maria del Fiore), Florence   Filippo Brunelleschi's dome has dominated the Florentine skyline for centuries. Beneath it are such masterpieces as the world's largest painting of the *Last Supper* and the magnificently decorated doors of the Baptistery. Piazza del Duomo; ✆ 055-2302885; www.duomofirenze.it.

Milan

Duomo, Milan   The fourth-largest church in the world is a monument to Gothic architecture, a marvel of pinnacles and statues—with, as an added attraction, terrific views of the Alps from the roof. Piazza del Duomo; ✆ 02-86463456.

Rome
Basilica di San Pietro   Designed by Bramante, decorated by Bernini, crowned with a dome by Michelangelo, and graced with such treasures as the *Pietà*, this monument to Italian art and architecture is also the epicenter of the Roman Catholic Church. Piazza San Pietro; ✆ **06-69881662**.

Sicily
Cattedrale di Monreale, Sicily   The interior is carpeted with 311,077 sq. ft. (28,900 sq. m) of glittering 12th-century mosaics and serene cloisters, revealing a heady blend of Sicilian and Arab influences. Piazza Buono; ✆ **091-6404413**.

Venice
Basilica di San Marco, Venice   Onion-domed and covered in glittering mosaics, this creation of the Venetian Republic is one of the most exotic churches in Christendom—especially when admired from the piazza it commands, one of the most breathtaking sights you're ever going to lay eyes on. Piazza San Marco; ✆ **041-5225205**; www.basilicasanmarco.it.

ESCORTED CULTURE TOURS

Cooking
Giuliano Bugialli (✆ **646/638-0883**; www.bugialli.com), a well-known chef and cookbook author, teaches 1-week courses in his native Florence. At **Divina Cucina,** Via Taddea 31, Florence (✆ **925/939-6346**; www.divinacucina.com), American chef **Judy Witts Fancini,** also a longtime resident of Florence, provides hands-on lessons that begin with shopping in the city's Central Market.

Biking & Walking
Ciclismo Classico (www.ciclismoclassico.com) specializes in Italy, with a long list of tours in different parts of the country, from the Alps to Sicily, geared to participants at varying levels of fitness.

General Interest

Perillo Tours (© 800/431-1515; www.perillotours.com) is a well-seasoned tour operator with a proven track record, as is **Trafalgar Tours** (www.trafalgartours.com), one of Europe's largest tour companies.

Seniors

Saga Holiday Tours (www.saga.co.uk) is a long-established specialist in escorted tours for travelers 50 and older. Breaking away from the 10-day, 10-cities approach, they offer tours that focus on a single region, such as the Lake District or Southern Italy. **Elderhostel** (© 877/426-8056; www.elderhostel.org) offers study programs for travelers age 50 and older, with modest accommodations and in-depth visits to different parts of Italy—such as 2 weeks in Sorrento, exploring the Bay of Naples, and 2 weeks in Siena, with excursions to the Tuscan hill towns. **ElderTreks** (© 800/741-7956; www.eldertreks.com) offers a variety of itineraries—from sailboating and hiking around the Gulf of Trieste to making a classical music circuit of Rome, Florence, and Venice.

Specialty Travel Resources

Info Hub Specialty Travel Guide (www.infohub .com) will help you find an Italian tour to match your interests. Select from a long list of activities—say, cooking or hiking—and the site brings up tours to match. **Specialty Travel Index** (www.specialtytravel.com) and **Shaw Guides** (www.shawguides. com) are two other good resources for specialty tours.

Travelers with disabilities should contact the **Society for Accessible Travel and Hospitality** (© 212/447-7284; www.sath.org) for information on access, destinations, tour operators, and other resources.

Gay and lesbian travelers can find tour operators, travel agents, and other resources at **International Gay and Lesbian Travel Association** (IGLTA; © 800/448-8550 or **954/776-2626**; www.iglta.org).

CULTURE

WHAT TO ASK BEFORE YOU SIGN UP FOR A TOUR

- Is a deposit required? How much is it? Is it refundable?
- Can the operator cancel a trip if an insufficient number of people sign up? Do you get a full refund if they do?
- Can you cancel? How soon before departure? Do you get a full refund if you cancel?
- What's the schedule and how much time do you have on your own to relax?
- How big is the group and what are the demographics? Gender breakdown? Singles or couples?
- What are the accommodations like? What is their government rating?
- What exactly is included in the price? Meals? Transfers? Tips?
- Are there extra charges, such as admission fees and single supplements?

HOW TO AVOID THE LINES

Through booking agencies, you can reserve tickets in advance for admission to many museums for designated days and times. For museums in Venice, Milan, Florence, Rome, and Naples, check out **Goporta** (www.goporta.com). For Florence's treasure trove of museums, contact **Firenze Musei** (© **055-294-883**; www.firenzemusei.it). These services add at least 1.50€ per reservation to the ticket price, but they can spare you high-season waits of up to three hours or more to see *The Last Supper* in Milan or to get into the Uffizi and Accademia Galleries in Florence or the Vatican Museums in Rome. Do not, however, book all your museum tickets through these services, since you'll be pleasantly surprised to learn that you can get into many museums without a wait, and crowds even at such tourist magnets as the Uffizi thin out between October and March.

CHAPTER EIGHT

SHOPPING

This chapter covers the phrases you'll need to shop in a variety of settings: from the mall to the town square artisan market. We also threw in the terminology for a visit to the barber or hairdresser.

For coverage of food and grocery shopping, see Chapter Four, Dining.

GENERAL SHOPPING TERMS

Please tell me ____	**Può dirmi per favore ____** *PWOH DEER-mee pehr fah-VOH-reh*
how to get to a mall?	**come si arriva ad un centro commerciale?** *KOH-meh see ahr-REE-vah ahd oon CHEHN-troh kohm-mehr-CHAH-leh*
the best place for shopping?	**il posto migliore per fare compere?** *eel POHS-toh meel-LYOH-reh pehr FAH-reh KOHM-peh-reh*
how to get downtown?	**come si arriva in centro?** *KOH-meh see ahr-REE-vah een CHEHN-troh*

Closed for August

Cities grow hot and steamy in summer, so Italians head for the hills—or the beach. Shops begin closing on August 1st, as well as supermarkets, banks, restaurants, and tourist attractions. The exodus peaks on August 15th, Ferragosto *fehr-rah-GOHS-toh* (Assumption Day), which celebrates the Virgin Mary's ascent to heaven.

Where can I find a _____   **Dove trovo _____**
DOH-veh TROH-voh

antiques shop?   **un negozio di antichità?**
oon neh-GOH-tsyoh dee
ahn-tee-kee-TAH

bookstore?   **una libreria?**
OO-nah lee-breh-REE-ah

cigar shop?   **un tabaccaio?**
oon tah-bahk-KAH-yoh

clothing store for men /   **un negozio di abbigliamento per**
women / children?   **uomo / donna / bambini?**
oon neh-GOH-tsyoh dee
ahb-beel-lyah-MEHN-toh pehr
WOH-moh / DOHN-nah /
bahm-BEE-nee

designer fashion shop?   **una boutique di moda firmata?**
OO-nah boutique dee MOH-dah
feer-MAH-tah

jewelry store?   **una gioielleria?**
OO-nah joh-yehl-leh-REE-ah

shoe store?   **un negozio di scarpe?**
oon neh-GOH-tsyoh dee
SKAHR-peh

souvenir shop?   **un negozio di souvenir?**
oon neh-GOH-tsyoh dee
souvenir

stationery store?   **una cartoleria?**
OO-nah kahr-toh-leh-REE-ah

toy store?   **un negozio di giocattoli?**
oon neh-GOH-tsyoh dee
joh-KAHT-toh-lee

vintage clothing store?   **un negozio di abiti usati?**
oon neh-GOH-tsyoh dee
AH-bee-tee oo-ZAH-tee

Where can I find a flea market?	**Dove trovo un mercatino delle pulci?** *DOH-veh TROH-voh oon mehr-kah-TEE-noh DEHL-leh POOL-chee*

CLOTHES SHOPPING

I'd like to buy ____	**Vorrei comprare ____** *vohr-RAY kohm-PRAH-reh*
children's clothes.	**dei vestiti per bambini.** *day vehs-TEE-tee pehr bahm-BEE-nee*
men's shirts.	**delle camicie da uomo.** *DEHL-leh kah-MEE-cheh dah WOH-moh*
toys.	**dei giocattoli.** *day joh-KAHT-toh-lee*
women's shoes.	**delle scarpe da donna.** *DEHL-leh SKAHR-peh dah DOHN-nah*

For a full listing of numbers, see p7.

I'm looking for a size ____	**Cerco una taglia ____** *CHEHR-koh OO-nah TAHL-lyah*
extra-small.	**molto piccola.** *MOHL-toh PEEK-koh-lah*
small.	**piccola.** *PEEK-koh-lah*
medium.	**media.** *MEH-dyah*
large.	**grande.** *GRAHN-deh*
extra-large.	**molto grande.** *MOHL-toh GRAHN-deh*
I'm looking for ____	**Cerco ____** *CHEHR-koh*
cashmere.	**qualcosa in cashmere.** *kwahl-KOH-zah een cashmere*

gli orecchini
la collana
il vestito
l'orologio
itacci alto

la camicia
la cravatta
la giacca
la cintura
i pantaloni
le scarpe

a coat.	**una giacca.** *OO-nah JAHK-kah*
cotton pants.	**dei pantaloni di cotone.** *day pahn-tah-LOH-nee dee* *koh-TOH-neh*
a hat.	**un cappello / berretto.** *oon kahp-PEHL-loh /* *behr-REHT-toh*
a silk blouse.	**una camicia di seta.** *OO-nah kah-MEE-chah dee* *SEH-tah*
socks.	**dei calzini.** *day kahl-TSEE-nee*
sunglasses.	**degli occhiali da sole.** *DEHL-lyee OHK-kyah-lee dah* *SOH-leh*
sweaters.	**delle maglie.** *DEHL-leh MAHL-lyeh*
a swimsuit.	**un costume da bagno.** *oon kohs-TOO-meh dah* *BAHN-nyoh*

gli ochialli

la maglietta

i jeans

le scarpe da tennis

underwear.	**della biancheria intima.**
	DEHL-lah byahn-keh-REE-ah
	EEN-tee-mah
May I try it on?	**Posso provarlo?**
	POHS-soh proh-VAHR-loh
Where can I try this on?	**Dove posso provarlo?**
	DOH-veh POHS-soh proh-
	VAHR-loh
This is ____	**Questo è ____**
	KWEHS-toh EH
too tight.	**troppo stretto.**
	TROHP-poh STREHT-toh
too loose.	**troppo largo.**
	TROHP-poh LAHR-goh
too long.	**troppo lungo.**
	TROHP-poh LOON-goh
too short.	**troppo corto.**
	TROHP-poh KOHR-toh
This fits great!	**È perfetto!**
	EH pehr-FEHT-toh

SHOPPING

Thanks, I'll take it.	**Grazie, lo prendo.** *GRAH-tsyeh loh PREHN-doh*
Do you have that in ____	**Ce l'ha in ____** *cheh LAH een*
a smaller / larger size?	**una taglia più piccola / grande?** *OO-nah TAHL-lya PYOO* *PEEK-koh-lah / GRAHN-deh*
a different color?	**un altro colore?** *oon AHL-troh koh-LOH-reh*
How much is it?	**Quanto costa?** *KWAHN-toh KOHS-tah*

ARTISAN MARKET SHOPPING

Is there a craft / artisan market?	**C'è un mercato di artigianato?** *ch-EH oon mehr-KAH-toh dee* *ahr-tee-jah-NAH-toh*
That's beautiful. May I look at it?	**Che bello. Posso vederlo?** *keh BEHL-loh POHS-soh* *veh-DEHR-loh*
When is the farmers' market open?	**Quando apre il mercato di frutta e verdura?** *KWAHN-doh AH-preh eel* *mehr-KAH-toh deeFROOT-tah eh* *vehr-DOO-rah*

For full coverage of time, see p12.

Is that open every day of the week?	**È aperto tutti i giorni della settimana?** *EH ah-PEHR-toh TOOT-tee ee* *JOHR-nee DEHL-lah* *seht-tee-MAH-nah*

For full coverage of days of the week, see p14.

How much does that cost?	**Quanto costa?** *KWAHN-toh KOHS-tah*
That's too expensive.	**È troppo caro.** *EH TROHP-poh KAH-roh*

Venditori di falsi (fake designer goods)

Beware unscrupulous vendors who attempt to sell you illegal, contraband, or fake goods. Recent laws penalize buyers as well as sellers.

How much for two?	**Quanto per due?** *KWAHN-toh pehr DOO-eh*
Do I get a discount if I buy two or more?	**Mi fa lo sconto se ne compro due o più?** *mee fah loh SKOHN-toh seh neh KOHM-proh DOO-eh oh PYOO*
Do I get a discount if I pay in cash?	**Mi fa lo sconto se pago in contanti?** *mee fah loh SKOHN-toh seh PAH-goh een kohn-TAHN-tee*
No thanks. Maybe I'll come back.	**No grazie. Magari torno.** *noh GRAH-tsyeh mah-GAH-ree TOHR-noh*
Would you take € ____?	**Vanno bene ___ euro?** *VAHN-noh BEH-neh ___ EH-oo-roh*

For a full list of numbers, see p7.

That's a deal!	**Affare fatto!** *ahf-FAH-reh FAHT-toh*
Do you have a less expensive one?	**Ne ha uno meno caro?** *neh AH OO-noh MEH-no KAH-roh*
Is there tax?	**C'è l'IVA?** *ch-EH LEE-vah*
May I have the VAT forms? (Europe only)	**Posso avere un modulo per il rimborso dell'IVA?** *POHS-soh ah-VEH-reh oon MOH-doo-loh pehr eel reem-BOHR-soh dehl-LEE-vah*

BOOKSTORE / NEWSSTAND SHOPPING

Is there a ___ nearby?	**C'è ___ qui vicino?**
	ch-EH ___ kwee vee-CHEE-noh
bookstore	**una libreria**
	OO-nah lee-breh-REE-ah
newsstand	**un'edicola**
	oon-eh-DEE-koh-lah
Do you have ___ in English?	**Avete ___ in inglese?**
	ah-VEH-teh ___ een een-GLEH-seh
books	**libri**
	LEE-bree
books about local history	**libri di storia locale**
	LEE-bree dee STOH-ryah loh-KAH-leh
magazines	**riviste**
	ree-VEES-teh
maps	**cartine**
	kahr-TEE-neh
newspapers	**giornali**
	johr-NAH-lee
picture books	**libri illustrati**
	LEE-bree eel-loos-TRAH-tee
travel guides	**guide turistiche**
	GWEE-deh too-REES-tee-keh

SHOPPING FOR ELECTRONICS

With some exceptions, shopping for electronic goods in Italy is generally not recommended. The PAL encoding system for DVDs and VHS is different from NTSC and would not work in the United States or Canada.

Can I play this in the U.S.?	**Funziona questo negli Stati Uniti?** *foon-TSYOH-nah KWEHS-toh NEHL-lyee STAH-tee oo-NEE-tee*
Will this game work on my game console in the U.S.?	**Questo gioco funziona su una console americana?** *KWEHS-toh JOH-koh foon-TSYOH-nah soo OO-nah kohn-SOHL ah-meh-ree-KAH-nah*
Do you have this in a U.S. market format?	**C'è questo in formato americano?** *ch-EH KWEHS-toh een fohr-MAH-toh ah-meh-ree-KAH-noh*
Can you convert this to a U.S. market format?	**Si può convertire questo in formato americano?** *see PWOH kohn-vehr-TEE-reh KWEHS-toh een fohr-MAH-toh ah-meh-ree-KAH-noh*
Will this work with a 110V AC adaptor?	**Questo funziona con un adattatore da 110 volts?** *KWEHS-toh foon-TSYOH-nah kohn oon ah-daht-tah-TOH-reh dah CHEHN-toh-DYEH-chee volts*
Do you have an adaptor plug for 110 to 220 volts?	**Avete un adattatore da 110 a 220 volts?** *Ah-VEH-teh oon ah-daht-tah-TOH-reh dah CHEHN-toh-DYEH-chee ah doo-eh-CHEHN-toh-VEHN-tee volts*

Do you sell electronic adaptors here?	**Vendete adattatori per sistemi elettronici?**
	vehn-DEH-teh ah-daht-tah-TOH-ree pehr sees-TEH-mee eh-leht-TROH-nee-chee
Is it safe to use my laptop with this adaptor?	**Posso usare il computer portatile con questo adattatore?**
	POHS-soh oo-ZAH-reh eel com puter pohr-TAH-tee-leh kohn KWEHS-toh ah-daht-tah-TOH-reh
If it doesn't work, may I return it?	**Se non funziona, posso portarlo indietro?**
	seh nohn foon-TSYOH-nah POHS-soh pohr-TAHR-loh een-DYEH-troh
May I try it here in the store?	**Posso provarlo qui in negozio?**
	POHS-soh proh-VAHR-loh kwee een neh-GOH-tsyoh

AT THE BARBER / HAIRDRESSER

Do you have a style guide?	**Ha un catalogo dei vari stili?**
	AH oon kah-TAH-loh-goh day VAH-ree STEE-lee
A trim, please.	**Una spuntatina, per favore.**
	OO-nah spoon-tah-TEE-nah pehr fah-VOH-reh
I'd like it bleached.	**Vorrei ossigenarli.**
	vohr-RAY ohs-see-jeh-NAHR-lee
Would you change the color _____	**Mi fa il colore _____**
	mee fah eel koh-LOH-reh
darker?	**più scuro?**
	PYOO SKOO-roh
lighter?	**più chiaro?**
	PYOO KYAH-roh

For a full list of personal descriptors, see p133.
For a full list of colors, see English / Italian dictionary.

Would you just touch it up a little? | **Me li sistema un po'?**
meh lee see-STEH-mah oon POH

I'd like it curled. | **Li vorrei arricciati.**
lee vohr-RAY ahr-reet-CHAH-tee

Do I need an appointment? | **Ci vuole un appuntamento?**
chee VWOH-leh oon ahp-poon-tah-MEHN-toh

May I make an appointment? | **Posso prendere un appuntamento?**
POHS-soh PREHN-deh-reh oon ahp-poon-tah-MEHN-toh

Wash, dry, and set. | **Lavaggio, asciugatura, e messa in piega.**
lah-VAHD-joh ah-shoo-gah-TOO-rah eh MEHS-sah een PYEH-gah

Do you do permanents? | **Fate permanenti?**
FAH-teh pehr-mah-NEHN-tee

Please use low heat. | **Lo usi tiepido, per favore.**
loh OO-zee TYEH-pee-doh pehr fah-VOH-reh

Please don't blow dry it. | **Non li asciughi col phon, per favore.**
nohn lee ah-SHOOG-ee kohl fohn pehr fah-VOH-reh

Please dry it curly / straight. | **Li asciughi arricciandoli / stirandoli, per favore.**
lee ah-SHOO-gy ahr-reet-CHAHN-doh-lee / stee-RAHN-doh-lee pehr fah-VOH-reh

Would you fix my braids? | **Mi fa le trecce?**
mee fah leh TREHT-cheh

Would you fix my highlights? | **Mi fa i colpi di sole?**
mee fah ee KOHL-pee dee SOH-leh

Do you wax? | **Fate la ceretta?**
FAH-teh lah cheh-REHT-tah

Please wax my ___	**Mi faccia la ceretta ___ per favore.** *mee FAHT-chah lah cheh-REHT-tah ___ pehr fah-VOH-reh*
legs.	**alle gambe** *AHL-leh GAHM-beh*
bikini line.	**alla zona bikini** *AHL-lah DZOH-nah bikini*
eyebrows.	**alle sopracciglia** *AHL-leh soh-praht-CHEEL-lyah*
under my nose.	**sotto il naso** *SOHT-toh eel NAH-zoh*
Please trim my beard.	**Mi spunti la barba, per favore.** *mee SPOON-tee lah BAHR-bah pehr fah-VOH-reh*
A shave, please.	**Mi faccia la barba, per favore.** *mee FAHT-chah lah BAHR-bah pehr fah-VOH-reh*
Use a fresh blade, please.	**Usi una lametta nuova, per favore.** *OO-zee OO-nah lah-MEHT-tah NWOH-vah pehr fah-VOH-reh*
Sure, cut it all off.	**Certo, la tagli tutta.** *CHEHR-toh lah TAHL-lyee TOOT-tah*

BEST MARKETS

Most Italian towns host an outdoor market—usually held weekly or twice weekly in smaller towns, and daily in larger towns and cities. Most markets sell a good selection of food, including fresh produce and regional cheeses, and an unexciting range of cheaply made clothing, kitchen utensils, and other run-of-the-mill household items. For genuine crafts, antiques, and other finds, you'll need to stumble into the larger markets or a *Mercantino dell'Antiquariato* (Antiques Fair), which many towns host periodically. Here are some especially well-stocked and lively markets well worth seeking out in your travels.

Florence

Mercato San Lorenzo   One of Europe's largest markets stretches for blocks. Artful shoppers may turn up decent deals on leather goods and crafts items. Florence's bustling 19th-century cast-iron-and-glass Mercato Centrale, the main food market, rises above the stalls. *Around the church of San Lorenzo. Mon–Fri 7am–2pm, also Sat 4–8pm, June–Sept.*

Milan

Via Papiniano   Milanese in the know scour the stalls of the fashion capital's largest street market for designer seconds, last-year's styles, and decent imitations. Ticinese/Navigli district, near Sant'Agostino metro. *Tues 8am–1pm, Sat 9am–7:30pm.*

Rome

Porta Portese   Italy's best-stocked bazaar is a giant garage sale, where some shrewd wheeling and dealing could land anything from a used high-fashion suit to an antique candlestick. *Piazza Ippolito. Sun 7am–2pm.*

Campo de'Fiore   One of Rome's loveliest squares is the backdrop for a colorful swirl of stalls selling flowers, fruit, and vegetables. *Mon–Sat 10am–2pm.*

Venice

Rialto Market   The mainstays are glow-in-the-dark gondolas and tacky T-shirts. For a real show, follow your nose through the throngs to the Pescheria, the city's centuries-old fish market. *On the Grand Canal, near the west end of Rialto Bridge. Tues–Sun.*

BEST BUYS

Antiques

Where to Buy It   Almost all Italian cities are graced with venerable shops selling antique furniture, glass, jewelry, and ornaments, but bargains are hard to find. **Via Coronari** in **Rome** is especially good turf for antiques browsing. You'll also find a good selection of interesting pieces, sometimes at moderate prices, at a *Mercatino dell'Antiquariato* (Antiques Fair); cities around the country host these exhibitions seasonally. Italy's largest antiques fair sprawls across the **Piazza Duomo** in **Arezzo,** in Tuscany, the first weekend of every month. In **Venice,** more than a hundred vendors gather in **Campo San Maurizio** three times a year (at varying dates, usually early Apr, mid-Sept, and just before Christmas) to sell Murano glass, antique lace, old advertising posters, and larger pieces. **Florence** hosts a biannual **International Antiques Show** (for 2 weeks in Sept in odd-numbered years) at the Palazzo Strozzi.

Ceramics

Where to Buy It   Almost every Italian region produces distinctive ceramics. The pottery in **Faenza,** Emilia-Romagna specializes in *majolica* (also known, after the town, as faience)— a type of hand-painted, glazed, and heavily ornamented earthenware. Ceramics is a 500-year-old industry in **Vietri sul Mare,** Campagna, at the south end of the Amalfi Drive. A cluster of shops sells especially attractive glazed plates and bowls. **Deruta,** Umbria, is another town famed for its *majolica*, decorated in traditional and contemporary designs.

Fashion

Where to Buy It   Italian designers have been giving the French fashion monopoly a run for its money since the end of World War II. In **Milan,** the so-called Golden Triangle—four adjoining streets north of the Duomo: Via Montenapoleone, Via Spiga, Via Borgospesso, and Via Sant'Andrea. In **Florence,** on Via dei Tornabuoni and Via della Vigna Nuova. In **Rome,** around the Spanish steps, especially on the Via dei Condotti.

Gold

Where to Buy It   Italians have been goldsmiths since the Etruscan days 28 centuries ago, and the tradition is going strong.

The shop-lined Ponte Vecchio in **Florence** is the first stop for buyers seriously considering an investment in beautiful 18-karat gold jewelry.

Lace

Where to Buy It   Italy has long been known for its exquisite and delicate lace, often made by cloistered nuns. There are fewer such devotees of the craft around these days, but lacemakers still turn out intricate collars, handkerchiefs, doilies, and other wares. **Burano,** in the Venetian Lagoon, has been famous for its lace for centuries. These days the island often slips cheap imports into its shop windows; look for a lacemaker at work and buy from her.

Leather

Where to Buy It   Italian tanneries have been turning out some of the finest leather goods in the world since the Middle Ages. Careful shoppers will find a good selection of purses, wallets, boots, sandals, and other goods at moderate to high-but-worth-it prices in just about any Italian town or city. But **Florence** still holds the title for best leather shopping. A good place to start is the Leather School in the Church of Santa Croce, Piazza Santa Croce. If you don't mind wading through piles of mediocre merchandise, you may be able to find some decent leather goods in the Mercato San Lorenzo.

Religious Objects & Vestments

Where to Buy It   The religious objects industry in Italy—from cardinals' birettas and rosaries to religious art and vestments—is big and bustling. The biggest concentration of shops is in **Rome,** near the Vatican, around the Church of Santa Maria Sopra Minerva.

Venetian Glass

Where to Buy It   Tacky products have given Venice's centuries-old craft a bad name, but master craftspeople still have the touch and wield a mean torch. In **Murano,** gawdiness abounds, but several venerable workshops flourish on the Fondamenta dei Vetrai, Fondamenta Cavour, and surrounding streets and alleys.

UNDERSTANDING THE VAT

For most purchases you make in Italy, a value-added tax (VAT) of 17.36 % will be built into the price. Non-E.U. citizens are entitled to a refund of this tax if they spend more than 155€ ($186) at any one store. To claim a refund, present the invoice to the Customs office (*dogana*) at the airport and have it stamped. (Make sure not to pack the goods in your luggage, because you may need to show them.) You can then go to a tax-free booth and get your refund, minus a commission. For more information, check out www.globalrefund.com.

Another option is to keep the stamped form until you're back home, then mail it back to the store within 90 days of purchase, and the store will send you a refund check. Many shops are now part of the Tax Free for Tourists Network (look for a sticker in the window) and will issue you a check at the time of purchase.

CHAPTER NINE
SPORTS & FITNESS

STAYING FIT

Is there a gym nearby?
C'è una palestra qui vicino?
*ch-EH OO-nah pah-LEHS-trah
kwee vee-CHEE-noh*

Do you have free
weights?
Avete pesi liberi?
ah-VEH-teh PEH-zee LEE-beh-ree

I'd like to go for a swim.
Vorrei andare a nuotare.
*vohr-RAY ahn-DAH-reh ah
nwoh-TAH-reh*

Do I have to be a
member?
Devo essere socio?
DEH-voh EHS-seh-reh SOH-choh

May I come here for
one day?
Posso venire qui per un giorno?
*POHS-soh veh-NEE-reh kwee
pehr oon JOHR-noh*

How much does a
membership cost?
Quanto costa associarsi?
*KWAHN-toh KOHS-tah
ahs-soh-CHAHR-see*

I need to get a locker,
please.
**Mi serve un armadietto, per
favore.**
*mee SEHR-veh oon ahr-mah-
DYEHT-toh pehr fah-VOH-reh*

193

Do you have locks?	**Avete dei lucchetti?**
	Ah-VEH-teh day look-KEHT-tee
Do you have ____	**Avete ____**
	ah-VEH-teh
a treadmill?	**il treadmill?**
	eel treadmill
a stationary bike?	**la cyclette?**
	lah see-KLEHT
handball / squash courts?	**campi da pallamano / squash?**
	KAHM-pee dah PAHL-lah-MAH-noh / squash
Are they indoors?	**Sono campi interni?**
	SOH-noh KAHM-pee een-TEHR-nee
I'd like to play tennis.	**Vorrei giocare a tennis.**
	vohr-RAY joh-KAH-reh ah tennis
Would you like to play?	**Vuole giocare?**
	VWOH-leh joh-KAH-reh
I'd like to rent a racquet.	**Vorrei noleggiare una racchetta.**
	vohr-RAY noh-lehd-JAH-reh OO-nah rahk-KEHT-tah
I need to buy some ____	**Devo comprare ____**
	DEH-voh kohm-PRAH-reh
new balls.	**delle palle nuove.**
	DEHL-leh PAHL-leh NWOH-veh
safety glasses.	**degli occhiali di sicurezza.**
	DEHL-lyee ohk-KYAH-lee dee see-koo-REHT-sah
May I reserve a court for tomorrow?	**Posso prenotare un campo per domani?**
	POHS-soh preh-noh-TAH-reh oon KAHM-poh pehr doh-MAH-nee
May I have clean towels?	**Posso avere asciugamani puliti?**
	POHS-soh ah-VEH-reh ah-shoo-gah-MAH-nee poo-LEE-teh

Where are the showers / locker-rooms?	**Dove sono le docce / gli spogliatoi?** *DOH-veh SOH-noh leh DOHT-cheh / lyee spohl-lyah-TOY*
Do you have a workout room for women only?	**Avete un locale per l'allenamento riservato alle donne?** *ah-VEH-teh oon loh-KAH-leh pehr lahl-leh-nah-MEHN-toh ree-sehr-VAH-toh AHL-leh DOHN-neh*
Do you have aerobics classes?	**Avete corsi di aerobica?** *Ah-VEH-teh KOHR-see dee ah-eh-ROH-bee-kah*
Do you have a women's pool?	**Avete una piscina per donne?** *Ah-VEH-teh OO-nah pee-SHEE-nah pehr DOHN-neh*
Let's go for a jog.	**Andiamo a fare jogging.** *anh-DYAH-moh ah FAH-reh jogging*
That was a great workout!	**Che bell'allenamento!** *keh BEHL-lahl-leh-nah-MEHN-toh*

CATCHING A GAME

Where is the stadium?	**Dov'è lo stadio?** *doh-VEH loh STAH-dyoh*
Who is the best goalie?	**Qual è il portiere più bravo?** *kwah-LEH eel pohr-TYEH-reh PYOO BRAH-voh*

Are there any women's teams?

Ci sono squadre femminili?
chee SOH-noh SKWAH-dreh fehm-mee-NEE-lee

Do you have any amateur / professional teams?

Ci sono squadre dilettanti / professioniste?
chee SOH-noh SKWAH-dreh dee-leht-TAHN-tee / proh-fehs-syoh-NEES-teh

Is there a game I could play in?

C'è una partita in cui posso partecipare?
ch-EH OO-nah paar-TEE-tah een KOO-ee POHS-soh pahr-teh-chee-PAH-reh

Which is the best team?

Qual è la squadra migliore?
kwah-LEH lah SKWAH-drah meel-LYOH-reh

Will the game be on television?

Sarà in TV questa partita?
sah-RAH een tee-VOO KWEHS-tah paar-TEE-tah

Where can I buy tickets?

Dove si comprano i biglietti?
DOH-veh see KOHM-prah-noh ee beel-LYEHT-tee

The best seats, please.

I posti migliori, per favore.
ee POHS-tee meel-LYOH-ree pehr fah-VOH-reh

The cheapest seats, please.

I posti più economici, per favore.
ee POHS-tee PYOO eh-koh-NOH-mee-chee pehr fah-VOH-reh

How close are these seats?

Quanto distano questi posti?
KWAHN-toh DEES-tah-noh KWEHS-tee POHS-tee

May I have box seats?

Posso avere dei posti sul palco?
POHS-soh ah-VEH-reh day POHS-tee sool PAHL-koh

Wow! What a game!	**Wow! Che partita!**
	wow keh paar-TEE-tah
Go! Go! Go!	**Vai, vai, vai! / Dai, dai, dai!**
	VAH-ee / DAH-ee
Oh, no!	**Oh, no!**
	oh no
Give it to them!	**Schiacciateli!**
	skyaht-CHAH-teh-lee
Go for it!	**Forza! Vai!**
	FOHR-tsah VAH-ee
Score!	**Gol!**
	gol
What's the score?	**Qual è il punteggio?**
	kwah-LEH eel poon-TEHD-joh
Who's winning?	**Chi sta vincendo?**
	kee stah veen-CHEHN-doh

HIKING

Where can I find a guide to hiking trails?	**Dove trovo una guida ai sentieri per escursioni a piedi?**
	DOH-veh TROH-voh OO-nah GWEE-dah eye sehn-TYEH-ree pehr ehs-koor-SYOH-nee ah PYEH-dee
Do we need to hire a guide?	**Dobbiamo noleggiare una guida?**
	dohb-BYAH-moh noh-lehd-JAH-reh OO-nah GWEE-dah
Where can I rent equipment?	**Dove si possono noleggiare attrezzature?**
	DOH-veh see POHS-soh-noh noh-lehd-JAH-reh aht-treht-tsah-TOO-reh
Do they have rock climbing there?	**Si possono fare arrampicate qui?**
	see POHS-soh-noh FAH-reh ahr-rahm-pee-KAH-teh kwee

We need more ropes and carabiners.	**Ci servono altre corde e moschettoni.** *chee SEHR-voh-noh AHL-treh KOHR-deh eh mohs-keht-TOH-nee*
Where can we go mountain climbing?	**Dove si può andare a fare scalate?** *DOH-veh see PWOH ahn-DAH-reh ah FAH-reh skah-LAH-teh*
Are the routes ____	**I sentieri sono ____** *ee sehn-TYEH-ree SOH-noh*
well marked?	**ben marcati?** *behn mahr-KAH-tee*
in good condition?	**in buone condizioni?** *een BWOH-neh kohn-dee-TSYOH-nee*
What is the altitude there?	**Che l'altitudine c'è là?** *keh ahl-tee-TOO-dee-neh ch-EHLAH*
How long will it take?	**Quanto tempo ci vorrà?** *KWAHN-toh TEHM-poh chee vohr-RAH*
Is it very difficult?	**È molto difficile?** *EH MOHL-toh deef-FEE-chee-leh*
Is there a fixed-protection climbing path?	**C'è una via ferrata?** *CHEH OO-nah VEE-ah fehr-RAH-tah*

I want to hire someone to carry my excess gear.	**Vorrei noleggiare un aiuto che mi porti l'attrezzatura extra.**
	VOHR-ray noh-lehd-JAH-reh oon ah-YOO-toh keh mee POHR-tee laht-treht-tsah-TOO-rah extra
We don't have time for a long route.	**Non c'è tempo per un percorso lungo.**
	nohn ch-EH TEHM-poh pehr- oon pehr-KOHR-soh LOON-goh
I don't think it's safe to proceed.	**Non mi pare sicuro avanzare.**
	nohn mee PAH-reh see-KOO-roh ah-vahn-TSAH-reh
Do we have a backup plan?	**Abbiamo un piano alternativo?**
	ahb-BYAH-moh oon PYAH-noh ahl-tehr-nah-TEE-voh
If we're not back by tomorrow, send a search party.	**Se non torniamo entro domani, mandate una squadra di ricerca.**
	seh nohn tohr-NYAH-moh EHN-troh doh-MAH-nee mahn-DAH-teh OO-nah SKWAH-drah dee ree-CHEHR-kah
Are the campsites marked?	**I siti del campeggio sono marcati?**
	ee SEE-tee dehl kahm-PEHD-joh SOH-noh mahr-KAH-tee
Can we camp off the trail?	**Possiamo campeggiare fuori del sentiero?**
	pohs-SYAH-moh kahm-pehd-JAH-reh FWOH-ree dehl sehn-TYEH-roh
Is it okay to build fires here?	**Si possono fare fuochi qui?**
	see POHS-soh-noh FAH-reh FWOH-kee kwee
Do we need permits?	**Ci servono permessi?**
	chee SEHR-voh-noh pehr-MEHS-see

For more camping terms, see p87.

BOATING OR FISHING

When do we sail?
Quando salpiamo?
KWAHN-doh sahl-PYAH-moh

Where are the life preservers?
Dove sono i salvagenti?
DOH-veh SOH-noh ee sahl-vah-JEHN-tee

Can I purchase bait?
Posso acquistare esche?
POHS-soh ah-kwees-TAH-reh EHS-keh

Can I rent a pole?
Posso noleggiare una canna da pesca?
POHS-soh noh-lehd-JAH-reh OO-nah KAHN-nah dah PEHS-kah

How long is the voyage?
Quanto dura l'escursione?
KWAHN-toh DOO-rah lehs-koor-SYOH-neh

Are we going up river or down?
Andiamo a monte o a valle del fiume?
ahn-DYAH-moh ah MOHN-teh oh ah VAHL-leh dehl FYOO-meh

How far out are we going?
Quanto al largo andiamo?
KWAHN-toh ahl LAHR-goh ahn-DYAH-moh

How deep is the water here?
Quanto è profonda l'acqua qui?
KWAHN-toh EH proh-FOHN-dah LAHK-wah kwee

I got one!
L'ho preso!
LOH PREH-zoh

I can't swim.
Non so nuotare.
nohn soh nwo-TAH-reh

Can we go ashore? | **Possiamo sbarcare?**
pohs-SYAH-moh zbahr-KAH-reh

DIVING

I'd like to go snorkeling. | **Vorrei fare snorkeling.**
vohr-RAY FAH-reh snorkeling

I'd like to go scuba diving. | **Vorrei andare in immersione.**
vohr-RAY ahn-DAH-reh een eem-mehr-SYOH-neh

I have a NAUI / PADI certification. | **Ho il certificato NAUI / PADI.**
OH eel chehr-tee-fee-KAH-toh NAUI / PADI

I need to rent gear. | **Devo noleggiare dell'attrezzatura.**
DEH-voh noh-lehd-JAH-reh DEHL-laht-treht-tsah-TOO-rah

We'd like to see some shipwrecks, if we can. | **Vorremmo vedere dei relitti di navi se possibile.**
vohr-REHM-moh veh-DEH-reh day reh-LEET-tee dee NAH-vee seh pohs-SEE-bee-leh

Are there any good reef dives? | **Si possono fare belle immersioni lungo la scogliera?**
see POHS-soh-noh FAH-reh BEHL-leh eem-mehr-SYOH-nee LOON-goh lah skohl-LYEH-rah

I'd like to see a lot of sea-life. | **Vorrei vedere tanta fauna marina.**
vohr-RAY veh-DEH-reh TAHN-tah FOW-nah mah-REE-nah

Are the currents strong? | **Sono forti le correnti?**
SOH-noh FOHR-tee leh kohr-REHN-tee

How clear is the water? | **È limpida l'acqua?**
EH LEEM-pee-dah LAHK-wah

I want / don't want to go with a group. | **Voglio / Non voglio andare in gruppo.**
VOHL-lyoh / nohn VOHL-lyoh ahn-DAH-reh een GROOP-poh

Can we charter our own boat?	**Possiamo noleggiare la barca per uso privato?** *pohs-SYAH-moh noh-lehd-JAH-reh lah BAHR-kah pehr OO-zoh pree-VAH-toh*

AT THE BEACH

I'd like to rent a _____ for a day / half a day.	**Vorrei noleggiare ___ per un giorno / mezza giornata.** *vohr-RAY noh-led-JAH-reh ___ pehr oon JOHR-noh / MED-zah johr-NAH-tah*
a chair	**una sedia a sdraio** *OO-nah SEH-dyah ah ZDRAH-yoh*
an umbrella	**un ombrellone** *oon ohm-brehl-LOH-neh*
Is there space ___	**C'è posto ___** *CHEH POHS-toh*
closer to the water?	**più vicino all'acqua?** *PYOO vee-CHEE-noh ahl-LAHK-wah*
away from the disco music?	**lontano dalla musica?** *lohn-TAH-noh DAHL-lah MOO-zee-kah*

Equipped Beaches

Equipped beaches are more common than free ones, and they may charge an admission fee, plus additional fees for chair and umbrella rental.

Do you have ___	**Avete ___** *ah-VEH-teh*
a bar?	**un bar?** *oon bar*
a restaurant?	**un ristorante?** *oon rees-toh-RAHN-teh*
games?	**dei giochi?** *day JOH-kee*
a lifeguard?	**un bagnino?** *oon bahn-NYEE-noh*
a kid's club?	**animazioni per bambini?** *ah-nee-mah-TSYOH-nee pehr bahm-BEE-nee*
pedal boats for rent / hire?	**pedalò a noleggio?** *peh-dah-LOH ah noh-LED-joh*
Is there a free beach nearby?	**C'è una spiaggia libera qui vicino?** *ch-EH OO-nah SPYAD-jah LEE-beh-rah kwee vee-CHEE-noh*
How are the currents?	**Come sono le correnti?** *KOH-meh SOH-noh leh kohr-REHN-tee*
I'd like to go windsurfing.	**Vorrei fare del windsurf.** *vohr-RAY FAH-reh dehl windsurf*
Can I rent equipment?	**Posso noleggiare dell'attrezzatura?** *POHS-soh noh-lehd-JAH-reh DEHL-laht-treht-sah-TOO-rah*

GOLFING

I'd like to reserve a tee-time.

Vorrei prenotare un tee time.
vohr-RAY preh-noh-TAH-reh oon tee time

Do we need to be members to play?

Dobbiamo essere soci per giocare?
dohb-BYAH-moh EHS-seh-reh SOH-chee pehr joh-KAH-reh

How many holes is your course?

Quante buche ha il vostro campo da golf?
KWAHN-teh BOO-keh AH eel VOHS-troh KAHM-poh dah golf

What is par for the course?

Qual è la norma per il campo?
kwah-LEH lah NOHR-mah pehr eel KAHM-poh

I need to rent clubs.

Devo noleggiare delle mazze.
DEH-voh noh-lehd-JAH-reh DEHL-leh MAHT-seh

I need to purchase a sleeve of balls.

Devo acquistare una confezione di palline.
DEH-voh ah-kwees-TAH-reh OO-nah kohn-feh-TSYOH-neh dee pahl-LEE-neh

Do you require soft spikes?

Ci vogliono i soft spikes?
chee VOHL-lyoh-noh ee soft spikes

Do you have carts?

Avete i golf carts?
ah-VEH-teh ee golf carts

I'd like to hire a caddy.

Vorrei noleggiare un caddy.
vohr-RAY noh-lehd-JAH-reh oon caddy

Do you have a driving range?

Avete un driving range?
ah-VEH-teh oon driving range

How much are the greens fees?

Quanto sono le green fees?
KWAHN-toh SOH-noh leh green fees

Can I book a lesson with the pro?

Posso prenotare una lezione col professionista?
POHS-soh preh-noh-TAH-reh OO-nah leh-TSYOH-neh kohl proh-fehs-syoh-NEES-tah

I need to have a club repaired.

Devo far riparare una mazza.
DEH-voh fahr ree-pah-RAH-reh OO-nah MAHT-sah

Is the course dry?

È asciutto il campo?
EH ah-SHOOT-toh eel KAHM-poh

Are there any wildlife hazards?

Ci sono pericoli da animali selvatici?
chee SOH-noh peh-REE-koh-lee dah ah-nee-MAH-lee sehl-VAH-tee-chee

How many meters is the course?

Quanti metri misura il campo?
KWAHN-tee MEH-tree mee-ZOO-rah eel KAHM-poh

THE BEST ACTIVE SPORTS

Cycling Urban cyclists will enjoy **Ferrara,** a delightful Renaissance city of rose-colored brick in the Emilia-Romagna region, where the bicycle is the preferred mode of transport. The palace-lined streets are thick with bikers of all ages, as is the path that circumnavigates the city's massive medieval walls, wide enough to be topped by trees and lawns. Most hotels in town lend guests bikes, which are also available for rent at several outlets, including one just outside the train station (© 0532-772-190).

Hiking In 520,000-hectare (1.3-million-acre) **Parco Nazionale della Stelvio,** outside Merano (in the South Tyrol), a network of trails crisscrosses almost virgin wilderness where elk and chamois roam the mountainsides. Nearby **Parco Nazionale di Tessa** is a pleasant terrain of meadows and gentle, forest-clad slopes; and a relatively easy path, the southern route of the Meraner Hohenweg, allows even the most inexperienced hikers to cross the park effortlessly. The path is conveniently interspersed with restaurants and farmhouses offering rooms. The tourist office in Merano, Freiheistrasse 35 (© 0473-235-223; www.meraninfo.it), dispenses maps and lists of hiking trails, *rifugi*, and other accommodations for hikers.

The **Cinque Terre** has some of Italy's most popular hiking terrain. Trails plunge through vineyards and groves of olive and lemon trees, and hug seaside cliffs—affording heart-stopping views of the coast and connecting the five romantic villages from which the region takes its name. Depending on your pace and how long you stop in each village for a fortifying glass of *sciacchetrà*, the local sweet wine, you can make the trip between Monterosso, at the northern end of the Cinque Terre, and Riomaggiore, at the southern end, in about 5 hours. Since all the villages are linked by rail, you can hike as many portions of the itinerary as you wish and take the train to your next destination. Trails also cut through the forested, hilly terrain inland from the coast, much of which is protected as a nature preserve. The tourist office in **Monterosso,** on Via Fegina 8 (© **0187-817506**), provides maps and details; also visit www.cinqueterrenet.com.

Parco Nazionale di Gran Paradiso, in the Valle d'Aosta, encompasses 1,400 sq. miles (3,626 sq. km) of forests, pasturelands, and alpine meadows laced with hiking trails. The tourist office in the village of Cogne, at the edge of the park, at Piazza Chanoux 34-36 (© **0165-74040**; www.cogne.org), supplies maps and information. Also visit www.pngp.it.

Skiing   Cortina d'Ampezzo, Italy's leading ski resort, in the Dolomites, lives up to its reputation with eight exceptional ski areas. Two of the best, **Tofana-Promedes** and **Faloria-Tondi,** are accessible by funiculars that lift off from the edges of town. You can enjoy these facilities economically with one of the comprehensive **Dolomiti Superski passes,** which provide unlimited skiing (including all chairlift and funicular fees, as well as free shuttle bus service to and from Cortina and the ski areas) at Cortina's ski areas and those at outlying resorts. For more information, contact the tourist office, Palazzo San Francesco 8 (© **0436/3231**), or Dolomiti Superski, Via d. Castello 33 (© **0436-862-171** or **0471-795-397**; www.dolomitisuperski. com).

Monte Plose, outside Bressanone, is not as glamorous as Cortina, but the skiing is excellent and much less expensive. The tourist board in Bressanone, Via Stazione 9 (© **047-836401**; www.brixen.org), supplies maps and information on skiing and lodging in this mountain wilderness.

The best downhill runs in the Valle d'Aosta are those at **Breuvil-Cervinia,** on the flanks of the Matterhorn (Monte Cervino in Italian), and Courmayeur; for information, contact the tourist board in Breuvil-Cervinia, Via Guido Rey 17 (© **0166-949-136**; www.montecervino.it). Nearby Cogne is surrounded by more than 30 miles (48km) of cross country trails; for maps and information, contact the tourist office, Piazza Chanoux 34-36 (© **0165-74040**; www.cogne.org).

BEST BEACHES

Much of Italy's coast is rocky, but most of the beaches are jam-packed in summer. Aside from a suit and towel, bring euros, because many beaches are lined with bathing establishments that charge about 10€ for admission; the fee usually includes use of the facilities, a lounge chair, and an umbrella.

For the past 2,000 years, the best beach on the flashy resort island of Capri has been the **Bagni di Tiberio,** about a 20-minute walk west of Marina Grande; a crumbling wall of a Roman bathing establishment reminds you that the Emperor Tiberius allegedly liked to dip his toes into the water here, too. **Punta Carena,** outside Annacapri, is a lovely cove, with swimming off a pebbly beach. The rocky strands at **Punta Tragara,** below Capri town, take the prize for best scenery—they are framed by the famous *faraglioni,* rocks rising out of the sea.

The only sandy beach at Cinque Terre, Liguria, is the crowded strand in Monterosso, which you'll pay to use. Hike on: You'll find long, pebbly, and isolated strands just to the north and to the south of Corniglia, and a tiny crescent-shaped pebble beach reached by stone steps near the harbor in Riomaggiore.

The fashionable seaside getaway of **Lido,** Venice, with its crowded strands washed by polluted Adriatic waters, may disappoint beachgoers. Avoid the busy public beaches near the town center and head instead to quieter beaches on the south end of the island at Malamocco and Alberoni.

Beach life in Positano, Campagna, centers around the chic and always crowded Spiaggi Grande, much of which is taken up with bathing establishments; Formillo, on the other side of the headland, is calmer and less trendy.

At the pleasant little **Lido delle Bionde** beach in Sirmione, Lombardy, you can enjoy the clean waters of Lake Garda.

Italy's famous resort of **Taormina, Sicily,** sits high above beaches that stretch for miles around Mazzarò, at the base of the cliffs. You'll be surrounded by crowds, but on the peninsula of Isola Bella, you can enjoy the crystalline waters of a lovely cove at Lido Mendolia Beach Club (© **0942-625-258**).

SPECTATOR SPORTS

Car Racing   The **Italian Grand Prix** takes place in September outside Milan at Monza, one of the world's leading Formula 1 tracks (www.italiangp.it). During the first 2 weeks of October, drivers in the **San Remo Car Rally** race around the town and through the surrounding hills on a course that extends into neighboring Piemonte and covers 861 miles (1,389km); for more information, go to **www.sanremoguide.com**.

Cycling   In May and sometimes early June, the **Giro d'Italia,** Italy's version of the Tour de France, covers some 2,108 miles (3,400km) of terrain, much of it mountainous. For more information, visit **www.ilgiroditalia.com**.

Football (Soccer)   The season runs from September through June. Most coverage is in the Italian-language press, but one way to keep up with **Coppa Italia (Italian Cup)** standings, and get some insight into the national pastime, is to visit the website of Juventus, the Turin team, at **www.juventus.com** (see the English-language version). Italy's football obsession can be traced back to Calcio Fiorentino, a medieval version of the modern game that is still played in Florence during a series of matches around the feast day of San Giovanni, June 24; for information, call © **055-23320**.

CHAPTER TEN

NIGHTLIFE

For coverage of movies and cultural events, see p168, Chapter Seven, "Culture."

CLUB HOPPING

Where can I find_____	**Dove posso trovare _____** *DOH-veh POHS-soh troh-VAH-reh*
a good nightclub?	**un bel locale notturno / night-club?** *oon behl loh-KAH-leh noht-TOOR-noh / night club*
a club with a live band?	**un locale con musica dal vivo?** *oon loh-KAH-leh kohn MOO-zee-kah dahl VEE-voh*
a reggae club?	**un locale con musica reggae?** *oon loh-KAH-leh kohn MOO-zee-kah reggae*
a hip hop club?	**un locale con musica hip hop?** *oon loh-KAH-leh kohn MOO-zee-kah hip hop*
a techno club?	**un locale con musica techno?** *oon loh-KAH-leh kohn MOO-zee-kah techno*
a gay / lesbian club?	**un locale gay?** *oon loh-KAH-leh gay*
a club where I can dance?	**una discoteca?** *OO-nah dees-koh-TEH-kah*
a club with Italian music?	**un locale con musica italiana?** *oon loh-KAH-leh kohn MOO-zee-kah ee-tah-LYAH-nah*
the most popular club in town?	**il locale più frequentato in città?** *eel loh-KAH-leh PYOO freh-kwehn-TAH-toh een cheet-TAH*

a piano bar?	**un piano bar?** *oon piano bar.*
the most upscale club?	**il locale più di lusso?** *eel loh-KAH-leh PYOO dee LOOS-soh*
What's the hottest bar these days?	**Qual è il bar più di moda al momento?** *kwah-LEH eel bar PYOO dee MOH-dah ahl moh-MEHN-toh*
What's the cover charge?	**Quant'è il coperto?** *kwahn-TEH eel koh-PEHR-toh*
Do I need a membership?	**Bisogna essere soci?** *bee-ZOHN-nyah EHS-seh-reh SOH-chee*
Do they have a dress code?	**Che abbigliamento è richiesto?** *keh ahb-beel-lyah-MEHN-toh EH ree-KYEHS-toh*
Is it expensive?	**È caro?** *EH KAH-roh*
What's the best time to go?	**A che ora è meglio andarci?** *ah keh OH-rah EH MEHL-lyoh ahn-DAHR-chee*
What kind of music do they play there?	**Che tipo di musica c'è?** *keh TEE-poh dee MOO-zee-kah ch-EH*
Is smoking allowed?	**Si può fumare?** *see PWOH foo-MAH-reh*
I'm looking for a tobacconist.	**Cerco un tabaccaio.** *CHEHR-koh oon tah-bahk-KAH-yoh*

I'd like a pack of cigarettes.	**Vorrei un pacchetto di sigarette.**
	vohr-RAY oon pahk-KEHT-toh dee see-gah-REHT-teh
I'd like ____, please.	**Vorrei ____, per favore.**
	vohr-RAY ____ pehr fah-VOH-reh
a drink	**qualcosa da bere**
	kwahl-KOH-zah dah BEH-reh
a bottle of beer	**una bottiglia di birra**
	OO-nah boht-TEEL-lyah dee BEER-rah
a beer on tap	**una birra alla spina**
	OO-nah BEER-rah AHL-lah SPEE-nah
a shot of ____	**un ____**
	oon ____

For a full list of drinks, see p100.

Make it a double, please!	**Doppio, per favore!**
	DOHP-pyoh pehr fah-VOH-reh
With ice, please.	**Con ghiaccio, per favore.**
	kohn GYAT-choh pehr fah-VOH-reh
And one for the lady / the gentleman!	**E uno / a per la signora / il signore!**
	eh OO-noh pehr lah seen-NYOH rah / eel seen-NYOH reh
How much for a bottle / glass of beer?	**Quanto costa la birra alla bottiglia / al bicchiere?**
	KWAHN-toh KOHS-tah lah BEER-rah AHL-lah boht-TEEL-lyah / ahl beek-KYEH-reh

I'd like to buy a drink for that girl / guy over there.

Vorrei offrire da bere a quella ragazza (signora) / quel ragazzo (signore) là.

vohr-RAY ohf-FREE-reh dah BEH-reh ah KWEHL-lah rah-GAHT-sah (seen-NYOH-rah) / kwehl rah-GAHT-soh (seen-NYOH-reh) LAH

May I run a tab?

Posso aggiungere al conto?

POHS-soh ahd-JOON-jeh-reh ahl KOHN-toh

What's the cover?

Quant'è il coperto?

kwahn-TEH eel koh-PEHR-toh

ACROSS A CROWDED ROOM

Excuse me, may I buy you a drink?

Mi scusi, posso offrirle qualcosa da bere?

mee SKOO-zee POHS-soh ohf-FREER-leh kwahl-KOH-zah dah BEH-reh

You look amazing.

Lei è affascinante.

lay EH ahf-fah-shee-NAHN-teh

| You look like the most interesting person in the room. | **Lei mi sembra la persona più interessante in questo posto.** |
| | *lay mee SEHM-brah lah pehr-SOH-nah PYOO een-teh-rehs-SAHN-teh een KWEHS-toh POHS-toh* |

Would you like to dance?	**Le va di ballare?**
	leh vah dee bahl-LAH-reh
Do you like to dance fast or slow?	**Le piace il ballo veloce o lento?**
	leh PYAH-cheh eel BAHL-loh veh-LOH-cheh oh LEHN-toh

Here, give me your hand.	**Venga, mi dia la mano.**
	VEHN-gah mee DEE-ah lah MAH-noh
What would you like to drink?	**Cosa le va di bere?**
	KOH-zah leh vah dee BEH-reh
You're a great dancer.	**Come balla bene.**
	KOH-meh BAHL-lah BEH-neh

| I don't know that dance! | **Non conosco quella danza!** |
| | *nohn koh-NOHS-koh KWEHL-lah DAHN-tsah* |

| Do you like this song? | **Le piace questa canzone?** |
| | *leh PYAH-cheh KWEHS-tah kahn-TSOH-neh* |

| You have nice eyes! | **Che begli occhi che ha!** |
| | *kee BEHL-lyee OHK-kee keh AH* |

For a list of features, see p134.

| May I have your phone number? | **Posso avere il suo numero di telefono?** |
| | *POHS-soh ah-VEH-reh eel SOO-oh NOO-meh-roh dee teh-LEH-foh-noh* |

GETTING CLOSER

You're very attractive.

Sei molto bello -a.
say MOHL-toh BEHL-loh -ah

I like being with you.

Mi piace stare con te.
mee PYAH-cheh STAH-reh kohn teh

I like you.

Mi piaci.
mee PYAH-chee

I want to hold you.

Voglio tenerti fra le braccia.
VOHL-lyoh teh-NEHR-tee frah leh BRAHT-chah

Kiss me.

Baciami.
BAH-chah-mee

May I give you a hug / a kiss?

Posso abbracciarti / baciarti?
POHS-soh ahb-braht-CHAHR-tee / bah-CHAHR-tee

Would you like a back rub?

Vuoi che ti massaggi la schiena?
VWOH-ee keh tee mahs-SAHD-jee lah SKYEH-nah

Would you like a massage?

Ti piacerebbe un massaggio?
tee pyah-CHEH-rehb-beh oon mahs-SAHD-joh

NIGHTLIFE

Don't mix the message

Ti desidero / Ti voglio. *tee deh-ZEE-deh-roh /* *tee VOHL-lyoh*	I desire you / I want you. These are pretty much physical, erotic expressions, much as in English.
Ti amo. *tee AH-moh*	This means "I love you" and is used seriously.

SEX

Would you like to come inside?	**Vuoi entrare?** *VWOH-ee ehn-TRAH-reh*
May I come inside?	**Posso entrare?** *POHS-soh ehn-TRAH-reh*
Let me help you out of that.	**Ti aiuto a toglierlo.** *tee ah-YOO-toh ah TOHL-lyehr-loh*
Would you help me out of this?	**Mi aiuti a toglierlo?** *mee ah-YOO-tee ah TOHL-lyehr-loh*
You smell so good.	**Hai un buon profumo.** *eye oon bwon proh-FOO-moh*
You're beautiful / handsome.	**Sei bellissima / bellissimo.** *say behl-LEES-see-mah /* *beh-LEES-see-moh*
May I?	**Posso?** *POHS-soh*
OK?	**Va bene?** *vah BEH-neh*
Like this?	**Così?** *koh-ZEE*
How?	**Come?** *KOH-meh*

HOLD ON A SECOND

Please don't do that.	**No, per favore, non farlo.**
	noh pehr fah-VOH-reh nohn
	FAHR-loh
Stop, please.	**Smetti, per favore.**
	ZMEHT-tee pehr fah-VOH-reh
Do you want me to stop?	**Vuoi che smetta?**
	VWOH-ee keh ZMEHT-tah
Let's just be friends.	**Restiamo solo amici.**
	reh-STYAH-moh SOH-loh
	ah-MEE-chee
Do you have a condom?	**Hai un preservativo?**
	eye oon preh-sehr-vah-TEE-voh
Are you on birth control?	**Prendi la pillola?**
	PREHN-dee lah PEEL-loh-lah
I have a condom.	**Ho un preservativo.**
	OH oon preh-sehr-vah-TEE-voh
Do you have anything you should tell me first?	**Hai qualcosa da dirmi prima di continuare?**
	eye kwahl-KOH-zah dah
	DEER-mee PREE-mah dee
	kohn-tee-NWAH-reh

NIGHTLIFE

BACK TO IT

That's it.	**Ecco, sì.**
	EHK-koh SEE
That's not it.	**No, non così.**
	noh nohn koh-ZEE
Here.	**Qui.**
	kwee
There.	**Lì.**
	LEE
More.	**Ancora.**
	ahn-KOH-rah
Harder.	**Più forte.**
	PYOO FOHR-teh
Faster.	**Più veloce.**
	PYOO veh-LOH-cheh
Deeper.	**Più profondo.**
	PYOO proh-FOHN-doh
Slower.	**Più lento.**
	PYOO LEHN-toh
Easy / slowly.	**Piano.**
	PYAH-noh
Enough.	**Basta.**
	BAHS-tah

For a full list of features, see p134.
For a full list of body parts, see p230.

COOLDOWN

You're great.	**Sei fantastico -a.** *say fahn-TAHS-tee-koh -ah*
That was great.	**È stato bellissimo.** *EH STAH-toh behl-LEES-see-moh*
Would you like ____	**Vuoi ____** *VWOH-ee*
a drink?	**qualcosa da bere?** *kwahl-KOH-zah dah BEH-reh*
a snack?	**qualcosa da mangiare?** *kwahl-KOH-zah dah mahn-JAH-reh*
a shower?	**fare la doccia?** *FAH-reh lah DOHT-chah*
May I stay here?	**Posso stare qui?** *POHS-soh STAH-reh kwee*
Would you like to stay here?	**Vuoi stare qui?** *VWOH-ee STAH-reh kwee*
I'm sorry. I have to go now.	**Mi dispiace. Ora devo andare.** *mee dee-SPYAH-cheh OH-rah DEH-voh ahn-DAH-reh*
Where are you going?	**Dove vai?** *DOH-veh VAH-ee*
I have to work early.	**Devo alzarmi presto per andare al lavoro.** *DEH-voh ahl-TSAHR-mee PREHS-toh pehr ahn-DAH-reh ahl lah-VOH-roh*
I'm flying home in the morning.	**Torno a casa domani mattina.** *TOHR-noh ah KAH-zah doh-MAH-nee maht-TEE-nah*
I have an early flight.	**Il mio volo parte presto.** *eel MEE-oh VOH-loh PAHR-teh PREHS-toh*

I think this was a mistake.	**Credo che questo sia stato un errore.**
	KREH-doh keh KWEHS-toh SEE-ah STAH-toh oon ehr-ROH-reh
Will you make me breakfast too?	**Puoi preparare la colazione anche per me?**
	pwoy preh-pah-RAH-reh lah koh-lah-TSYOH-neh AHN-keh pehr meh
Stay, I'll make you breakfast.	**Stai qui, ti preparo la colazione.**
	STAH-ee kwee tee preh-PAH-roh lah koh-lah-TSYOH-neh

IN THE CASINO

How much is this table?	**Quanto costa questo tavolo?**
	KWAHN-toh KOHS-tah KWEHS-toh TAH-voh-loh
Deal me in.	**Entro in gioco.**
	EHN-troh een JOH-koh
Put it on red!	**Sul rosso!**
	sool ROHS-soh
Put it on black!	**Sul nero!**
	sool NEH-roh
Let it ride!	**Lascialo girare!**
	LAH-shah-loh jee-RAH-reh
21!	**Ventuno!**
	vehn-TOO-noh
Snake-eyes!	**Due uno!**
	DOO-eh OO-noh
Seven.	**Sette.**
	SEHT-teh

For a full list of numbers, see p7.

Damn, eleven.	**Accidenti, undici.**
	at-chee-DEHN-tee OON-dee-chee
I'll pass.	**Passo.**
	PAHS-soh
Hit me!	**Carte!**
	KAHR-te

Watch that stress!

The meaning of **casinò** (*kah-zee-NOH*) is different from that of **casino** (*kah-ZEE-noh*)! **Casinò** means the gambling house, while **casino** means a mess, a screwed up situation, or . . . "a lot", as in **Mi dispiace un casino** (I'm mad about something or someone).

Split.	**Metà e metà.**
	meh-TAH eh meh-TAH
Are the drinks complimentary?	**Le bevande sono gratis?**
	leh beh-VAHN-deh SOH-noh gratis
May I bill it to my room?	**Posso addebitarlo alla mia stanza?**
	POHS-soh ahd-deh-bee-TAHR-loh AHL-lah MEE-ah STAHN-tsah
I'd like to cash out.	**Vorrei incassare la vincita.**
	vohr-RAY een-kahs-SAH-reh lah VEEN-chee-tah
I'll hold.	**Va bene.**
	vah BEH-neh
I'll see your bet.	**Vedo.**
	VEH-doh
I call.	**Chlamo.**
	KYAH-moh
Full house!	**Full!**
	full
Royal flush.	**Scala reale.**
	SKAH-lah reh-AH-leh
Straight.	**Scala.**
	SKAH-lah

ENTERTAINMENT CALENDAR

January

Umbria Jazz Winter, Orvieto (℡ 075-5732432; www. umbriajazz.com). Jazz greats descend upon this beautiful medieval city for concerts in the 13th-century Palazzo del Sette and other evocative venues. *New Year's Weekend.*

February

Carnevale, Venice (℡ 041-5225150; www.carnivalofvenice .com). The sight of masked characters wafting through the city is spectacle enough, but concerts (from chamber music to reggae), masked balls, and other events are staged throughout the city. *Two weeks before Shrove Tuesday.*

March

Festival della Canzone Italiana (Festival of Italian Popular Song), San Remo (www.sanremostory.it). Major European artists perform the latest Italian song releases. *Early March.*

April

Festa Della Primavera (Feast of Spring), Rome (℡ 06-48899253; www.romaturismo.com). The Spanish Steps are decked out with azaleas and the Church of Trinità dei Monti, at the top of the steps, is the setting for orchestral and choral concerts. *End of the month or early May.*

May

Maggio Musicale Fiorentino (Florentine Musical May), Florence (℡ 055-213535; www.maggiofiorentino.com). Italy's oldest and most prestigious music festival includes concerts, dance, theater, and opera at Teatro Communale and other venues; some concerts are performed for free in Piazza della Signoria. *Through the end of June.*

June

Festival di Ravenna, Emilia-Romagna (© **0544-249211**; www.ravennafestival.org). Some of the most renowned classical performers gather for a program of operas, ballet, theater, symphonic music concerts, solo and chamber pieces, oratorios, and sacred music. *Through late July.*

Festival di Spoleto, Umbria (© **0743-45028**; www.spoletofestival.it). Since 1958, international performers have converged on this medieval hill town for 3 weeks of dance, drama, opera, and classical concerts. *Late June–early July.*

Biennale d'Arte (International Exposition of Modern Art), Venice (© **041-5218711**; www.labiennale.org). One of the most famous art events in Europe takes place on odd-numbered years. *Through mid-October.*

Heineken Jammin' Festival, Emilia-Romagna (www.heineken.it). Rock, hip-hop, and pop in a 3-day, outdoor concert that recalls the Woodstock days. *June.*

Ravello Classical Music Festival, Campagnia (© **089-858149**; www.rcs.amalficoast.it). Chamber music is performed in gardens, and other venues in a beautiful town on the Amalfi coast. *Through September.*

July

Festival Shakespeariano, Verona, the Veneto (© **045-8077111**). A week of performances by the Royal Shakespeare Company is often part of an agenda that includes ballet, drama, and jazz, all performed in the Teatro Romano. *Through August.*

Arena di Verona (Arena Outdoor Opera Season) Verona, the Veneto (© **045-8005151**; www.arena.it). The 20,000-seat Roman amphitheater, one of the world's best preserved ancient arenas, is the setting for a round of operas, many by Verdi, sung by some of the world's best voices. *Through late August.*

Umbria Jazz, Perugia, Umbria (© **075-5732432**; www.umbriajazz.com). All the big names in jazz converge for jam sessions and concerts. *Mid-July.*

NIGHTLIFE

Festival Internazionale di Musica Antica, Urbino, the Marches (✆ 0722-2613). Renaissance and baroque music is the focus.

Arezzo Wave, Tuscany (www.arezzowave.com). A blow-out rock-and-blues extravaganza. *Mid-July.*

August

Torre del Lago Puccini, near Lucca, Tuscany (✆ 0584-359-322). Puccini operas are performed in this Tuscan lakeside town's open-air theater, near the villa where the celebrated, Lucca-born composer spent his summers and is buried. *Through August.*

Rossini Opera Festival, Pesaro, Italian Riviera (✆ 0721-3800294; www.rossinioperafestival.it). The world's top *bel canto* specialists gather in Rossini's birthplace to perform his operas and choral works. *Through August.*

Venice International Film Festival (✆ 041-2424; www.labiennale.org). Stars and filmmakers from all over the world crowd the Palazzo del Cinema on the Lido; mere mortals can attend the screenings. *Late August through September.*

Stresa Musical Weeks, Stresa, Lombardy (✆ 0323-31095; settimanemusicali.net). Classical musicians gather in this pretty lakeside town for 3 weeks of concerts. *Aug–Sept.*

September

Independent Days Festival, Bologna (✆ 0434-208631; www.indipendente.com). An independent music festival, with bands ranging from the obscure to the ultra-famous. *Early September.*

October

Festa di San Francesco (Feast of Saint Francis), Asissi (www.assisionline.com). The birthplace of Italy's patron saint is the setting for processions and church music, as well as dance performances and concerts of popular song, commemorating the death of Francis. *October 3-4.*

EuroChocolate Festival, Perugia (www.chocolate.perugia. it). Italy's chocolate capital is the setting for a week of sweet entertainment, when artists sculpt masterpieces out of 1,000-kilogram blocks of chocolate as enthusiastic crowds eat the shavings, nude models dip themselves in tubs of chocolate, and other activities take place. *Mid-late October.*

December–November

La Scala Opera Season, Teatro alla Scala, Milan (© **02-7200-3744**; www.teatroallascala.org). Tickets are scarce at the most famous opera house of them all, but the thrill of seeing a performance here makes the effort of getting a seat worthwhile. *Year-round; season opens early December.*

ADVANCE TICKET RESERVATIONS

If you want to reserve seats for performances before you leave home, contact **www.culturalitaly.com**, a Web-based company that dispenses tickets to concerts, music festivals, and other events. But there's a rub: a 10€ booking fee per ticket. Another source is www.globaltickets.com/GTS/INDEX.htm. You can also ask your hotel concierge to reserve tickets for you when you book your room (with the promise of a tip to follow).

For a list of upcoming events around the world, try the invaluable site, **www.whatsonwhen.com**.

NATIONAL FEASTS & HOLIDAYS

Offices and shops are closed on the following national holidays:

January 1   New Year's Day

Easter Monday

April 25   Liberation Day

May 1   Labor Day

August 15   Assumption of the Virgin

November 1   All Saints' Day

December 8   Feast of the Immaculate Conception

December 25   Christmas Day

December 26   Feast of Santo Stefano

NIGHTLIFE

CHAPTER ELEVEN
HEALTH & SAFETY

This chapter covers the terms you'll need to maintain your health and safety—including the most useful phrases for the pharmacy, the doctor's office, and the police station.

AT THE PHARMACY

Please fill this prescription.	**Mi servono questi farmaci, per favore.** *mee SEHR-voh-noh KWEHS-tee FAHR-mah-chee pehr fah-VOH-reh*
Do you have something for ____	**Ha qualcosa per ____** *AH kwahl-KOH-zah pehr*
a cold?	**il raffreddore?** *eel rahf-frehd-DOH-reh*
a cough?	**la tosse?** *lah TOHS-seh*
I need something for ____	**Mi serve qualcosa per ____** *mee SEHR-veh kwahl-KOH-zah pehr*
acne.	**l'acne.** *LAHK-neh*
congestion.	**la congestione.** *lah kohn-jehs-TYOH-neh*
constipation.	**la costipazione.** *lah kohs-tee-pah-TSYOH-neh*
corns.	**i calli.** *ee KAHL-lee*
diarrhea.	**la diarrea.** *lah dyahr-REH-ah*
indigestion.	**l'indigestione.** *leen-dee-jehs-TYOH-neh*
motion sickness.	**il mal d'auto.** *eel mahl DOW-toh*

nausea.	**la nausea.**
	lah NOW-zeh-ah
seasickness.	**il mal di mare.**
	eel mahl dee MAH-reh
warts.	**le verruche.**
	leh vehr-ROO-keh
to help me sleep.	**aiutarmi a dormire.**
	ah-yoo-TAHR-mee ah
	dohr-MEE-reh
to help me relax.	**aiutarmi a rilassarmi.**
	ah-yoo-TAHR-mee ah
	ree-lahs-SAHR-mee
I want to buy ____	**Vorrei ____**
	vohr-RAY
antibiotic cream.	**una crema antibiotica.**
	OO-nah KREH-mah
an antihistamine.	**un antistaminico.**
	oon ahn-tees-tah-MEE-nee-koh
	ahn-tee-BYOH-tee-kah
aspirin.	**dell'aspirina.**
	dehl-lahs-pee-REE-nah
condoms.	**dei preservativi.**
	day preh-sehr-vah-TEE-vee
insect repellant.	**un insetto-repellente.**
	oon een-seht-toh
	reh-pehl-LEHN-teh
medicine with codeine.	**un farmaco con codeina.**
	oon FAHR-mah-koh kohn
	koh-deh-EE-nah
non-aspirin pain	**un analgesico senza aspirina.**
reliever.	*oon ah-nahl-JEH-zee-koh*
	SEHN-tsah ahs-pee-REE-nah

AT THE DOCTOR'S OFFICE

I would like to see ____   **Vorrei vedere ____**
vohr-RAY veh-DEH-reh

a doctor.   **un medico.**
oon MEH-dee-koh

a chiropractor.   **un chiroterapeuta.**
oon kee-roh-teh-rah-PEHoo-tah

a gynecologist.   **un ginecologo.**
oon jee-neh-KOH-loh-goh

an eye / ears / nose /   **un otorinolaringoiatra.**
throat specialist.   *oon oh-toh-REE-noh-lah-REEN-*
goh-YAH-trah

a dentist.   **un dentista.**
oon dehn-TEES-tah

an optometrist.   **un optometrista.**
oon ohp-toh-meh-TREES-tah

Do I need an   **Mi serve un appuntamento?**
appointment?   *mee SEHR-veh oon*
ahp-poon-tah-MEHN-toh

I have an emergency.   **È un'emergenza.**
EH oon-eh-mehr-JEHN-tsah

I need an emergency   **Mi servono questi farmaci urgenti.**
prescription refill.   *mee SEHR-voh-noh KWEHS-tee*
FAHR-mah-chee oor-JEHN-tee

Please call a doctor.   **Chiami un medico, per favore.**
KYAH-mee oon MEH-dee-koh
pehr fah-VOH-reh

I need an ambulance.   **Mi serve un'ambulanza.**
mee SEHR-veh
oon-ahm-boo-LAHN-tsah

SYMPTOMS

For a full list of body parts, see p230.

My ____ hurts.	**Mi fa male ____.**
	mee fah MAH-leh
My ____ is stiff.	**____ è rigido -a.**
	____ EH REE-jee-doh -ah
I think I'm having a heart attack.	**Credo sia un attacco cardiaco.**
	KREH-doh SEE-ah oon aht-TAHK-koh kahr-DEE-ah-koh
I can't move.	**Non riesco a muovermi.**
	nohn ree-EHS-koh ah MWOH-vehr-mee
I fell.	**Sono caduto -a.**
	SOH-noh kah-DOO-toh -ah
I fainted.	**Sono svenuto -a.**
	SOH-noh zveh-NOO-tohlah
I have a cut on my ____.	**Ho un taglio su ____.**
	OH oon TAHL-lyoh soo
I have a headache.	**Ho mal di testa.**
	OH mahl dee TEHS-tah
My vision is blurry.	**La vista è annebbiata.**
	lah VEES-tah EH ahn-nehb-BYAH-tah
I feel dizzy.	**Mi gira la testa.**
	mee JEE-rah lah TEHS-tah
I think I'm pregnant.	**Credo di essere incinta.**
	KREH-doh dee EHS-seh-reh een-CHEEN-tah
I don't think I'm pregnant.	**Non credo di essere incinta.**
	nohn KREH-doh dee EHS-seh-reh een-CHEEN-tah
I'm having trouble walking.	**Faccio fatica a camminare.**
	FAHT-choh fah-TEE-kah ah kahm-mee-NAH-reh
I can't get up.	**Non riesco ad alzarmi.**
	nohn ree-EHS-koh ahd ahl-TSAHR-mee

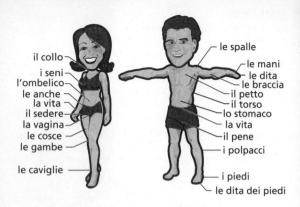

il collo
i seni
l'ombelico
le anche
la vita
il sedere
la vagina
le cosce
le gambe
le caviglie

le spalle
le mani
le dita
le braccia
il petto
il torso
lo stomaco
la vita
il pene
i polpacci
i piedi
le dita dei piedi

See p134 for facial features.

See p134 for facial features.

I was mugged.	**Sono stato aggredito -a.** *SOH-noh STAH-toh ahg-ghreh-DEE-toh -ah*
I was raped.	**Sono stato violentato -a.** *SOH-noh STAH-toh vyo-lehn-TAH-toh -tah*
A dog attacked me.	**Un cane mi ha aggredito -a.** *oon KAH-neh mee AH ahg-ghreh-DEE-toh -ah*
A snake bit me.	**Mi ha morso un serpente.** *mee AH MOHR-soh oon sehr-PEHN-teh*
I can't move my ____ without pain.	**Mi fa male quando muovo ____.** *mee fah MAH-leh KWAHN-doh MWOH-voh*
I think I sprained my ankle.	**Credo di essermi slogato la caviglia.** *KREH-doh dee EHS-sehr-mee zloh-GAH-toh lah kah-VEEL-lyah*

MEDICATIONS

I need morning-after pills.	**Mi servono delle pillole del giorno dopo.**
	mee SEHR-voh-noh DEHL-leh PEEL-loh-leh dehl JOHR-noh DOH-poh
I need birth control pills.	**Mi servono pillole anticoncezionali.**
	mee SEHR-voh-noh PEEL-loh-leh anti-kohn-CHEH-tsyoh-NAH-lee
I need erectile dysfunction pills.	**Mi servono pillole per la disfunzione erettile.**
	mee SEHR-voh-noh PEEL-loh-leh pehr lah dees-foon-TSYOH-neh eh-REHT-tee-leh
I lost my eyeglasses and need new ones.	**Ho perso gli occhiali da vista e me ne servono di nuovi.**
	OH PEHR-soh lyee ohk-kee-AH-lee dah VEES-tah eh meh neh SEHR-voh-noh dee NWOH-vee
I need new contact lenses.	**Mi servono lenti a contatto nuove.**
	mee SEHR-voh-noh LEHN-tee ah kohn-TAHT-toh NWOH-veh
It's cold in here!	**Fa freddo qui!**
	fah FREHD-doh kwee
I am allergic to ____	**Sono allergico -a ____**
	SOH-noh ahl-LEHR-jee-koh -ah
penicillin.	**alla penicillina.**
	AHL-lah peh-nee-cheel-LEE-nah
antibiotics.	**agli antibiotici.**
	AHL-lyee ahn-tee-BYOH-tee-chee
sulfa drugs.	**ai sulfonamidi.**
	eye sool-foh-NAH-mee-dee
steroids.	**agli steroidi.**
	AHL-lee steh-ROY-dee
I have asthma.	**Soffro d'asma.**
	SOHF-froh DAHZ-mah

DENTAL PROBLEMS

Where can I find a dentist?	**Dove posso trovare un dentista?** *DOH-veh POHS-soh troh-VAH-reh oon dehn-TEES-tah*
I have a toothache.	**Mi fa male un dente.** *mee fah MAH-leh oon DEHN-teh*
I chipped a tooth.	**Mi si è rotto un dente.** *mee see EH ROHT-toh oon DEHN-teh*
My bridge came loose.	**Mi si è allentato il ponte.** *mee see EH ahl-lehn-TAH-toh eel POHN-teh*
I lost a crown.	**Ho perso una capsula.** *OH PEHR-soh OO-nah KAHP-soo-lah*
I lost a denture plate.	**Ho perso una piastra della dentiera.** *OH PEHR-soh OO-nah PYAHS-trah DEHL-lah dehn-TYEH-rah*

AT THE POLICE STATION

I'm sorry, did I do something wrong?	**Scusi, ho fatto qualcosa di male?** *SKOO-zee OH FAHT-toh kwahl-KOH-zah dee MAH-leh*
I am _____	**Sono _____** *SOH-noh*
American.	**americano -a.** *ah-meh-ree-KAH-noh -ah*
Canadian.	**canadese.** *kah-nah-DEH-zeh*
European.	**europeo -a.** *eh-oo-roh-PEH-oh -ah*
Australian.	**australiano -a.** *ow-strah-LYAH-noh -ah*
New Zealandese.	**neozelandese.** *neh-oh-dzeh-lahn-DEH-zeh*

For a full listing of nationalities, see English / Italian dictionary.

Listen Up: Police Lingo

Favorisca la patente, il libretto e l'assicurazione. *fah-voh-REES-kah lah pah-TEHN-teh eel lee-BREHT-toh eh LAHS-see-koo-raht-SYOH-neh*	Your license, registration and insurance, please.
La multa è di dieci euro. Può pagarla direttamente a me. *lah MOOL-tah EH dee DYEH-chee EH-oo-roh PWOH pah-GAH-reh dee-reht-tah-MEHN-teh ah meh*	The fine is €10. You can pay me directly.
Il suo passaporto, per favore. *eel SOO-oh pahs-sah-POHR-toh pehr fah-VOH-reh*	Your passport, please.
Dov'è diretto? *dohv-EH dee-REHT-toh*	Where are you going?
Perchè tanta fretta? *pehr-KEH TAHN-tah FREHT-tah*	Why are you in such a hurry?

The car is a rental.	**L'auto è a noleggio.** *LOW-toh EH ah noh-LEHD-joh*
Do I pay the fine to you?	**Devo pagare la multa a lei?** *DEH-voh pah-GAH-reh lah MOOL-tah ah lay*
Do I have to go to court?	**Devo andare in tribunale?** *DEH-voh ahn-DAH-reh een tree-boo-NAH-leh*
When?	**Quando?** *KWAHN-doh*

I'm sorry, my Italian isn't very good.	**Scusi, non parlo bene l'italiano.** *SKOO-zee nohn PAHR-loh* *BEH-neh lee-tah-LYAH-noh*
I need an interpreter.	**Mi serve un interprete.** *mee SEHR-veh* *oon-een-TEHR-preh-teh*
I'm sorry, I don't understand the ticket.	**Scusi, non capisco la multa.** *SKOO-zee nohn kah-PEES-koh lah* *MOOL-tah*
May I call my embassy?	**Posso chiamare la mia ambasciata?** *POHS-soh kyah-MAH-reh lah* *MEE-ah ahm-bah-SHAH-tah*
I was robbed.	**Mi hanno derubato.** *mee AHN-noh deh-roo-BAH-toh*
I was mugged.	**Sono stato -a aggredito -a.** *SOH-noh STAH-toh -ah ahg-ghreh-* *DEE-toh -ah*
I was raped.	**Sono stato violentato -a.** *SOH-noh STAH-toh vyo-lehn-* *TAH-toh -tah*
May I make a report?	**Posso sporgere denuncia?** *POHS-soh SPOHR-jeh-reh deh-* *NOON-chah*
Somebody broke into my room.	**Qualcuno è entrato nella mia stanza.** *kwahl-KOO-noh EH ehn-TRAH-toh* *NEHL-lah MEE-ah STAHN-tsah*
Someone stole my purse / wallet.	**Qualcuno mi ha rubato la borsetta / il portafoglio.** *kwahl-KOO-noh mee AH* *roo-BAH-toh lah bohr-SEHT-tah /* *eel pohr-tah-FOHL-lyo*

HEALTH FAST FACTS

Drugstores Pharmacies are easy to spot by the green crosses in front. Most are well-stocked and staffed with knowledgeable personnel who will make a sincere effort to help you. Pharmacies remain open all night and on Sundays on a rotating basis; a sign on the door or window will indicate which pharmacy in the area is keeping these extended hours.

Emergencies Call ✆ 113 for medical assistance as well as the police and fire brigade.

Precautions Travelers to Italy do not require shots, and food and tap water are generally safe (though Italians usually drink bottled mineral water). Vegetarians will soon discover that fresh vegetables and meatless pasta sauces are in ready supply.

If you suffer from epilepsy, diabetes, or heart problems, wear a **MedicAlert** identification tag (✆ 888/633-4298; www.medicalert.org), which will immediately alert doctors to your condition. Pack prescription medications in your carry-on luggage, and carry prescription medications in their original containers (to show customs officials as well as physicians, if necessary). Bring enough medications to last the duration of your trip, and don't forget your sunglasses and an extra pair of contact lenses or prescription glasses. Bring along the generic name of medications, as the Italian pharmacist may not be familiar with a particular brand.

What to Do If You Get Sick Your hotel should be able to recommend a doctor. If not, contact your embassy or consulate. Many hospitals have walk-in clinics for emergency cases that are not life-threatening. **International Association for Medical Assistance to Travelers** (**IAMAT**; iamat.org) has a full listing of English-speaking doctors around the world.

SAFETY FAST FACTS

Crime   The biggest threat to your safety in Italy is petty crime—Rome, Naples, Florence, Palermo, and some other cities are plagued with purse snatchers and pickpockets. You can protect yourself with a few precautions:

- Carry money in a front pocket or in a money belt.
- Don't wear expensive jewelry or flash money and other valuables.
- Keep large amounts of cash, extra credit cards, and your passport in the safe in your room or with the front desk. Keep credit card and passport numbers there, too, as well as contact information, in case the originals get lost.
- Don't leave anything of value on view in a parked car. It's best to rent a car with a trunk (rather than a wagon or SUV), so you can keep your luggage hidden in the trunk.

Driving Breakdowns   Foreign motorists can call ✆ **803-116** (24-hour nationwide telephone service, usually in English). For road information, itineraries, and all sorts of travel assistance, call ✆ **06-514971**.

Drugs & Alcohol   Italian authorities take a hard line on drugs, and drunk driving is considered a serious offense, too. Should you be held for any drug or alcohol-related charges, contact your embassy or consulate. Officials there will not interfere with the Italian legal process, but they probably will help put you in touch with an attorney.

Embassies & Consulates   In general, consulates are geared to deal with the public, while embassies work with diplomats. Even so, embassy personnel can put you in touch with the right office to handle a given problem. And in case of emergencies, embassies have a 24-hour referral service.

The **U.S. Embassy** is in Rome at Via Vittorio Veneto 119A (✆ **06-46-741**; fax 06-48-82-672). There are **U.S. consulates** in Florence, at Lungarno Amerigo Vespucci 38 (© **055-266-951**; fax 055-284-088); in Milan, at Via Principe Amedeo 2-10 (© **02-29-03-51**; fax 02-2900-1165); in Naples on Piazza della Repubblica 1 (© **081-583-8111**; fax 081-761-1869); and in Genoa at Via Dante 2 (© **010-58-44-92**).

The **Canadian Embassy** in Rome is at Via G. B. de Rossi 27 (© **06-445-981**; fax 06-445-982912). The **Canadian Consulate** and **passport service** is in Rome at Via Zara 30 (© **06-445-981**). The **Canadian Consulate** in Milan is at V.V. Pisani 19 (© **02-67581**).

Women & Safety   Whistling and other unwanted attentions, even "bottom-pinching," are not uncommon in Italy, but serious aggression, including rape, is extremely rare. Women who don't want the attentions of would-be Casanovas should follow the example of their Italian counterparts and simply ignore them. Should that prove to be impossible, holler *Smettila!* (Stop it!) and try to enlist the aid of an Italian woman.

INSURANCE MATTERS

Check your existing insurance policies before you buy travel insurance; it's likely you already have partial or complete coverage for your trip.

Trip-cancellation insurance helps you get your money back if you have to back out of a trip, if you have to return home early, or if your travel supplier goes bankrupt. Permissible reasons for cancellation can range from sickness to natural disasters to the State Department declaring your destination unsafe for travel. Read the fine print—and make sure that your airline or cruise line is on the list of carriers covered in case of bankruptcy.

Protect yourself further by paying for the insurance with a credit card; by law, consumers can get their money back on goods and services not received if they report the loss within

60 days after the charge is listed on their credit card statement. For more information, contact one of the following recommended insurers (they also offer comprehensive packages covering medical and lost-baggage as well): **Access America** (© 866/807-3982; www.accessamerica.com); **Travel Guard International** (© 800/826-4919; www.travelguard.com); **Travel Insured International** (© 800/243-3174; www. travelinsured.com); and **Travelex Insurance Services** (© 888/457-4602; www.travelex-insurance.com).

Lost-luggage insurance is useful if you plan to check items worth more than the airlines' standard liability policy, which is limited to approximately $9.05 per pound, up to some $635 per checked bag on international flights (including U.S. portions of international trips). Lost luggage insurance is often part of the comprehensive travel-insurance packages offered by the companies listed above. Before purchasing, however, check to see if your valuables are covered by your homeowner's policy.

Medical insurance is a safety net, as most health plans (including Medicare and Medicaid) do not provide coverage for overseas treatment, and the ones that do often require you to pay for services up front and reimburse you only after you return home. If you feel you need travel health insurance as a backup, contact **MEDEX Assistance** (© 410/453-6300; www.medexassist.com) or **Travel Assistance International** (© 800/821-2828; www.travelassistance.com).

CHAPTER TWELVE

CULTURE GUIDE

HISTORIC TIMELINE

The Etruscans

Refugees from Mesopotamia travel west in **1200 B.C.** and within a few hundred years dominate the Italian peninsula. They introduce gold tableware and jewelry, bronze urns and terra-cotta statuary, and the best of Greek and Asia Minor art and culture.

Bronze Age   Celts, Teutonic tribes, and others from the Mediterranean and Asia Minor inhabit the Italian peninsula.

1000 B.C.   Large colonies of Etruscans settle in Tuscany and Campania, subjugating many Latin inhabitants of the peninsula.

800 B.C.   Rome begins to take shape, evolving from a strategically located shepherds' village into a magnet for Latin tribes fleeing the Etruscans.

600 B.C.   Etruscans occupy Rome, making it the capital of their empire. The city grows fast, and a major seaport opens at Ostia.

510 B.C.   Latin tribes, based in Rome, revolt against the Etruscans. Alpine Gauls attack from the north, and Greeks living in Sicily destroy the Etruscan navy. The Roman Republic is born and increases power through conquest, alliances, and colonization.

The Roman Empire

An all-powerful senate presides as Rome defeats rival powers and comes to dominate the Mediterranean. Beginning with the rule of the first emperor, Augustus, in **27 B.C.,** Rome enforces peace in the world for 2 centuries (the Pax Romana). But the emperors' autocratic power leads to corruption, and attacks by northern tribes increase until the last emperor is deposed in **476.**

250 B.C.   Romans, allied with Greeks, Phoenicians, and Sicilians, defeat the Etruscans. Rome begins to build a vast empire.

49 B.C.   Italy (through Rome) controls the Mediterranean world.

44 B.C.   Julius Caesar is assassinated. His successor, Augustus, transforms Rome from a city of brick into a city of marble.

3rd c. A.D.   Rome declines under a series of incompetent and corrupt emperors.

4th c. A.D.   Rome is fragmented politically as administrative capitals are established in such cities as Milan and Trier, Germany.

330   Constantine establishes a "New Rome" at Constantinople (Byzantium).

395   The empire splits into Eastern and Western parts. The Goths successfully invade Rome's northern provinces. Over the following decades, Rome is besieged by barbarians.

476   Rome falls, leaving only the primate of the Catholic Church in control. The pope slowly adopts many powers once reserved for the Roman emperor.

The Middle Ages

As Rome crumbles, the popes take on more imperial powers, yet there is no political unity in Italy. Warlords vie for power, the peninsula fragments into city-states, and the papacy succumbs to feudal landowners. By the end of the 11th century, the popes begin aggressively expanding church influence and acquisitions.

800   Pope Leo III crowns Charlemagne emperor; his legacy, the Holy Roman Empire, will last several hundred years.

Late 11th century   The popes function like secular princes with private armies.

1065   The Holy Land falls to the Muslim Turks; the Crusades are launched.

1303–77   The Papal Schism occurs; the pope and his entourage move from Rome to Avignon, France.

1377   The papacy returns to Rome.

The Renaissance

The great ruling families—especially the Medicis in Florence, the Gonzagas in Mantua, and the Estes in Ferrara—reform law and commerce and spark a "rebirth" in art.

1443 Brunelleschi's dome caps the Duomo in Florence as the Renaissance bursts into full bloom.

1469–92 Lorenzo il Magnifico rules in Florence as the Medici patron of the arts.

1499 Leonardo da Vinci completes *The Last Supper* in Milan.

1508 Michelangelo begins work on frescoes in the Vatican's Sistine Chapel.

1527 Rome is sacked by Charles V of Spain, who is crowned Holy Roman Emperor in 1528.

A United Italy

In the 19th century the last of the Renaissance city-states collapse. Political unrest becomes a fact of life in Italy, encouraged by rapid industrialization in the north and lack of economic development in the south.

1796–97 A series of invasions by Napoleon arouses Italian nationalism.

1861 The Kingdom of Italy is established.

1915–18 Italy enters World War I on the side of the Allies.

The Rise of Il Duce & World War II

In the early 1920s, with inflation soaring and workers striking, Victor Emmanuel III recognizes Benito Mussolini, who started his Fascist Party in 1919, as the new government leader.

1922 Fascists march on Rome; Mussolini becomes premier.

1929 A concordat between the Vatican and the Italian government is signed, delineating the rights and duties of each party.

1935 Italy invades Abyssinia (Ethiopia).

1936 Italy signs "Axis" pact with Germany.

1940 Italy invades Greece.

1943 U.S. Gen. George Patton seizes control of Sicily.

1945 Mussolini is killed by a mob in Milan. World War II ends.

The Postwar Years

Disaffected with the monarchy and its ties to the fallen Fascist dictatorship, Italy's citizens vote to establish a republic. The country quickly succeeds in rebuilding its economy and becomes one of the world's leading industrialized nations.

1946 The Republic of Italy is established.

1957 The Treaty of Rome, establishing the European Community (EC), is signed by six nations.

1960s The country's economy grows under the EC, but the impoverished south lags behind.

1970s Italy is plagued by left-wing terrorism; former premier Aldo Moro is kidnapped and killed.

1980s Political changes in Eastern Europe induce Italy's strong Communist Party to modify its program and even to change its name; the Socialists head their first post-1945 coalition government.

The 1990s & Into the New Millennium

In the early 1990s, many leading Italian politicians are accused of corruption. Economic problems increase, and politicians take measures to put the country on a sound footing.

1994 A conservative coalition, led by media magnate Silvio Berlusconi, wins general elections.

1995 Berlusconi resigns; treasury minister Lamberto Dini is named prime minister to head the transitional government.

1996 Dini steps down as prime minister, and President Oscar Scalfaro dissolves both houses of parliament. In general elections, the center-left Olive Tree coalition sweeps the Senate and the Chamber of Deputies.

1997–1998 Twin earthquakes hit Umbria, killing 11 people and destroying precious frescoes in Assisi's basilica. Prime minister Romano Prodi survives a neo-Communist challenge and presses for budget cuts in an effort to "join Europe."

1999 The euro becomes the official currency of Italy and other European Union nations.

2001   Berlusconi is elected prime minister, winning by a landslide and leading the right wing to sweeping victory.

2002   Euro notes are introduced, and lire begin to be withdrawn from circulation over a transition period.

2003   Italy assumes presidency of the European Union.

2004   Corruption charges against Berlusconi are dismissed.

2005   Pope John Paul II dies; Benedict XVI succeeds him.

ITALIAN ART HISTORY

Classical Greeks, Etruscans & Romans (5th c. B.C.–5th c. A.D.)

Three major cultures influenced early art on the Italian peninsula:

* **Greeks** settled Sicily and southern Italy centuries before the Romans expanded south. Greek temples stand at Segesta, Selinunte, and Agrigento in Sicily. The world's best surviving ancient Greek murals are displayed in the museum in Paestum.

* The **Etruscans** arrived from Asia Minor around 1000 B.C., bringing their own styles in statuary, tableware, and jewelry. By the 6th century B.C. they were borrowing from Greek sculpture and importing Attic vases painted in the style of ancient Greece. The best works remain in Volterra's Guarnacci Museum and Rome's Villa Giulia and Vatican Museums.

* In ancient **Rome,** bucolic frescoes adorned the walls of the wealthy. Sculptures, which often copied Greek originals, idealized emperors and the human form. Look for the marble **bas-reliefs** on Rome's Arch of Constantine, the sculpture and mosaic collections at the Museo Nazionale Romano, and the gilded equestrian statue of Marcus Aurelius at the Capitoline Museums. Sicily's Piazza Armerina has the world's most extensive Roman mosaics. Pompeii's Villa dei Misteri frescoes are expertly wrought and preserved. Don't miss the Alexander mosaic from Pompeii at the archaeological museum in Naples.

Byzantine & Romanesque (5th–13th c.)

Artistic expression in medieval Italy was largely church-related. Because Mass was recited in Latin, images were used to communicate the Bible lessons to the illiterate masses. Bas-reliefs around the churches' main doors, and wall paintings and altarpieces inside, told key tales to inspire faith in God and fear of sin.

The Byzantine style of painting and mosaic was stylized and static, in an iconographic tradition imported from the eastern part of the Roman Empire centered at Byzantium. Faces and eyes were almond-shaped with pointed chins, noses were long, and folds in robes (always blue over red) were represented by stylized cross-hatching in gold leaf.

Romanesque sculpture was more fluid but far from naturalistic. Often childlike in its narrative simplicity, it frequently mixes biblical scenes with myths and motifs from local pagan traditions. Romanesque art survives mostly in scraps, as column capitals or carvings set above church doors, all across Italy. These are some prime examples of Byzantine and Romanesque art:

- **Ravenna.** The churches of Italy's Byzantine capital are covered in stylized Byzantine mosaics, especially at San Vitale, Sant'Appollinare in Classe, and Sant'Appollinare Nuovo.

- **Basilica di San Marco, Venice.** Venice's basilica is a late Byzantine monument of domes and mosaics.

- **Duomo di Monreale, Sicily.** This hillside hamlet has a cathedral filled with Byzantine mosaics. Its cloister columns are topped with some of Italy's best Romanesque carved capitals.

- **Basilica San Zeno Maggiore, Verona.** The 48 relief panels of the bronze doors, some of Italy's most important Romanesque sculptures, were cast between the 9th and 11th centuries and are flanked by strips of 12th-century stone reliefs.

- **Baptistry, Parma.** Romanesque allegorical friezes by Benedetto Antelami adorn the exterior. He also carved the statues inside. Anonymous 13th-century Romanesque artists painted the frescoes of the interior.
- **Collegiata dei Santi Pietro e Orso, Aosta.** This Romanesque church preserves part of an 11th-century fresco cycle and 40 remarkable 12th-century carved column capitals in the cloisters.

International Gothic (Late 13th–Early 15th c.)

Late medieval Italian art continued to be largely ecclesiastical. Statues and carvings festooned church facades and pulpits. The colors used in painting were more rich and varied than in the Romanesque period, and sculptural figures tended to be more natural but highly stylized and rhythmic, with features and gestures exaggerated for symbolic or emotional emphasis. Late Gothic painters such as Giotto introduced more realism, depth, and emotion—characteristics that would later define the Renaissance.

- **Pisano Pulpits (1255–1311).** The Pisanos, father Nicola (1200–1284) and son Giovanni (1245–1320), carved four pulpits: in Pisa's Baptistry and Duomo, and in Siena's Duomo.
- **Andrea Orcagna (1344–1368),** a painter, sculptor, and architect, left many works in Florence: frescoes in Basilica di Santa Croce, the Strozzi altarpiece in Santa Maria Novella, the tabernacle in Orsanmichele, and the Loggia della Signoria.
- **Ambrogio Lorenzetti (ca. 1290–ca. 1348)** is best known for *Allegory of Good and Bad Government* (1338), a complex Gothic painting full of details from daily Sienese life; it hangs in Siena's National Picture Gallery, and his gorgeous *Presentation at the Temple* (1342) is in Florence's Uffizi Gallery.
- **Giotto (1266–1337),** the greatest Gothic artist, laid the groundwork for Renaissance realism and perspective. His

best works are frescoes in Assisi's Basilica di San Francesco, Padua's Chapel of the Scrovegni, and Florence's Basilica di Santa Croce. See also his *Ognissanti Maestà* (1310) in the Uffizi Gallery.

Renaissance & Mannerism (Early 15th to Mid–17th c.)

From the 14th to the 16th century, the humanist philosophy prompted princes and prelates to patronize a generation of innovative young artists, given rise to the **Renaissance** ("rebirth") of art. Painters, sculptors, and architects broke with static medieval traditions to pursue expressiveness and naturalism. They developed techniques such as linear perspective, pioneered by architect Brunelleschi and sculptors Donatello and Ghiberti.

Eventually the High Renaissance began to stagnate, producing technically perfect but vapid works. One attempt to counter the downward spiral was Mannerism, reflected in the extreme torsion of Michelangelo's figures and his unusual use of oranges, greens, and other nontraditional colors.

* **Lorenzo Ghiberti (1378–1455),** a sculptor, completed two sets of doors full of relief panels for Florence's baptistery. One of them, noted for its studied naturalism and dynamic action, is now in Florence's Bargello Museum.

* **Donatello (ca. 1386–1466),** the first full-fledged Renaissance sculptor, used a *schiacciato* technique of warping low-relief surfaces and etching backgrounds to create a sense of deep space. His bronze and marble figures are some of the most expressive and psychologically probing of the Renaissance. He cast the first free-standing nude (the Bargello Museum's *David*) since antiquity. His works are in Florence's Bargello Museum, Duomo Museum, Basilica di San Lorenzo, and Palazzo Vecchio; and in Siena's Duomo, Baptistry, and Duomo Museum.

* **Masaccio (1401–1427)** produced the first example of painted perspective in the *Trinità* fresco (1427) in Florence's

Basilica di Santa Maria Novella, as well as the fresco cycle in Florence's Brancacci Chapel (1424–27) of Santa Maria del Carmine. His work was studied by such masters as Michelangelo.

* **Sandro Botticelli (1444–1510)** is known for his courtly, graceful paintings populated by languid figures which are among the most beloved of the Early Renaissance. His masterpieces *The Birth of Venus* (ca. 1485) and *Allegory of Spring* (ca. 1481) are in Florence's Uffizi Gallery.

* **Leonardo da Vinci (1452–1519)** dabbled in everything from art to philosophy to science. Little of his remarkable painting survives, because he experimented with new pigment mixes that lacked staying power. Leonardo invented *sfumato*, which softens outlines and blurs background details to create a sense of realism and distance within a painting. The best example of this effect—*The Last Supper* (1495–1497) fresco in Milan— is sadly deteriorated; see his earlier *Annunciation* (1481) in Florence's Uffizi for a better preserved example.

* **Raphael (1483–1520),** one of Western art's greatest draftsmen, ignited European painters for centuries to come. See his Madonnas and papal portraits in Florence's Uffizi and Palazzo Pitti and in Rome's National Gallery of Ancient Art. The Vatican holds his ethereal *Transfiguration* (1520) and his greatest work: a series of frescoes (1508–1520) that includes *School of Athens*—portraits of Leonardo, Michelangelo, Raphael, and the architect Bramante, posing as Greek philosophers.

* **Michelangelo (1475–1564)**—a genius of sculpture, painting, architecture, and poetry—marked the apogee of the Renaissance. Pope Julius II commissioned many of his projects, including the Sistine Chapel frescoes (ceiling 1508–1512; *Last Judgment* 1535–1541), *Moses* (1513–1515), in Rome's San Pietro in Vincoli, and the *Slaves* (1513–1516), in Florence's Galleria dell'Accademia. The Medicis also

commissioned work, including the family tombs in Florence's Medici Chapels (1531–1533).

Michelangelo saw the male nude as the ultimate form and used *torsion* (twisting the body in one direction) or *contraposto* (twisting the body in contradictory directions) to bring out its musculature. When forced against his will to paint the Sistine Chapel, he broke almost all the rules and sent painting in a new direction (Mannerism), marked by nonprimary colors and twisting, elongated figures.

Of Michelangelo's painting, Italy has only *Sacra Famiglia* (1504) in Florence's Uffizi. Of his sculpture, Florence preserves the famous *David* (1502–1504) in the Galleria dell'Accademia and several early pieces in the Bargello Museum and Buonarroti's House. He sculpted three *Pietàs* over his long life—the first (1500) is in Rome's St. Peter's Basilica and the second (1550–1553) in Florence's Duomo Museum. He was working on the elongated *Rondanini Pietà*, now in Milan's Museum of Ancient Art, when he died.

- **Titian (1485–1576)** loved color and tonality and exploring the effects of light on darkened scenes. In Venice, his works are everywhere, from canvases in the Academy Galleries to altarpieces in churches such as Santa Maria Gloriosa dei Frari and his early *Battle* (1513) in the Ducal Palace's Maggior Consiglio. Fine works in Florence include the Uffizi's luminous *Flora* (1520) and the famous *Venus of Urbino* (1538), and the Palazzo Pitti's *Mary Magdalene* (1548) and *The Concert* (1510).

- **Mannerist Artists.** Artists who took Michelangelo's ideas to their logical limits include painters **Andrea del Sarto** (1486–1530) and his students **Rosso Fiorentino** (1494–1540) and **Pontormo** (1494–1556). The three are well represented in Florence's Uffizi Gallery and Palazzo Pitti. **Il Parmigianino**'s *Madonna of the Long Neck* (1534), in the Uffizi, is exemplary of the style, featuring a waifish

Virgin. Sculptors fared better with the Mannerism idea, producing statues that need to be viewed from multiple angles; a good example is **Giambologna**'s (1529–1608) *Rape of the Sabines* (1583) under Florence's Loggia della Signoria.

Baroque & Rococo (Late 16th–18th c.)

The **baroque,** a more theatrical and decorative take on the Renaissance, mixes a kind of super-realism based on using peasants as models and an exaggerated use of light and dark, called chiaroscuro, with compositional complexity and explosions of dynamic fury, movement, color, and figures. The even more dramatic **rococo** is later baroque art gone awry, frothy, and chaotic.

- **Michelangelo da Caravaggio (1571–1610)** used peasants as models and depicted the earthy facts of their lives. His chiaroscuro technique played areas of harsh light off deep, black shadows. Among his masterpieces are the *St. Matthew* (1599) cycle in Rome's San Luigi dei Franccsi, paintings in Rome's Galleria Borghese, the *Deposition* (1604) in the Vatican Museums, works in Florence's Uffizi Gallery and Palazzo Pitti, and in Naples's National Museum & Gallery of the Capodimonte.

- **Gian Bernini (1598–1680)** was the greatest baroque sculptor, a fantastic architect, and an accomplished painter. His finest sculptures are in the Galleria Borghese in Rome: *Aeneas and Anshises* (1613), *Apollo and Daphne* (1624), *The Rape of Persephone* (1621), and *David* (1623–24). His other masterpiece is the *Fountain of the Four Rivers* (1651), in Piazza Navona.

- **Giovanni Battista Tiepolo (1696–1770),** arguably the best rococo artist, specialized in ceiling frescoes and canvases painted with frothy, cloud-filled heavens of light, angels, and pale, early-morning colors. He created many works for Veneto villas and traveled through Europe on long commissions; his work in Würzburg, Germany, is the largest ceiling fresco in the world.

Late 18th Century to Today

Italy ran out of steam with the baroque, leaving countries such as France to develop the heights of **neoclassicism** and, in the late 19th century, Impressionism. Italy had its own version of the latter, called the *Macchiaioli*, in Tuscany.

- **Antonio Canova (1757–1822),** Italy's top neoclassical sculptor, was popular for his mythological figures and Bonaparte portraits. See his work in Venice's Correr Civic Museum, Rome's Galleria Borghese, Florence's Palazzo Pitti, and Milan's Brera Picture Gallery.

- **Giovanni Fattori (1825–1908)** painted battle scenes and landscapes populated by the Maremma's long-horned white cattle. His works grace Florence's Palazzo Pitti, Milan's Brera Picture Gallery, and Rome's National Gallery of Modern Art.

- **Amadeo Modigliani (1884–1920),** known for his elongated, mysterious heads and rapidly painted nudes, helped reinvent the portrait in painting and sculpture after he moved to Paris in 1906. Check out his work at Milan's Brera Picture Gallery and Rome's National Gallery of Modern Art.

- **Futurist Artists.** Part of the early-20th-century's futurist movement, **Umberto Boccioni** (1882–1916) painted in a style similar to cubism. His work can be seen in Milan's Brera Picture Gallery and Rome's National Gallery of Modern Art. **Gino Severini** (1883–1966) employed sophisticated colors that also inspired the core cubists; see his works in Milan's Civic Gallery of Modern Art and Rome's National Gallery of Modern Art.

- **Giorgio de Chirico (1888–1978)** founded *Pittura Metafisica* ("Metaphysical Painting"), a forerunner of Surrealism in which figures and objects are stripped of their usual meaning through odd juxtapositions, warped perspective, unnatural shadows, a general spatial emptiness, and other bizarre effects. Look for them at Milan's Brera

Picture Gallery and Rome's National Gallery of Modern Art and Collection of Modern Religious Art in the Vatican Museums.

- **Giorgio Morandi (1890–1964).** With his eerily minimalist, highly modeled, quasi-monochrome still lifes, Morandi was influenced by *Pittura Metafisica*. His paintings decorate Bologna's Palazzo Comunale, Milan's Brera Picture Gallery, and Rome's National Gallery of Modern Art and Collection of Religious Art in the Vatican Museums.

ITALIAN ARCHITECTURAL HISTORY

Classical: Greeks & Romans (6th c. B.C.–4th c. A.D.)

The **Greeks** settled Sicily and southern Italy, leaving behind some of the world's best-preserved ancient temples. The **Romans** made use of certain architectural Greek innovations. They adopted post-and-lintel construction (essentially, a weight-bearing frame, like a door) and then added the load-bearing arch. Roman builders were inventive engineers, developing a hoisting mechanism and a specially trained workforce.

Column design, characterized by capital-type, is important to Greek and Roman architecture: Doric columns have a plain capital, Ionic have a scrolled capital, and Corinthian have a capital with acanthus leaves. Less ornate capitals were used on the ground level and more ornate ones on upper levels.

Although marble is traditionally associated with Roman architecture, Roman engineers also worked with bricks and concrete—concrete seating made possible such enormous theaters as Rome's 2.4-hectare (6-acre), 45,000-seat Colosseum.

Where to See Classical Architecture Most **Greek temples** in southern Italy were built in the 5th century B.C., Doric style, including those at **Paestum** south of Naples, and in Sicily at **Segesta** and **Agrigento,** including the remarkably preserved Temple of Concord. **Greek theaters** survive in Sicily at Taormina, Segesta, and Syracuse (the largest in the ancient world).

CULTURE GUIDE

Examples of most major public buildings still exist in Rome: the Colosseum (1st c. A.D.); Hadrian's marvel of engineering, the Pantheon (1st c. A.D.); the brick public Baths of Caracalla (3rd c. A.D.); and the Basilica of Constantine and Maxentius in the Roman Forum (4th c. A.D.). Roman basilicas, which housed law courts, were rectangular structures supported by arches atop columns along the sides of the interior, with an apse at one or both ends; Christians adopted this form for their first grand churches.

You can visit three preserved Roman cities with street plans and some buildings intact: doomed Pompeii and its neighbor Herculaneum (both buried by Vesuvius's 79 A.D. eruption), and Rome's ancient seaport Ostia Antica.

Romanesque (A.D. 800–1300)

The Romanesque style took its inspiration and rounded arches from ancient Rome. Romanesque architects built large churches with wide aisles to accommodate the masses, who came to hear priests say Mass and to worship at the altars of various saints. To support all that masonry, walls had to be thick and solid (with only a few small windows), resting on huge piers, giving churches a dark, somber, mysterious, and often oppressive feeling.

- **Rounded arches.** These load-bearing architectural devices allowed architects to open up wide naves and spaces, channeling the weight of stone walls and ceilings across the curve of the arch and into the ground, via columns or pilasters.

- **Blind arcades.** A range of arches was carried on piers or columns and attached to a wall. Set into each arch's curve was often a lozenge, a diamond-shaped decoration, sometimes inlaid with colored marbles.

- **Stacked facade arches.** A tall facade was often created by stacking small, open-air loggias with columns of different styles on top of one another to a height of three to five levels.

Where to See the Romanesque   Modena's Duomo (12th c.) marks one of the earliest appearances of rounded arches, and its facade is covered with Romanesque reliefs. **Abbazia di Sant'Antimo** (1118), outside **Montalcino,** is a beautiful example of French Romanesque style. The tiered loggias and arcades of **Milan's Basilica di San Ambrogio** (11th–12th c.) became hallmarks of the Lombard Romanesque.

Pisa's Cathedral group (1153–1360s) is typical of the Pisan-Romanesque style, with stacked arcades of mismatched columns in the cathedral's facade (and wrapping around the famous Leaning Tower of Pisa) and blind arcading set with lozenges. **Lucca's Cattedrale di San Martino** and **San Michele** in Foro (11th–14th c.) are also prime examples of the style.

Gothic (Late 12th–Early 15th c.)

By the late 12th century, engineering developments freed architecture from the heavy, thick walls of the Romanesque and allowed ceilings to soar, walls to thin, and windows to proliferate.

In place of the dark, somber, relatively unadorned Romanesque interiors that forced the eyes of the faithful toward the altar, the Gothic interior enticed the churchgoers' gaze upward to high ceilings filled with light. Peasants could "read" the Gothic comic books of stained-glass windows.

The style began in France and was popular in Italy only in the northern region. From Florence south, most Gothic churches were built by the preaching orders of friars (Franciscans and Dominicans) as cavernous, barnlike structures.

- **Pointed arches.** The most significant development of the Gothic era was the discovery that pointed arches could carry far more weight than rounded ones.

Colosseum, Rome

- **Cross vaults.** Instead of being flat, the square patch of ceiling between four columns arches up to a point in the center, creating four sail shapes. The "X" separating these four sails is often reinforced with ridges called ribbing. Four-sided cross vaults later became multi-sided.

- **Tracery.** These lacy webs of carved stone grace the pointed ends of windows and sometimes the spans of ceiling vaults.

- **Flying buttresses.** These free-standing exterior pillars, connected by thin arms of stone, channel the weight of the building and its roof out and down into the ground. To help counter the cross forces, the piers of buttresses were often topped by heavy pinnacles in the form of minispires or statues.

- **Stained glass.** Because pointed arches carry more weight than rounded ones, windows could be larger and more numerous. They were often filled with Bible stories and symbolism written in the colorful patterns of stained glass.

Where to See Gothic Architecture The only truly French-style Gothic church in Italy is **Milan's massive Duomo and Baptistry** (begun ca. 1386), a lacy festival of pinnacles, buttresses, and pointy arches. Siena's Duomo (1136–1382), though started in the late Romanesque, has enough Giovanni Pisano sculptures and pointy arches to be considered Gothic. **Florence** has two of those barnlike Gothic churches: **Basilica di Santa Maria Novella** (1279–1357) and **Basilica di Santa Croce** (1294). The decorations inside **Santa Maria Sopra Minerva** (1280–1370) (**Rome**'s only Gothic church) are newer, but the architecture itself is all pointed arches and soaring ceilings.

Renaissance (15th–17th c.)

Renaissance architectural rules stressed proportion, order, classical inspiration, and mathematical precision to create unified, balanced structures. It was probably the architect **Filippo Brunelleschi,** in the early 1400s, who first grasped "perspective" and laid ground rules for creating the illusion of three dimensions on a flat surface. He often worked in soft white plaster walls with architectural details and lines in pale gray *pietra serena* stone.

Cathedral, Pisa

Where to See Renaissance Architecture Brunelleschi's masterpieces in **Florence** include the **Basilica di Santa Croce's Pazzi Chapel** (1442–1446); the interior of the **Basilica di San Lorenzo** (1425–1446); and the ingenious **dome** capping **Il Duomo** (1420–1446)—the Renaissance's debt to the ancients.

   Bramante (1444–1514), from Urbino, was perhaps the most mathematical and classically precise of the early High Renaissance architects, as is evident in his plans for **Rome's St. Peter's Basilica** (his spiral staircase in the Vatican Museum has survived untouched). Also see his jewel of perfect Renaissance architecture, the **Tempietto** (1502) at San Pietro in Montorio on the slopes of Rome's Gianicolo Hill.

   Michelangelo (1475–1564) took up architecture late in life, designing **Florence's Medici Laurentian Library** (1524) and **New Sacristy** (1524–1534), which houses the Medici Tombs at Basilica di San Lorenzo. In Rome, he created the facade of the **Palazzo Farnese** (1566) and the dome of St. Peter's Basilica.

   The fourth great High Renaissance architect was **Andrea Palladio** (1508–1580), who worked in a more classical mode of columns, porticoes, pediments, and other features inspired by ancient temples. His masterpieces include **Villa Foscari** and the **Villa Rotonda,** both in the **Veneto** countryside around Vicenza. His final work is **Vicenza's Olympic Theater** (1580), an attempt to reconstruct a Roman theater stage. Other designs include the Venetian church of **San Giorgio Maggiore** (1565–1610).

Baroque & Rococo (17th–18th c.)

Architects in the **baroque** period aimed toward a seamless meshing of architecture and art. Stuccoes, sculptures, and paintings were carefully designed to complement each other and the space itself to create a unified whole. This whole was both aesthetic and narrative, with the various art forms working together to tell a single biblical story or relate the deeds of the commissioning patron to historic or biblical events. The **rococo** style, excessively complex and dripping with decorative tidbits, is a kind of a twisted version of the baroque.

- **Classical architecture rewritten with curves.** The baroque style is similar to that of the Renaissance, but many right angles and ruler-straight lines are exchanged for curves of complex geometry and an interplay of concave and convex surfaces. The overall effect is to lighten the appearance of structures and add movement of line and vibrancy.

- **Complex decoration.** Unlike the sometimes severe and austere designs of the Renaissance, the baroque was playful. Architects festooned exteriors and encrusted interiors with an excess of decorations intended to liven things up— ornate stucco work, pouty cherubs, airy frescoes, heavy gilding, twisting columns, and multicolored marbles.

- **Multiplying forms.** Why use one column when you can stack a half-dozen partial columns on top of each other, slightly offset? Architects in the baroque loved to pile up forms and elements to create a rich, busy effect, breaking a pediment curve into segments so that each would protrude farther out than the last, or building up an architectural feature by stacking short sections of concave walls, each one curving to a different arc.

Where to See the Baroque & Rococo   The baroque flourished across Italy. Though relatively sedate, Carlo Maderno's facade and Bernini's sweeping elliptical colonnade for **Rome's St. Peter's Square** make one of Italy's outstanding baroque assemblages. A quirky, felicitous baroque style flourished in the Apulian city **Leece.** When an earthquake decimated the Sicilian town of **Noto,** it was rebuilt from scratch on a complete baroque city plan.

For the rococo—more a decorative than architectural movement—look no further than **Rome's Spanish Steps** (1726), by architect de Sanctis, or the **Trevi Fountain** (1762), by Salvi.

Neoclassical to Modern (18th–21st c.)

As a backlash against the excesses of the baroque and rococo, architects turned to the simplicity and grandeur of the classical age and inaugurated the **neoclassical** style by the middle of the 18th century. Their work was inspired by the rediscovery of Pompeii and other ancient sites.

In the late 19th and 20th centuries, Italy's architectural styles went in several directions. The **Industrial Age** brought with it the first genteel shopping malls of glass and steel. The country's take on the Art Nouveau movement was called **Liberty Style**. Mussolini made an attempt to bring back ancient Rome in what can only be called **Fascist architecture.** Since then, Italy has built mostly concrete and glass **skyscrapers,** like the rest of the world.

- **Neoclassical.** The classical ideals of mathematical proportion and symmetry are the hallmark of every classically styled era. Neoclassicists reinterpreted ancient temples as buildings and as decorative, massive colonnade porticos.

- **Liberty Style.** Like Art Nouveau practitioners elsewhere, Italian decorators rebelled against mass production by stressing craft. They created asymmetrical, curvaceous designs based on organic inspiration (plants and flowers) and used wrought iron, stained glass, tile, and hand-painted wallpaper.

- **Fascist.** Buildings of this period are cold, imposing, stark, white marble structures surrounded by classical statuary.

Where to See the Neoclassical & Modern Architecture   Of the **neoclassical, Caserta's Royal Palace** (1752–1774), outside Naples, was an attempt to create a Versailles for the Bourbon monarchs. The huge (and generally derided) **Vittorio Emanuele Monument** (1884–1927) in Rome, has been compared to a Victorian typewriter.

Fascist architecture still infests corners of Italy, although most right-wing reliefs and repeated engravings of DVCE—Mussolini's nickname—have been chipped out. You can see it in Rome's planned satellite community **EUR,** which includes a multi-story "square Colosseum" that has been featured in many films and music videos, and in **Rome's Stadio Olimpico** complex.

The mid–20th century was dominated by **Pier Luigi Nervi** (1891–1979) and his reinforced concrete buildings, **Florence's Giovanni Berta Stadium** (1932), **Rome's Palazzo dello Sport stadium** (1960), and **Turin's Exposition Hall** (1949).

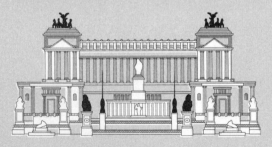

Vittorio Emanuele Monument, Rome

DICTIONARY KEY

n	noun	m	masculine
v	verb	f	feminine
adj	adjective	s	singular
prep	preposition	pl	plural
adv	adverb	pron	pronoun
interj	interjection		

All verbs are listed in infinitive (to + verb) form, cross-referenced to the appropriate conjugations page. Adjectives are listed first in masculine singular form, followed by the feminine ending.

For food terms, see the Menu Reader (p91) and Grocery Section (p100) in Chapter 4, Dining.

A

able, to be able to (can) v potere **p30**

above prep sopra

accept, to accept v accettare **p20**

Do you accept credit cards? Accettate la carta di credito?

accident n l'incidente m

I've had an accident. Ho avuto un incidente.

account n il conto m

I'd like to transfer to / from my checking account. Vorrei trasferire dei fondi al / dal mio conto corrente.

I'd like to transfer to / from my savings account. Vorrei trasferire dei fondi al / dal mio conto di risparmio.

acne n l'acne f

across prep attraverso, dall'altro lato di

across the street dall'altro lato della strada

actual adj reale

adapter plug n lo spinotto adattore m

address n l'indirizzo m

What's the address? Qual è l'indirizzo?

admission fee n il prezzo d'ingresso m

in advance in anticipo

African-American adj afroamericano -a

after prep dopo

afternoon n il pomeriggio m

in the afternoon nel / di pomeriggio

age n l'età f **p116**

What's your age? Quanti anni ha?

agency n l'agenzia f

(travel) l'agenzia viaggi m

agnostic adj agnostico -a

air conditioning n l'aria condizionata f
Would you lower / raise the air conditioning? Può abbassare / aumentare l'aria condizionata?
airport n l'aeroporto m
I need a ride to the airport. Ho bisogno di un passaggio all'aeroporto.
How far is it from the airport? Quanto dista dall'aeroporto?
airsickness bag n il sacchetto per il mal d'aria m
aisle (in store) n la corsia f
Which aisle is it in? In quale corsia si trova?
alarm clock n la sveglia f
alcohol n l'alcol m
Do you serve alcohol? Servite bevande alcoliche?
I'd like nonalcoholic beer. Vorrei una birra analcolica.
all n il tutto m
all of the time sempre
That's all, thank you. È tutto, grazie.
all adj tutto -a
allergic adj allergico -a See common allergens,
I'm allergic to ____. Sono allergico -a a ____.
altitude n l'altitudine f
aluminum n l'alluminio m
ambulance n l'ambulanza f
American adj americano -a
amount n la quantità f

angry adj arrabbiato -a
animal n l'animale m
another adj altro -a
answer n la risposta f
answer, to answer v rispondere **p20**
Answer me, please. Per cortesia, mi risponda.
antibiotic n l'antibiotico m
I need an antibiotic. Ho bisogno di un antibiotico.
antihistamine n l'antistaminico m
anxious adj ansioso -a
any adj qualsiasi
anything n qualsiasi cosa f
anywhere adv dovunque
appointment n l'appuntamento m
Do I need an appointment? Ho bisogno di un appuntamento?
April n aprile m
are See be, to be, p24
arm n il braccio m, le braccia f
arrival(s) n l'arrivo m / gli arrivi m pl
arrive, to arrive v arrivare **p20**
art n l'arte f
exhibit of art la mostra d'arte
art museum il museo d'arte
fine arts le belle arti
Renaissance art l'arte del Rinascimento
artist n l'artista m f
Asian adj asiatico -a

ask, to ask v chiedere, domandare **p20**

to ask for (to request) chiedere

to ask a question fare una domanda **p28**

aspirin n l'aspirina f

assist, to assist v assistere **p21**

assistance n l'assistenza f

asthma n l'asma f

  I have asthma. Ho l'asma.

at prep a, in

atheist adj, n ateo -a

ATM / cash machine n il bancomat m

  I'm looking for an ATM / cash machine. Sto cercando un bancomat.

attend, to attend v partecipare **p20**

audio adj, n l'audio m

August n agosto m

aunt n la zia f

Australia n l'Australia f

Australian adj australiano -a

autumn n l'autunno m

available adj disponibile

B

baby n il / la bambino -a m f

baby adj per bambini

  Do you sell baby food? Vendete cibi per bambini?

babysitter n il / la baby-sitter m f

  Do you have babysitters? Avete baby-sitter?

Do you have babysitters who speak English? Avete delle baby-sitter che parlano inglese?

back n la schiena f

  My back hurts. Mi fa male la schiena.

back rub n il massaggio alla schiena m

backed up (toilet) adj intasato m

  The toilet is backed up! Il gabinetto è intasato!

bag n la borsa f, il sacchetto m

  airsickness bag il sacchetto per il mal d'aria.

  My bag was stolen. La mia borsa è stata rubata.

  I lost my bag. Ho perso la mia borsa.

bag, to bag v mettere in borsa **p20**

baggage adj, n il bagaglio m

  baggage claim il recupero bagagli

bait n l'esca f

balance (on bank account) n il saldo m

balance, to balance v bilanciare **p20**

balcony n il balcone m

ball (sport) n la palla f

ballroom dancing n il ballo da sala m

band (musical ensemble) n il gruppo m

band-aid n il cerotto m

bank *n* la banca *f*

> **Do you know where I can find a bank?** Sa dov'è una banca?

bar *n* il bar *m*

barber *n* il barbiere *m*

bass (instrument) *n* il basso *m*

bath *n* il bagno *m*, la toilette *f*

bathroom (restroom) *n* il bagno *m*

> **Where is the nearest public bathroom?** Sa dov'è il bagno pubblico più vicino?

bathtub *n* la vasca da bagno *f*

bathe, to bathe *v* fare il bagno p28

battery (for flashlight) *n* la pila *f*

battery (for car) *n* la batteria *f*

bee *n* l'ape *f*

> **I was stung by a bee.** Mi ha punto un'ape.

be, to be *v* essere p26, stare p25

beach *n* la spiaggia *f*

beach, to beach *v* tirare a riva p20

beautiful *adj* bello -a

bed *n* il letto *m*

beer *n* la birra *f*

> **beer on tap** la birra alla spina

begin, to begin *v* cominciare, iniziare p20

behave, to behave *v* comportarsi p20, 35

behind *prep, adv* dietro -a

below *prep, adv* sotto -a

belt *n* la cintura *f*

> **conveyor belt** il nastro trasportatore

berth *n* la cuccetta *f*

best *adj* il / la migliore

bet *n* la scommessa *f*

> **I'll see your bet.** Eguaglio la sua scommessa.

bet, to bet *v* scommettere p20

better *adj* migliore

between *prep* fra, tra

big *adj* grande

bilingual *adj* bilingue

bill (currency) *n* la banconota *f*
(check) *n* il conto *m*
(utility bill) *n* la bolletta *f*

bill, to bill *v* mandare il conto p20

biography *n* la biografia *f*

biracial *adj* birazziale

bird *n* l'uccello *m*

birth control *n* la contraccezione *f*

birth control (contraceptive) *adj* anticoncezionale

> **I'm out of birth control pills.** Non ho più pillole anticoncezionali.
> **I need more birth control pills.** Ho bisogno di più pillole anticoncezionali.

bit (small amount) *n* un poco *m*

black *adj* nero -a

blanket *n* la coperta *f*

bleach *n* la candeggina *f*

blind *adj* cieco -a

block, to block *v* bloccare p20

ENGLISH—ITALIAN

blond(e) *adj, n* il / la biondo -a
blouse *n* la camicetta *f*
blue *adj* azzurro -a, blu
blurry *adj* annebbiato -a
board *n* l'asse *f*
   on board a bordo
board, to board *v* salire a
   bordo di **p21**
boarding pass *n* la carta
   d'imbarco *f*
boat *n* l'imbarcazione *f*
bomb *n* la bomba *f*
book *n* il libro *m*
bookstore *n* la libreria *f*
boss *n* il capo *m*
bottle *n* la bottiglia *f*
   May I heat this (baby) bot-
   tle someplace? Posso
   riscaldare questo biberon
   da qualche parte?
box (seat) *n* il palco *m*
box office *n* la biglietteria *f*
boy *n* il ragazzo *m*
boyfriend (friend, date) *n* il
   ragazzo *m*, boy-friend *m*
braid *n* la treccia *f*
braille, American *n* il braille
   americano *m*
brake *n* il freno *m*
   emergency brake il freno
   d'emergenza
brake, to brake *v* frenare **p20**
brandy *n* il brandy *m*
bread *n* il pane *m*
break, to break *v* rompere **p20**
breakfast *n* la colazione *f*
   What time is breakfast? A
   che ora è la colazione?

bridge (across a river, dental
   structure) *n* il ponte *m*
   I need a new bridge. Ho
   bisogno di un'altra protesi
   dentaria.
briefcase *n* la borsa portadocumenti *f*
bright *adj* brillante, luminoso -a
broadband *n* la banda larga *f*
bronze *adj* bronzo
brother *n* il fratello *m*
brown *adj* marrone
brunette *n* il / la bruno -a *m f*
Buddhist *adj* il / la buddista
budget *n* il bilancio *m*
buffet *n* il buffet *m*
bug *n* l'insetto *m*
burn, to burn *v* bruciare,
   incendiare **p20**
   Can I burn a CD here? Posso
   masterizzare un CD qui?
bus *n* l'autobus *m*
   Where is the bus stop?
   Dov'è la fermata degli
   autobus?
   Which bus goes to ____?
   Quale autobus va a ____?
business *n* l'attività *m*
business *adj* commerciale
   business center il centro
   affari
busy (restaurant) *adj* affollato -a **(phone)** *adj* occupato -a
butter *n* il burro *m*
buy, to buy *v* acquistare,
   comprare **p20**

C

café *n* il caffè *m*, il bar *m*
  Internet café il Internet café
call, to call (shout) *v* gridare (telephone) *v* chiamare **p20**
camp, to camp *v* campeggiare, fare campeggio **p20, 28**
camper (person) *n* il campeggiatore / la campeggiatrice
  Do we need a camping permit? Abbiamo bisogno d'un permesso di campeggio?
campsite *n* l'area di campeggio *f*
can *n* la scatola *f*, la lattina *f*
can (to be able to) *v* potere **p30**
Canada *n* il Canada *m*
Canadian *adj, n* canadese *m f*
cancel, to cancel *v* cancellare **p20**
  My flight was canceled. Il mio volo è stato cancellato.
canvas (art) *n* la tela *f*
car *n* l'auto *f*, la macchina *f*
  See car types, .
  car rental agency l'autonoleggio
  I need a rental car. Mi serve un'auto a noleggio.
card *n* la carta *f*
  Do you accept credit cards? Accettate le carte di credito?

  May I have your business card? Posso avere il suo biglietto da visita?
  I'd like a greeting card. Vorrei un biglietto d'auguri.
car seat (child's safety seat) *n* il sedile di sicurezza *m*
  Do you rent car seats for children? Noleggiate sedili di sicurezza per bambini?
car sickness *n* il mal d'auto *m*
cash *n* i contanti *m*, i soldi *m*
  cash only solo contanti
cash, to cash *v* incassare **p20**
  to cash out (gambling) incassare la vincita
cash machine / ATM *n* il bancomat *m*
cashmere *adj, n* il cashmere *m*
casino *n* il casinò *m*
cat *n* il / la gatto -a *m f*
Catholic *adj, n* cattolico -a
cavity (tooth) *n* la carie *f*
  I think I have a cavity. Credo di avere una carie.
CD *n* il CD *m*
CD player *n* il lettore di CD *m*
celebrate, to celebrate *v* celebrare **p20**
cell / mobile phone *n* il cellulare *m*
centimeter *n* il centimetro *m*
chamber music *n* la musica da camera *f*

change (money) n il resto m

I'd like change, please.
Vorrei degli spiccioli, per
cortesia.

**This isn't the correct
change.** Questo resto non
è esatto.

**change (to change money or
clothes)** v cambiare **p20**

changing room n il camerino m

charge, to charge (money) v
addebitare **(a battery)** v
caricare **p20**

charmed (greeting) piacere

charred (meat) adj bruciacchiato -a

charter, to charter v noleggiare **p20**

cheap adj economico a

check / money order n
l'assegno m

**Do you accept travelers'
checks?** Accettate i trav-
ellers' checks?

check, to check v verificare **p20**

checked (pattern) adj a
quadretti

check-in (airport) n il check-
in m

What time is check-in? A
che ora è il check-in?

check-out (hotel) n la
partenza f

check-out time l'orario di
partenza

What time is check-out? A
che ora è la partenza?

**check out, to check out
(hotel)** v pagare il conto
dell'albergo **p20**

cheese n il formaggio m

chicken n il pollo m

child n il / la bambino -a m f

children n i / le bambini -e m f

Are children allowed? Sono
ammessi i bambini?

**Do you have children's pro-
grams?** Avete dei pro-
grammi per bambini?

**Do you have a children's
menu?** Avete un menu per
bambini?

Chinese adj cinese m f

chiropractor n il chiropratico m

chrysanthemum n il crisan-
temo m

church n la chiesa f

cigarette n la sigaretta f

a pack of cigarettes un pacchetto di sigarette m

cinema n il cinema m

city n la città f

claim n il reclamo m

I'd like to file a claim. Vorrei
fare un reclamo.

clarinet n il clarinetto m

class n la classe f

business class la classe business

economy class la classe economica

first class la prima classe

classical (music, taste) adj
classico -a

clean *adj* pulito -a

clean, to clean *v* pulire **p21**

Please clean the room today. Per favore, oggi pulisca la camera.

clear *adj* chiaro -a

climb, ascent *n* la scalata *f*

climb, to climb *v* scalare, salire **p20, 21**

(a mountain) scalare una montagna **p20**

(stairs) salire le scale

close, to close *v* chiudere **p20**

close (near) *adj* vicino -a

closed *adj* chiuso -a

cloudy *adj* nuvoloso -a

clover *n* il trifoglio *m*

go clubbing, to go clubbing *v* andare per locali notturni **p27**

coat *n* il cappotto *m*

coffee *n* il caffè *m*

iced coffee il caffè freddo

cognac *n* il cognac *m*

coin *n* la moneta *f p*

cold *adj* freddo -a

cold *n* il freddo *m*

I'm cold. Ho freddo.

It's cold. Fa freddo.

cold (infection) *n* il raffreddore *m*

I have a cold. Ho il raffreddore.

Coliseum *n* il Colosseo *m*

collect *adj* a carico del destinatario

I'd like to place a collect call. Vorrei fare una telefonata a carico del destinatario.

collect, to collect *v* raccogliere **p20**

college *n* l' università *f*

color *n* il colore *m*

color, to color *v* colorare **p20**

common *adj* comune

computer *n* il computer *m*

concert *n* il concerto *m*

condition *n* la condizione *f*

in good / bad condition in buone / cattive condizioni

condom *n* il condom *m*

Do you have a condom? Hai un condom?

Not without a condom. Non senza un condom.

confirm, to confirm *v* confermare **p20**

I'd like to confirm my reservation. Vorrei confermare la mia prenotazione.

confused *adj* confuso -a

congested *adj* congestionato -a

connection speed *n* la velocità di connessione *f*

constipated *adj* stitico -a

I'm constipated. Sono stitico -a.

contact lenses *n* le lenti a contatto *f pl*

I lost my contact lenses. Ho perso le mie lenti a contatto.

continue, to continue v continuare **p20**

convertible n la ecappottibile f

cook, to cook v cucinare **p20**

I'd like a room where I can cook. Vorrei una stanza con uso cucina.

cookie n il biscotto m

copper adj rame

corner n l'angolo m

on the corner all'angolo

correct, to correct v correggere **p20**

correct adj giusto -a

Am I on the correct train? Mi trovo sul treno giusto?

cost, to cost v costare **p20**

How much does it cost? Quanto costa?

costume n il costume m

cotton n il cotone m

cough n la tosse f

cough, to cough v tossire **p21**

counter (board) n il banco m

court (legal) n il tribunale m

court (sport) n il campo m

courteous adj cortese

cousin n il / la cugino -a m f

cover charge (bar, restaurant) n il coperto m

cow n la mucca f

crack (glass) n l'incrinatura f

craftsperson n l'artigiano -a m f

cream n la crema f

credit card n la carta di credito f

Do you accept credit cards? Accettate carte di credito?

crib n la culla f

crown (dental) n la capsula f

curb n il bordo del marciapiede m

curl n il riccio m

curly adj riccio -a

currency exchange n il cambio di valuta m

Where is the nearest currency exchange? Sa dove si trova il cambio di valuta più vicino?

current (water, electricity) n la corrente f

customs n la dogana f

cut (wound) n la ferita f

I have a bad cut. Ho una brutta ferita.

cut, to cut v tagliare **p20**

cybercafé n l'Internet café m

Where can I find a cybercafé? Sa dove posso trovare un Internet café?

D

damaged adj danneggiato -a

Damn! expletive Dannazione!

dance, to dance v ballare **p20**

danger n il pericolo m

dark adj scuro -a

dark n il buio m

daughter n la figlia f

day n il giorno m

the day before yesterday
ieri l'altro

these last few days questi
ultimi giorni

dawn *n* l'alba *f*

at dawn all'alba

deaf *adj* sordo -a

deal (bargain) *n* l'affare *m*

What a great deal! Che
affarone!

deal, to deal (cards) *v* dare le
carte **p28**

Deal me in. Dia le carte
anche a me.

December *n* dicembre *m*

declined *adj* rifiutato -a

**Was my credit card
declined?** La mia carta di
credito è stata rifiutata?

declare, to declare *v*
dichiarare **p20**

I have nothing to declare.
Non ho niente da
dichiarare.

deep *adj* profondo -a

delay *n* il ritardo *m*

How long is the delay?
Quanto dura il ritardo?

delighted *adj* felicissimo -a

democracy *n* la democrazia *f*

dent, to dent *v* ammaccare
p20

He / She dented the car. Lui
/ Lei ha ammaccato la
macchina.

dentist *n* il dentista *m f*

denture *n* la dentiera *f*

denture plate la piastra
dentale

departure *n* la partenza *f*

designer *n* lo / la stilista *m f*

dessert *n* il dolce *p*

dessert menu la lista dei
dolci

destination *n* la destinazione *f*

diabetic *adj* diabetico -a

dial, to dial (phone number)
v fare il numero **p28**

dial direct fare il numero
diretto

diaper *n* il pannolino *m*

**Where can I change a dia-
per?** Dove posso cambiare
il pannolino?

diarrhea *n* la diarrea *f*

dictionary *n* il dizionario *m*

different (other) *adj* diverso -a,
altro -a

difficult *adj* difficile

dinner *n* la cena *f*

directory assistance (phone)
n l'assistenza telefonica *f*

disability *n* l'invalidità *f*

disappear, to disappear *v*
sparire **p21**

disco *n* il disco *m*

disconnect, to disconnect *v*
staccare **p20**

disconnected *adj* staccato -a

**Operator, I was discon-
nected.** Centralino, è
caduta la linea.

discount n lo sconto m
Do I qualify for a discount?
Posso ricevere uno sconto?
dish n il piatto m
dive, to dive v tuffarsi **p35**
scuba dive l'immersione sub-acquea con le bombole
divorced adj divorziato -a
dizzy adj stordito -a
do, to do v fare **p28**
doctor n il medico m f
doctor's office n lo studio del medico m
dog n il cane m
service / guide dog il cane guida
dollar n il dollaro m
door n la porta f
double adj doppio -a
double bed il letto a due piazze
double vision la visione doppio
down adv giù
download, to download v scaricare **p20**
downtown n il centro città m
dozen n la dozzina f
drain n lo scarico m
drama n il dramma m
drawing (art) n il disegno m
dress (garment) n il vestito m
dress (general attire) n l'abbigliamento m
What's the dress code?
Come ci si deve vestire?

dress, to dress v vestirsi **p35**
Should I dress up for that affair? Dovrei vestirsi bene per quella festa?
dressing (salad) n il condimento m
dried adj secco -a
drink n la bevanda f
I'd like a drink. Vorrei una bibita.
drink, to drink v bere **p29**
drip, to drip v sgocciolare **p20**
drive, to drive v guidare **p20**
driver n l'autista m f
drum n il tamburo m
dry adj secco -a, asciutto -a
This towel isn't dry. Questo asciugamano non è asciutto.
dry, to dry v asciugarsi **p20**
I need to dry my clothes.
Devo asciugarmi i vestiti.
dry cleaner n la lavanderia a secco f
dry cleaning n il lavaggio a secco m
duck n l'anatra f
duty-free adj esente tasse, duty-free
duty-free shop n il negozio duty-free m
DVD n il DVD m
Do the rooms have DVD players? C'è il lettore di DVD nelle stanze?

Where can I rent DVDs or videos? Sa dove posso noleggiare DVD o video?

E

early *adv* presto
It's early. E' presto.
eat, to eat *v* mangiare p20
to eat out *v* mangiare fuori
economy *n* l'economia *f*
editor *n* il redattore *m*, la redattrice *f*
educator *n* l'educatore *m*, l'educatrice *f*
eight *adj* otto
eighteen *adj* diciotto
eighth *adj* ottavo -a
eighty *adj* ottanta
election *n* l'elezione *f*
electrical hookup *n* il collegamento elettrico *m*
elevator *n* l'ascensore *m*
eleven *adj* undici
e-mail *n* l'e-mail *f*
May I have your e-mail address? Posso avere il suo indirizzo di e-mail?
e-mail message il messaggio e-mail
e-mail, to send e-mail *v* inviare un'e-mail p20
embarrassed *adj* imbarazzato -a
embassy *n* l'ambasciata *f*
emergency *n* l'emergenza *f*
emergency brake *n* il freno d'emergenza *m*

emergency exit *n* l'uscita d'emergenza *f*
employee *n* il / la dipendente *m f*
employer *n* il datore di lavoro / la datrice di lavoro *m f*
engine *n* il motore *m*
engineer *n* l'ingegnere *m f*
England *n* l'Inghilterra *f*
English *n, adj* inglese *m f*
Do you speak English? Parla inglese?
enjoy, to enjoy *v* piacere p33
enter, to enter *v* entrare p20
Do not enter. Vietato l'ingresso.
enthusiastic *adj* entusiasta
entrance *n* l'entrata *f*
envelope *n* la busta *f*
environment *n* l'ambiente *m*
escalator *n* la scala mobile *f*
espresso *n* il caffè *m*
evening *n* la sera *f*
exchange rate *n* il cambio *m*
What is the exchange rate for U.S. / Canadian dollars? Qual è il cambio del dollaro USA / canadese?
excuse, to excuse (pardon) *v* scusare p20
Excuse me. Mi scusi.
(to get through) Permesso.
exhausted *adj* esausto -a
exhibit *n* la mostra *f*
exit *n* l'uscita *f*
not an exit senza uscita
exit, to exit *v* uscire p32

ENGLISH—ITALIAN

expensive adj caro -a
explain, to explain v spiegare p20
express adj espresso -a
express check-in il check-in espresso
extra (additional) adj extra / in più
extra-large adj extra-large
eye n l'occhio m
eyebrow n il sopracciglio m
eyeglasses n gli occhiali m
eyelashes n le ciglia f pl

F

fabric n il tessuto m
face n il viso m
faint, to faint v svenire p21
fall (season) n l'autunno m
fall, to fall v cadere p20
family n la famiglia f
fan n il ventilatore m
far adj lontano -a
  How far is it to _____?
  Quanto dista _____?
fare n la tariffa f
fast adj veloce
fat adj grasso -a
fat n il grasso m
father n il padre m
faucet n il rubinetto m
fault n il torto m
  I'm at fault. E' colpa mia.
  It was his fault. E' colpa sua.
fax n il fax m
February n febbraio m
fee n l'onorario m, la tassa f

female adj femminile f
female n la donna / la femmina f
fiancé(e) n il / la fidanzato -a m f
fifteen adj quindici
fifth adj quinto -a
fifty adj cinquanta
find, to find v trovare p20
fine (traffic violation) n la multa f
fine adj bello -a
  I'm fine (well). Sto bene.
fire n il fuoco m
  Fire! Al fuoco!
first adj primo -a
fishing pole n la canna da pesca f
fitness center n il centro benessere m,
fit, to fit (size) v andare bene p27 **(looks)** v stare bene p25, 35
  This doesn't fit. Questo non mi va bene.
  Does this look like it fits? Sembra che mi stia bene?
fitting room n il camerino m
five adj cinque
flight n il volo
  Where do domestic flights arrive? Dove arrivano i voli nazionali?
  Where do domestic flights depart? Da dove partono i voli nazionali?

Where do international flights arrive? Dove arrivano i voli internazionali?

Where do international flights depart? Da dove partono i voli internazionali?

What time does this flight leave? A che ora parte questo volo?

flight attendant l'assistente di volo *m f*

floor *n* il piano *m* **(ground)** *n* il pavimento *m*

ground floor il pianoterra

first floor il primo piano

flower *n* il fiore *m*

flush (gambling) *n* il flush *m*

flush, to flush *v* tirare l'acqua del water **p20**

This toilet won't flush. Non si può tirare l'acqua a questo water.

flute *n* il flauto *m*

food *n* il cibo *m*

foot (body part) *n* il piede *m*

for *prep* per

forehead *n* la fronte *f*

format *n* il formato *m*

formula *n* la formula *f*

Do you sell infants' formula? Vendete il latte in polvere?

forty *adj* quaranta

forward *adv* avanti

four *adj* quattro

fourteen *adj* quattordici

fourth *adj* quarto -a

one fourth un quarto *m*

fragile *adj* fragile

freckle *n* la lentiggine *f*

French *adj* francese *m f*

fresh *adj* fresco -a

Friday *n* venerdì *m*

friend *n* l'amico -a, *m f*

from *prep* da

front *adj* anteriore *adv* davanti

front desk la reception

front door la porta principale

fruit *n* il frutto *m* **(collective)** *n* la frutta *f*

fruit juice *n* il succo di frutta *m See fruits, .*

full *adj* pieno -a

Full house! *n* Full house! *f*

fuse *n* la valvola fusibile *f*

G

garlic *n* l'aglio *m*

gas *n* il gas *m* **(fuel)** *n* la benzina *f*

gas gauge la spia del serbatoio

out of gas la benzina è finita

gate (at airport) *n* l'uscita *f*

German *adj, n* tedesco -a *m f*

gift *n* il regalo *m*

girl *n* la ragazza *f*

girlfriend *n* la ragazza *f*

give, to give *v* dare **p28**

glass (drinking) n il bicchiere m
Do you have it by the glass? Lo servite a bicchiere?
I'd like a glass please. Vorrei un bicchiere per favore.
glass (material) n il vetro m
glasses (spectacles) n gli occhiali m, pl
I need new glasses. Ho bisogno di nuovi occhiali.
glove n il guanto m
go, to go v andare p27
goal (sport) n il goal m
goalie n il portiere m
gold adj oro
golf n il golf m
golf, to go golfing v giocare a golf p20
good adj buono -a
goodbye n arrivederci m See common salutations, .
goose n l'oca f
grade (school) n la classe f
gram n il grammo m
grandfather n il nonno m
grandmother n la nonna f
grandparents n i nonni m pl
grape n l'uva f
gray adj grigio -a
Great! adj Eccellente!
Greek adj greco -a
Greek Orthodox adj greco-ortodosso -a
green adj verde
groceries n la spesa f
group n il gruppo m

grow, to grow (get larger) v crescere p20
Where did you grow up? Dov'è cresciuto -a?
guard n la guardia f
security guard la guardia di sicurezza
guest n l'ospite m f
guide (tour) n la guida f (publication) n la guida f
guide, to guide v guidare p20
guided tour n la gita guidata f
guitar n la chitarra m
gym n la palestra f
gynecologist n il / la ginecologo -a m f

H
hair n i capelli m pl
haircut n il taglio di capelli m
I need a haircut. Ho bisogno di un taglio ai capelli.
How much is a haircut? Quanto costa il taglio?
hairdresser n il / la parrucchiere -a m f
hair dryer n l'asciugacapelli m
half adj mezzo -a
half n la metà f
hallway n il corridoio m
hand n la mano f, le mani f, pl
handbag n la borsetta f
handicapped-accessible adj accessibile ai disabili
handle, to handle v maneggiare p20

Handle with care.
Maneggiare con cura.

handsome *adj* bello -a

hangout (hot spot) *n* il ritrovo *m*

hang out, to hang out (relax) *v* rilassarsi p20, 35

hang up, to hang up (end a phone call) *v* riattaccare p20

hanger *n* la gruccia *f*

happy *adj* felice

hard *adj* duro -a

hat *n* il cappello *m*, il berretto *m*

have, to have *v* avere p27

hazel *adj* color nocciola

hazel (nut) *n* la nocciola *f*

headache *n* il mal di testa *m*

headlight *n* il faro della macchina *m*

headphones *n* le cuffie *f pl*

hear, to hear *v* udire, sentire p21

hearing-impaired *adj* ipoudente

heart *n* il cuore *m*

heart attack *n* l'infarto *m*

hectare *n* l'ettaro *m* 10

Hello! *n* Salve! / Ciao! *See greetings,* .

Help! *n* Aiuto!

help, to help *v* aiutare p20

hen *n* la gallina *f*

her *pron* lei *f*

her, hers *adj, pron* suo -a, suoi / sue *pl*

herb *n* l'erbetta *f*

here *adv* qui, qua

high *adj* alto -a

highlights (hair) *n* i colpi di sole *m*

highway *n* l'autostrada *f*

hike, to hike *v* fare un'escursione a piedi p28

him *pron* lui *m*

Hindu *adj* indù

hip-hop *n* l'hip-hop *m*

his *adj, pron* suo -a, *sing,* suoi / sue *pl*

historical *adj* storico -a

history *n* la storia *f*

hobby *n* l'hobby *m*

hold, to hold *v* reggere p20

to hold hands tenersi per mano

Would you hold this for me? Può reggermi questo, per favore?

hold, to hold (wait) *v* aspettare p20

Hold on a minute! Aspetti un attimo!

I'll hold. Sì, attendo.

holiday *n* la festa *f*

to go on holiday andare in vacanza

home *n* la casa *f*

homemaker *n* il marito casalingo *m* / la casalinga *f*

horn *n* il corno *m*

horse *n* il cavallo *m*

hostel *n* l'ostello della gioventù *m*

hot *adj* caldo -a

hot chocolate *n* la cioccolata calda *f*

hotel *n* l'albergo, l'hotel *m*

Do you have a list of local hotels? Ha un elenco di alberghi locali?

hour *n* l'ora *f*

hours (schedule) *n* l'orario *m*

how *adv* come

humid *adj* umido -a

hundred *adj* cento

hurry, to hurry *v* aver fretta p27

I'm in a hurry. Ho fretta.

Hurry, please! Si sbrighi per favore!

hurt, to hurt *v* far male p28

Ouch! That hurts! Ahi! Fa male!

husband *n* il marito *m*

I

I *pron* io

ice *n* il ghiaccio *m*

identification *n* il documento di riconoscimento *m*

in *prep* in

indigestion *n* l'indigestione *f*

inexpensive *adj* economico -a

infant *n* il / la neonato -a *m f*

Are infants allowed? Si possono portare i neonati?

information *n* l'informazione *f*

information booth *n* il banco informazioni *f*

injury *n* la ferita *f*

insect repellent *n* l'insetto-repellente *m*

inside *adj* interno -a

inside *adv* dentro

insult, to insult *v* insultare p20

insurance *n* l'assicurazione *f*

intercourse (sexual) *n* il rapporto sessuale *m*

interest rate *n* il tasso d'interesse *m*

intermission *n* l'intervallo *m*

Internet *n* l'Internet *m*

High-speed Internet l'Internet ad alta velocità

Do you have Internet access? Avete l'accesso a Internet?

Where can I find an Internet café? Sa dove posso trovare un Internet café?

interpreter *n* l'interprete *m f*

I need an interpreter. Mi serve un interprete.

introduce, to introduce *v* presentare p20

I'd like to introduce you to _____. Ho il piacere di presentarle _____.

Ireland *n* l'Irlanda *f*

Irish *adj* irlandese *m f*

is See be, to be, p24.

Italian *adj* italiano -a

J

jacket *n* la giacca *f*

January *n* gennaio *m*

Japanese *adj* giapponese

jazz *n* il jazz *m*

Jewish *adj* ebreo -a

jog, to run *v* correre p20

juice *n* il succo *m*

July *n* luglio *m*

June *n* giugno *m*

K

keep, to keep *v* tenere, conservare p20

kid *n* il / la ragazzo -a *m f*

Are kids allowed? Sono ammessi i ragazzi?

Do you have kids' programs? Avete programmi per ragazzi?

Do you have a kids' menu? Avete un menu per i ragazzi?

kilo *n* il chilo *m*

kilometer *n* il chilometro *m*

kind (type) *n* il tipo *m*

(nice) *adj* gentile simpatico -a

What kind is it? Che tipo è?

kiss *n* il bacio *m*

kitchen *n* la cucina *f*

know, to know (something) *v* sapere p31

know, to know (someone) *v* conoscere p20

kosher *adj* kasher

L

lactose-intolerant *adj* intollerante al lattosio

land, to land *v* atterrare p20

landscape (painting) *n* il paesaggio *m*, **(land)** *n* il panorama *m*

language *n* la lingua *f*

laptop *n* il portatile *m*

large *adj* grande

last, to last *v* durare p20

last *adj* ultimo -a

late *adv* tardi

Please don't be late. Non ritardi per favore.

later *adv* più tardi

See you later. A più tardi.

lately *adv* di recente

laundry (shop) *n* la lavanderia *f*, **(clothes)** il bucato *m*

lavender *adj* lavande

law *n* la legge *f*

lawyer *n* l'avvocato *m* / l'avvocassa *f*

least *n* il minimo *m*, *adj* minimo -a

leather *n* la pelle *f*

leave, to leave (depart) *v* partire p21

left *adj* sinistro -a

on the left a sinistra

(remaining) rimasto -a

leg *n* la gamba *f*

lemonade *n* la limonata *f*

less *adv* meno

lesson *n* la lezione *f*

license *n* il permesso *m*

driver's license la patente *f*

life *n* la vita *f*

the good life la dolce vita *f*

life preserver *n* il salvagente *m*

light (brightness) *adj* luminoso -a

light *n* la luce *f*
  (for cigarette) l'accendino
  May I offer you a light? Posso offrirle da accendere?
  (lamp) la lampada *f*
  (weight) leggero -a

like, to like *v* piacere **p32**
  I would like ___. Mi piacerebbe / Vorrei ___.
  I like this place. Mi piace questo posto.

limo *n* la limousine *f*

liqueur *n* il liquore *m*

liquor *n* il liquore *m*

liter *n* il litro *m*

little *adj* piccolo -a

live, to live *v* vivere **p20**
  (dwell) *v* abitare **p20**
  Where do you live? Dove abita?
  What do you do for a living? Che mestiere fa?

local *adj* locale

lock *n* la serratura *f*

lock, to lock *v* chiudere a chiave **p20**
  I can't lock the door. Non riesco a chiudere la porta a chiave.
  I'm locked out. Sono rimasto chiuso fuori.

locker *n* l'armadietto *m*
  storage locker l'armadietto di deposito
  locker room lo spogliatoio

long (length) *adj* lungo -a *adv* lungo, molto tempo
  For how long? Per quanto tempo?
  long ago molto tempo fa

look, to look (to observe) *v* guardare, osservare **p20**
  I'm just looking. Sto solo guardando.
  Look here! Guarda qui!
  look (to appear) *v* sembrare **p20**
  How does this look? Come sembra questo?

look for, to look for (to search) *v* cercare **p20**
  I'm looking for a porter. Cerco un facchino.

loose *adj* sciolto -a

lose, to lose *v* perdere **p20**
  I lost my passport. Ho perso il mio passaporto.
  I lost my wallet. Ho perso il mio portafogli.
  I'm lost. Mi sono perso.

lost *adj* perso -a

loud *adj* rumoroso -a

loudly (voice) *adv* ad alta voce

lounge *n* la sala d'aspetto *f*

lounge, to lounge *v* bighellonare **p20**

love *n* l'amore *m*

love, to love *v* amare **p20**
  (family) voler bene
  (a friend) voler bene
  (a lover) amare

to make love fare l'amore
low *adj* basso -a
lunch *n* il pranzo *m*
luggage *n* il bagaglio *m*

> **Where do I report lost luggage?** Dove posso denunciare la perdita del bagaglio?
> **Where is the lost luggage claim?** Dov'è l'ufficio bagagli smarriti?

M

machine *m* la macchina *f*
made of *adj* fatto -a di
magazine *n* la rivista *f*
maid (hotel) *n* la cameriera *f*
maiden *adj* nubile *f*

> **That's my maiden name.** E' il mio nome da nubile.

mail *n* la posta *f*

> **air mail** la posta aerea
> **registered mail** posta assicurata

make, to make *v* fare **p28**
makeup *n* il trucco *m*
make up, to make up (apply cosmetics) *v* truccarsi **p20, 35**
make up, to make up (apologize) *v* fare la pace **p28**
male *adj* maschile *m*
male *n* il maschio *m*
mall *n* il centro commerciale *m*
man *n* l'uomo *m*
manager *n* il manager *m f*, il direttore / il direttrice *m f*
manual *n* il manuale *m*

many *adj* molti -e
map *n* la cartina *f*
March *n* marzo *m*
market *n* il mercato *m*

> **flea market** il mercatino delle pulci
> **open-air market** il mercato all'aperto

married *adj* sposato -a
marry, to marry *v* sposarsi **p20, 35**
massage, to massage *v* massaggiare **p20**
match (sport) *n* la partita *f*
(stick) il fiammifero

> **book of matches** una bustina di fiammiferi

match, to match *v* abbinare **p20**

> **Does this ____ match my outfit?** Questo -a ____ si abbina al mio completo?

May *n* maggio *m*
may *v* potere **p30**

> **May I ____?** Posso ____?

meal *n* il pasto *m*
meat *n* la carne *f*
meatball *n* la polpetta *f*
medication *n* il farmaco *m*
medium (size) *adj* medio -a
medium rare (meat) *adj* quasi al sangue
medium well (meat) *adj* ben cotto -a
member *n* il socio *m*
menu *n* il menu *m*

> **May I see a menu?** Posso vedere il menu?

children's menu il menu dei
  bambini
diabetic menu il menu per i
  diabetici
kosher menu il menu di
  piatti kasher
vegetarian menu il menu
  vegetariano
metal detector n il rivelatore
  di metalli m
meter n il metro m
middle adj medio -a
midnight n la mezzanotte f
mile n il miglio m
military n il militare m
milk n il latte m
  milk shake n il frappè m
milliliter n il millilitro m
millimeter n il millimetro m
minute n il minuto m
  in a minute fra un minuto
miss, to miss (a flight) v
  perdere p20
missing adj perso -a
mistake n l'errore m
moderately priced adj a
  prezzo modico m
mole (facial feature) n il neo m
Monday n lunedì m
money n il denaro m, i soldi
  m pl
  money transfer il trasferimento di valuta
month n il mese m
morning n il mattino m
  in the morning al mattino
mosque n la moschea f

mother n la madre f
mother, to mother v curare
  p20
motorcycle n la moto f
mountain n la montagna f
  mountain climbing scalata
  montana
mouse n il topo m
mouth n la bocca f
move (change position) v
  spostare, spostarsi p20, 35
  (relocate) v traslocare p20
movie n il film m
much adj molto -a
to get mugged essere vittima
  di un assalto p26
museum n il museo m
music n la musica f
  live music la musica dal vivo
musician n il musicista m f
Muslim adj musulmano -a
my / mine pron mio -a, miei
  m pl, mie f pl
mystery (novel) n il giallo m

N
name n il nome m
  My name is ____. Mi chiamo
  ____.
  What's your name? Come si
  chiama?
napkin n il tovagliolo m
narrow adj stretto -a
nationality n la nazionalità f
nausea n la nausea f
near adj vicino
nearby adv vicino

neat (tidy) *adj* ordinato -a

need, to need *v* bisognare **p20**

  I need ___ . Ho bisogno di ___ .

neighbor *n* il / la vicino -a *m f*

nephew *n* il nipote *m*

network *n* la rete *f*

new *adj* nuovo -a

newspaper *n* il giornale *m*

newsstand *n* l'edicola *f*

New Zealand *n* la Nuova Zelanda *f*

New Zealander *adj* neozelandese *m f*

next *adj* prossimo -a

  next to *prep* accanto a

  the next station la prossima stazione

nice *adj* simpatico -a

niece *n* la nipote *f*

night *n* la notte *f*

  at night di notte

  per night a notte

nightclub *n* il locale notturno *m*

nine *adj* nove

nineteen *adj* diciannove

ninety *adj* novanta

ninth *adj* nono -a

no *adv* no

noisy *adj* rumoroso -a

none *pron* nessuno

no smoking *adj* vietato fumare

  nonsmoking area la zona non-fumatori

  nonsmoking room la stanza per non-fumatori

noon *n* il mezzogiorno *m*

nose *n* il naso *m*

novel *n* il romanzo *m*

not *adv* non

nothing *n* il niente *m*

November *n* novembre *m*

now *adv* adesso

number *n* il numero *m*

  Which room number? Che numero di camera?

  May I have your phone number? Posso avere il suo numero di telefono?

nurse *n* l'infermiere -a *m f*

nurse, to nurse (breastfeed) *v* allattare **p20**

  Do you have a place where I can nurse? C'è un posto dove posso allattare?

nursery *n* l'asilo infantile *m*

  Do you have a nursery? Avete un asilo infantile?

nut *n* la noce *f*

O

o'clock *adv* in punto

  two o'clock le due in punto

October *n* ottobre *m*

of *prep* di

offer, to offer *v* offrire **p21**

officer *n* il poliziotto *m*

off-white *adj* bianco, sporco

oil *n* l'olio *m*

okay *adv* okay, va bene **p**

old *adj* vecchio -a

olive *n* l'oliva *f*

on *prep* su, sopra

one *adj* uno -a

one way (traffic sign) *n* il senso unico *m*

open (business) *adj* aperto -a

Are you open? Siete aperti?

opera *n* l'opera *f*

operator (phone) *n* il centralino *m* il / la operatore -trice *m f*

optometrist *n* l'optometrista *m*

orange *adj* arancio

orange juice *n* il succo d'arancia *m*

order, to order (demand) *v* ordinare (request) *v* chiedere **p20**

organic *adj* organico -a, (food) biologico -a

Ouch! *interj* Ahi!

ours *pron* nostro -a, nostri -e

out *adv* fuori

outside *adj* esterno -a

over *prep* sopra, su

overcooked *adj* troppo cotto -a

overheat, to overheat *v* surriscaldare **p20**

The car overheated. La macchina si è surriscaldata.

overflowing *adj* traboccante

oxygen tank *n* la bombola d'ossigeno *f*

P

package *n* il pacco *m*

pacifier *n* il ciuccio *m*

page, to page (someone) *v* far chiamare *v* **p28**

paint, to paint *v* dipingere **p20**

painting *n* il quadro *m*, la pittura *f*

pale *adj* pallido -a

paper *n* la carta *f*

parade *n* la parata *f*

parent *n* il genitore / la genitrice *m f*

park *n* il parco *m*

park, to park *v* parcheggiare **p20**

parking *n* il parcheggio *m*

no parking sosta vietata

parking fee la tariffa del parcheggio

parking garage il garage parcheggio

partner *n* il / la compagno -a *m f*

party *n* il party *m*, la festa *f*

political party il partito politico

pass, to pass *v* passare **p20**

I'll pass. Io passo.

passenger *n* il / la passeggero -a *m f*

passport *n* il passaporto *m*

I've lost my passport. Ho perso il mio passaporto.

password *n* la password *f*

past *adj* passato

past *n* il passato *m*

(in space) *prep* dopo, oltre

pay, to pay *v* pagare **p20**

peanut *n* l'arachide *f*

pedestrian *n* il pedone *m*

pediatrician *n* il / la pediatra *m f*

Can you recommend a pediatrician? Può consigliarmi un pediatra?

permit *n* il permesso *m*

Do we need a permit? Abbiamo bisogno di un permesso?

permit, to permit *v* permettere **p20**

petrol / gas *n* la benzina *f*

phone *n* il telefono *m*

Do you have a phone directory? Ha una guida telefonica?

May I have your phone number? Può darmi il suo numero di telefono?

Where can I find a public phone? Dove posso trovare un telefono pubblico?

phone operator il operatore *m*, la operatrice *f*

Do you sell prepaid phones? Vendete i telefonini prepagati?

phone call *n* la telefonata *f*

I need to make a collect phone call. Ho bisogno di fare una telefonata a carico del destinatario.

an international phone call una telefonata internazionale *f*

photocopy, to photocopy *v* fotocopiare **p20**

piano *n* il pianoforte *m*

pillow *n* il cuscino *m*

down pillow il cuscino di piuma *m*

pink *adj* rosa

pizza *n* la pizza *f*

place, to place *v* mettere **p20**

plastic *n* la plastica *f*

play *n* il gioco *m*

play, to play (a game) *v* giocare, **(an instrument)** *v* suonare **p20**

playground *n* il giardino di ricreazione *m*

Do you have a playground? Avete un giardino di ricreazione?

plaza *n* la piazza *f*

please (polite entreaty) *interj* per favore

please, to be pleasing to *v* accontentare **p20**

pleasure *n* il piacere *m*

It's a pleasure. E' un piacere.

plug (electrical) *n* la spina *f*

plug, to plug *v* inserire la spina **p21**

point, to point *v* indicare **p20**

Would you point me in the direction of ____? Può indicarmi la direzione per ____?

police *n* la polizia *f*

police station *n* la stazione di polizia *f*

pool *n* la piscina *f* **(game)** *n* il biliardo *m*

pop music *n* la musica pop *f*

popular *adj* popolare

port (beverage, harbor) *n* il porto *m*

porter *n* il facchino *m* il portiere **(concierge)** *m*

portion *n* la porzione *f*

portrait *n* il ritratto *m*

postcard *n* la cartolina *f*

post office *n* l'ufficio postale *m*

Where is the post office? Dov'è l'ufficio postale?

poultry *n* il pollame *m*

prefer, to prefer *v* preferire p32 (like uscire)

pregnant *adj* incinta *f*

prepared *adj* preparato -a

prescription *n* la ricetta *f*

price *n* il prezzo *m*

print, to print *v* stampare p20

private berth / cabin *n* la cabina privata *f*

problem *n* il problema *m*

process, to process *v* elaborare p20

product *n* il prodotto *m*

professional *adj* professionale

program *n* il programma *m*

May I have a program? Posso avere un programma?

Protestant *adj* protestante

publisher *n* l'editore *m* / l'editrice *f*

pull, to pull *v* tirare p20

pump *n* la pompa *f*

purple *adj* viola

purse *n* la borsetta *f*

push, to push *v* spingere p20

put, to put *v* mettere p20

Q

quarter *n* il quarto *m*

one-quarter un quarto *m*

quick *adj* veloce

quiet *adj* tranquillo

R

rabbit *n* il coniglio *m*

radio *n* la radio *f*

satellite radio la radio satellitare

rain, to rain *v* piovere p20

Is it supposed to rain? E' prevista pioggia?

rainy *adj* piovoso -a

It's rainy. Piove.

ramp *n* la rampa *f*

rare (meat) *adj* al sangue

rate (fee) *n* la tariffa *f*

What's the rate per day? Qual è la tariffa giornaliera?

What's the rate per week? Qual è la tariffa settimanale?

rate plan (cell phone) *n* il piano rateale *m*

rather *adv* preferibilmente

raven *n* il corvo *m*

read, to read *v* leggere p20

really *adv* davvero

receipt *n* la ricevuta *f*

receive, to receive *v* ricevere p20

recommend, to recommend *v* raccomandare, consigliare p20

red *adj* rosso -a

redhead *n* dai capelli rossi *m f*

reef *n* la scogliera *f*

refill, to refill (beverage) *v* riempire **p21**

refill (of prescription) la ripetizione di una ricetta

reggae *n* la musica reggae *f*

relative *n* il / la parente *m f*

remove, to remove *v* togliere **p20**

rent, to rent *v* noleggiare **p20**

I'd like to rent a car. Vorrei noleggiare un'auto.

repeat, to repeat *v* ripetere **p20**

Would you please repeat that? Può ripeterlo per favore?

reservation *n* la prenotazione *f*

I'd like to make a reservation for ___. Vorrei fare una prenotazione per ___. *See numbers,* .

restaurant *n* il ristorante *m*

Where can I find a good restaurant? Dove posso trovare un buon ristorante? *See restaurant types,* .

restroom *n* il bagno *m*

Do you have a public restroom / toilet ? C'è un bagno pubblico?

return, to return (to a place) *v* ritornare **p20**

return, to return (something to a store) *v* portare indietro **p20**

ride, to ride *v* viaggiare **p20**

right *adj* il / la destro -a

It is on the right. E' sulla destra.

Turn right at the corner. All'angolo, giri a destra.

rights *n* i diritti *m pl*

civil rights i diritti civili

river *n* il fiume *m*

road *n* la strada *f*

road closed sign *n* il segnale della strada bloccata *f*

rob, to rob *v* rubare **p20**

I've been robbed. Mi hanno derubato.

rock climbing *n* la scalata rocciosa *f*

rocks *n* le roccie *f*

I'd like it on the rocks. Lo gradirei con ghiaccio.

romance (novel) *n* il romanzo *m*

romantic *adj* romantico -a

room (hotel) *n* la camera, la stanza *f*

room for one / two la camera singola / doppia

room service il servizio in camera

rope *n* la fune *f*

rose *n* la rosa *f*

royal flush *n* il royal flush *m*

run, to run *v* correre **p20**

S

sad *adj* triste

safe (container) *n* la cassaforte *f*

  Do the rooms have safes?
  C'è una cassaforte nelle camere?

safe (secure) *adj* sicuro -a

  Is this area safe? Questa zona è sicura?

sail *n* la vela *f*

sail, to sail *v* navigare a vela p20

  When do we sail? Quando salpiamo?

salad *n* l'insalata *f*

salesperson *n* il / la commesso -a *m f*

salt *n* il sale *m*

  Is that low-salt? Questo è con poco sale?

satellite *n* il satellite *m*

  satellite radio la radio satellitare

  satellite tracking il tracking satellitare

Saturday *n* il sabato *m*

sauce *n* il sugo *m*

say, to say *v* dire p28

scan, to scan *v* (with a scanner) scannerizzare p20

schedule *n* l'orario *m*

school *n* la scuola *f*

scooter *n* il motorino *m*

score *n* il punteggio *m*

Scottish *adj* scozzese

scratch *n* il graffio *m*

scratch, to scratch *v* graffiare p20

scratched *adj* graffiato -a

  scratched surface superficie scalfita

scuba dive, to scuba dive *v* immergersi con le bombole d'ossigeno p20, 35

sculpture *n* la scultura *f*

seafood *n* i frutti di mare *m pl*

search *n* la ricerca *f*

  hand search la perquisizione manuale

search, to search *v* cercare p20

seasick *adj* che soffre il mal di mare

  I am seasick. Ho mal di mare.

seasickness pill *n* la pillola antinausea *f*

seat *n* il sedile *m*, il posto *m*

  child seat il sedile per bambini

second *adj* secondo -a

security *n* la sicurezza *f*

  security checkpoint il punto di controllo di sicurezza

  security guard la guardia di sicurezza

sedan *n* la berlina *f*

see, to see *v* vedere p20

  May I see it? Posso vederlo?

self-serve *n* il self-service *m f*

sell, to sell *v* vendere p20

seltzer *n* la soda *f*

send, to send *v* spedire, mandare, inviare **p20, 21**

separated (marital status) *adj* separato -a

September *n* settembre *m*

serve, to serve *v* servire **p21**

service *n* il servizio *m*

out of service fuori servizio

services (religious) *n* le funzioni religiose *f*

service charge / cover *n* il coperto *m*

seven *adj* sette

seventy *adj* settanta

seventeen *adj* diciassette

seventh *n adj* il / la settimo -a

sew, to sew *v* cucire **p21**

sex *n* il sesso *m*

sex, to have (intercourse) *v* avere rapporti sessuali **p27**

shallow *adj* poco profondo -a

sheet (bed linen) *n* il lenzuolo *m*, le lenzuola *f*
(paper) *n* il foglio *m*

shellfish *n* i crostacei *m pl*

ship *n* la nave *f*

ship, to ship *v* spedire **p21**

How much to ship this to _____? Quanto costa per spedire questo a _____?

shipwreck *n* il naufragio *m*

shirt *n* la camicia *f*

shoe *n* la scarpa *f*

shop *n* il negozio *m*

shop, to shop *v* fare compere **p28**

I'm shopping for mens' clothes. Sto cercando abbigliamento da uomo.

I'm shopping for womens' clothes. Sto cercando abbigliamento da donna.

I'm shopping for childrens' clothes. Sto cercando abbigliamento per bambini.

short *adj* basso -a

shorts *n* i calzoncini corti *m*

shot (liquor) *n* il bicchierino *m*

shout, to shout *v* gridare **p20**

show (performance) *n* lo spettacolo *m*

What time is the show? A che ora inizia lo spettacolo?

show, to show *v* mostrare **p20**

Would you show me? Può mostrarmelo?

shower *n* la doccia *f*

Does it have a shower? C'è una doccia?

shower, to shower *v* fare la doccia **p28**

shrimp *n* il gambero *m*

shuttle bus *n* l'autobus navetta *m*

sick *adj* malato -a

I feel sick. Mi sento male.

side *n* il lato *m*

on the side (separately) a parte

sidewalk *n* il marciapiede *m*

sightseeing *n* la gita turistica *f*

ENGLISH—ITALIAN

sightseeing bus n l'autobus per gite turistiche m

sign, to sign v firmare **p20**

  Where do I sign? Dove devo firmare?

silk n la seta f

silver n l'argento m

silver adj argento

sing, to sing v cantare **p20**

single (unmarried) adj single, celibe m, nubile f

  Are you single? E' single?

single (one) adj singolo -a

  single bed il letto ad una piazza

sink n il lavabo m

sister n la sorella f

sit, to sit v sedersi **p20, 35**

six adj sei

sixteen adj sedici

sixty adj sessanta

size (clothing) n la taglia f

  (shoes) n il numero m

skin n la pelle f

sleeping berth n la cuccetta f

slow adj lento -a

slow, to slow v rallentare **p20**

  Slow down! Rallenti!

slowly adv lentamente

  Please speak more slowly. Per favore parli più lentamente.

slum n i bassifondi m pl

small adj piccolo -a

smell, to smell v puzzare **p20**

smoke, to smoke v fumare **p20**

smoking n il fumo m

smoking area la zona fumatori

  No Smoking Vietato fumare

snack n lo spuntino m

Snake eyes! n Occhi di serpe!

snorkel, to snorkel v fare snorkeling **p28,**

soap n il sapone m

sock n il calzino m

soda n il selz m

  diet soda la bibita light

soft adj morbido -a

software n il software m

sold out adj tutto esaurito

some adj qualche

someone n qualcuno -a m f

something n il qualcosa f

son n il figlio m

song n la canzone f

sorry adj pentito -a

  I'm sorry. Mi dispiace.

soup n la minestra f

spa n le terme f pl

Spain n la Spagna f

Spanish adj spagnolo -a

spare tire n la ruota di scorta f

speak, to speak v parlare **p20**

  Do you speak English? Parla inglese?

  Would you speak louder, please? Può parlare a voce più alta, per favore?

  Would you speak slower, please? Per favore, può parlare più lentamente?

special (featured meal) n la specialità del giorno f

specify, to specify v specificare p20

speed limit n il limite di velocità m

What's the speed limit? Qual è il limite di velocità?

speedometer n il tachimetro m

spell, to spell v scrivere correttamente p20

How do you spell that? Come si scrive quello?

spice n la spezia f

spill, to spill v rovesciare p20

split (gambling) n la divisione f

sport n lo sport m

spring (season) n la primavera f

stadium n lo stadio m

staff (personnel) n il personale m

stamp (postage) n il francobollo m

stair n la scala f

Where are the stairs? Dove sono le scale?

Are there many stairs? Ci sono molte scale?

stand, to stand v stare in piedi p24, 25

start, to start (commence) v iniziare, cominciare p20

start, to start (a car) v accendere p20

state n lo stato m

station n la stazione f

Where is the nearest gas station? Dov'è il distributore di benzina più vicino?

Where is the nearest bus station? Dov'è la stazione degli autobus più vicina?

Where is the nearest subway station? Dov'è la stazione della metropolitana più vicina?

Where is the nearest train station? Dov'è la stazione dei treni più vicina?

stay, to stay v restare p20

We'll be staying for ____ nights. Pernotteremo per ____ notti.

steakhouse n il ristorante specializzato in bistecche m

steal, to steal v rubare p20

stolen adj rubato -a

stop n la fermata f

Is this my stop? E' questa la mia fermata?

I missed my stop. Ho passato la mia fermata.

stop, to stop v fermare p20

Please stop. Per favore si fermi.

Stop, thief! Fermo, al ladro!

store n il negozio m

straight adj diritto -a

straight ahead avanti diritto

(drink) liscio

Go straight (directions). Vada diritto.

straight (gambling) *n* la scala *f*

street *n* la via *f*, la strada *f*

across the street dall'altra parte della strada

down the street giù per la strada

Which street? Quale strada?

How many more streets? Ancora quante strade?

stressed *adj* stressato -a

striped *adj* a striscie

stroller *n* il passeggino *m*

Do you rent baby strollers? Noleggiate passeggini per bambini?

substitution *n* la sostituzione *f*

suburb *n* la periferia *f*

subway / underground *n* la metropolitana *f*, il metrò *m*

subway line la linea della metropolitana

subway station la stazione della metropolitana

Which subway do I take for ____? Che linea del metrò devo prendere per ____?

subtitle *n* il sottotitolo *m*

suitcase *n* la valigia *f*

suite *n* la suite *m*

summer *n* l'estate *f*

sun *n* il sole *m*

sunburn *n* la scottatura solare *f*

I have a bad sunburn. Ho una brutta scottatura.

Sunday *n* la domenica *f*

sunglasses *n* gli occhiali da sole *m pl*

sunny *adj* soleggiato -a

It's sunny out. C'è il sole fuori.

sunroof *n* il tettuccio apribile *m*

sunscreen / sunblock *n* la crema solare protettiva *f*

Do you have sunscreen / sunblock SPF ____? Avete la crema solare protettiva fattore ____?

supermarket *n* il supermarket *m*

surf, to surf *v* fare il surf p28

surfboard *n* la tavola da surf *f*

suspiciously *adv* in modo sospetto

swallow, to swallow *v* inghiottire p21

sweater *n* la maglia *f*

swim, to swim *v* nuotare p20

Can one swim here? Si può nuotare qui?

swimsuit il costume da bagno

swim trunks i calzoncini da bagno

symphony *n* la sinfonia *f*

T

table *n* il tavolo *m*

table for two un tavolo per due

tailor n il sarto m

Can you recommend a good tailor? Può consigliarmi un buon sarto?

take, to take v portare p20

Take me to the station. Mi porti alla stazione.

How much to take me to ____? Quanto costa per portarmi a ____?

takeout / takeaway menu n il menu da asporto m

talk, to talk v parlare p20

tall adj alto -a

tan adj marroncino

tanned adj abbronzato -a

taste (flavor) n il sapore m, il gusto m

taste (discernment) n il gusto m

taste, to taste v assaggiare p20

tax n la tassa f

value-added tax (VAT) l'imposta sui valori aggiunti (IVA)

taxi n il taxi / il tassì m

Taxi! Taxi!

Would you call me a taxi? Mi chiama un taxi per favore?

tea n il tè m

team n la squadra f

techno n la musica techno f

television n la televisione f

temple n il tempio m

ten adj dieci

tennis n il tennis m

tennis court il campo da tennis

tent n la tenda f

tenth n adj il / la decimo -a

terminal (airport) n il terminal m

Thank you. interj Grazie.

that adj quello -a, quelli -e pl

theater n il teatro m

their(s) pron di loro; il / la / i / le loro m f

them pron loro m f

there (demonstrative) adv là

Is / Are there ____? C'è / Ci sono ____?

It's there. E' là.

these adj questi -e m f

thick adj spesso -a

thin adj sottile

third adj terzo -a

thirteen adj tredici

thirty adj trenta

this adj questo -a

those adj quelli -e

thousand adj mille

three adj tre

Thursday n il giovedì m

ticket n il biglietto m

ticket counter la biglietteria

one-way ticket un biglietto di sola andata

round-trip ticket un biglietto di andata e ritorno

tight adj stretto -a

time n il tempo m, l'ora f

Is it on time? E' in orario?

At what time? A che ora?

What time is it? Che ora è?

timetable (train) n l'orario m

tip (gratuity) n la mancia f

tire n la gomma f

I have a flat tire. Ho una gomma a terra.

tired adj stanco -a

to prep a, per

today adv oggi

toilet n il gabinetto m, la toiletta f

The toilet is overflowing. Il gabinetto trabocca.

The toilet is backed up. Il gabinetto è intasato.

toilet paper n la carta igienica f

You're out of toilet paper. E' finita la carta igienica.

toiletries n articoli da toletta m pl

toll n il pedaggio m

tomorrow adv domani

ton n la tonnellata f

too (excessively) adv troppo

too (also) adv anche

tooth n il dente m

I lost my tooth. Ho perso un dente.

toothache n il mal di denti m

I have a toothache. Ho il mal di denti.

total n il totale m

What is the total? Qual è il totale?

tour n la gita f

Are guided tours available? Ci sono gite guidate?

Are audio tours available? Ci sono gite con audioguida?

towel n l'asciugamano m

May we have more towels? Possiamo avere altri asciugamani?

toy n il giocattolo m

toy store il negozio di giocattoli

Do you have any toys for the children? Avete dei giocattoli per i bambini?

traffic n il traffico m

How's traffic? Com'è il traffico?

Traffic is terrible. Il traffico è orribile.

traffic rules le regole del traffico f

trail n il sentiero m

Are there trails? Ci sono dei sentieri?

train n il treno m

express train l'espresso

local train il locale

Does the train go to ____? Questo treno va a ____?

May I have a train schedule? Posso avere un orario del treno?

Where is the train station? Dov'è la stazione dei treni?

train, to train v addestrare **p20**

transfer, to transfer v trasferire **p32** (like uscire)

I need to transfer funds. Devo trasferire del denaro.

transmission *n* il cambio *m*

automatic transmission il cambio automatico

standard transmission il cambio manuale

travel, to travel *v* viaggiare p20

traveler's check *n* il traveller's cheque *m*

Do you cash travelers' checks? Cambiate i traveller's cheque?

trim, to trim (hair) *v* spuntare p20

trip *n* il viaggio *m*

triple *adj* triplo -a

trumpet *n* la tromba *f*

trunk / boot (car) *n* il bagagliaio *m*

try, to try (attempt) *v* cercare di **(clothing)** *v* provare **(food)** *v* assaggiare p20

Tuesday *n* il martedì *m*

turkey *n* il tacchino *m*

turn, to turn *v* girare p20

to turn left / right girare a sinistra / destra p20

to turn off / on spegnere / accendere p20

twelve *adj* dodici

twenty *adj* venti

twine *n* lo spago *m*

two *adj* due

U

umbrella *n* l'ombrello *m*

uncle *n* lo zio *m*

under *prep* sotto

undercooked *adj* crudo -a

understand, to understand *v* capire p32 (like uscire)

I don't understand. Non capisco.

Do you understand? Capisce? / Capite?

underwear *n* la biancheria intima *f*

university *n* l'università *f*

up *adv* su, sopra

update, to update *v* aggiornare p20

upgrade *n* la categoria superiore *f*

upload, to upload *v* caricare p20

upscale *adj* di lusso

us *pron* noi

USB port *n* la porta USB *f*

use, to use *v* usare p20

V

vacation *n* la vacanza *f*

on vacation in vacanza

to go on vacation andare in ferie p27

vacancy *n* la disponibilità *f*

van *n* il furgoncino *m*

VCR *n* il videoregistratore *m*

Do the rooms have VCRs? C'è il videoregistratore nelle camere?

vegetable *n* la verdura *f*

vegetarian *adj* vegetariano -a

vending machine *n* il distributore automatico *m*

version *n* la versione *f*

very *adj* molto -a

video *n* il video *m*

Where can I rent videos or DVDs? Dove posso noleggiare video o DVD?

view *n* la vista *f*

beach view la vista della spiaggia

city view la vista della città

vineyard *n* il vigneto *f*

vinyl *n* il vinile *m*

violin *n* il violino *m*

visa *n* il visto *m*

Do I need a visa? Ho bisogno del visto?

vision *n* la visione *f*

visit, to visit *v* visitare **p20**

visually impaired *n* l'ipovedente *m*

vodka *n* la vodka *f*

voucher *n* il buono *m*

W

wait, to wait *v* attendere **p20**

Please wait. Per favore attenda.

wait *n* attesa *f*

How long is the wait? Quanto è lunga l'attesa?

waiter *n* il / la cameriere -a *m f*

waiting area *n* la sala d'aspetto *m*

wake-up call *n* la chiamata sveglia *f*

wallet *n* il portafogli *m*

I lost my wallet. Ho perso il mio portafogli.

Someone stole my wallet. Mi hanno rubato il portafogli.

walk, to walk *v* camminare **p20**

walker (device) *n* il girello *m*

walkway *n* il passaggio pedonale *m*

moving walkway la passerella mobile

want, to want *v* volere **p31**

war *n* la guerra *f*

warm *adj* caldo -a

watch, to watch *v* guardare **p20**

water *n* l'acqua *f*

Is the water potable? L'acqua è potabile?

Is there running water? C'è l'acqua corrente?

wave, to wave *v* salutare con la mano **p20**

waxing *n* la depilazione con ceretta *f*

weapon *n* l'arma *f*

wear, to wear *v* indossare **p20**

weather forecast *n* le previsioni del tempo *f pl*

Wednesday *n* il mercedì *m*

week *n* la settimana *f*

this week questa settimana

last week la settimana scorsa

next week la settimana prossima

last week la settimana scorsa

weigh, to weigh v pesare **p20**

I weigh ____ kilos. Peso ____ chili.

It weighs ____. Pesa ____

weights n i pesi m pl

welcome adv benvenuto -a

You're welcome. Prego.

well adv bene

well done (meat) ben cotto -a

well done (task) ben fatto -a

I don't feel well. Non mi sento bene.

western adj il western

whale n la balena f

what adv che

What sort of ____? Che tipo di ____?

What time is ____? Che ora è ____?

wheelchair n la sedia a rotelle f

wheelchair access l'accesso alle sedie a rotelle

wheelchair ramp la rampa delle sedie a rotelle

power wheelchair la sedia a rotelle motorizzata

when adv quando

where adv dove

Where is it? Dov'è? / Dove si trova?

which adv quale

Which one? Quale?

white adj bianco -a

who adv chi

whose adj di chi

wide adj largo -a

widow, widower n la / il vedova -o m f

wife n la moglie f

wi-fi n il wi-fi m

window n la finestra f

drop-off window il finestrino di consegna

pick-up window il finestrino di raccolta

windshield / windscreen n il parabrezza m

windshield wiper n il tergi-cristallo m

windsurf, to windsurf v fare il windsurf **p28**

windy adj ventoso -a

wine n il vino m

winter n l'inverno m

wiper n il tergicristallo m

with prep con

withdraw, to withdraw v riti-rare **p20**

I need to withdraw money. Ho bisogno di prelevare dei soldi.

without prep senza

woman n la donna f

work, to work v lavorare **p20**

This doesn't work. Questo non funziona.

workout n l'esercizio fisico m

worse adj peggiore

worst adj il peggiore

write, to write *v* scrivere **p20**
Would you write that down for me? Me lo può scrivere per favore?
writer *n* lo scrittore *m*, la scrittrice *f*

X
x-ray machine *n* l'apparecchiatura per i raggi X *f*

Y
yellow *adj* giallo -a
yes *interj* sì
yesterday *adv* ieri
the day before yesterday ieri l'altro
yield sign *n* il segnale di precedenza *m*

you (sing. informal) tu
you (sing. formal) Lei
you (pl informal) voi
you (pl formal) Loro, Voi
your(s) (informal) *pron* tuo -a *m f*, tuoi *m pl*, tue *f pl*
your(s) (pl informal) *pron* vostro -a *m f*, vostri -e *m f pl*
yours (formal) *pron* di lei; suo -a *m f*, suoi *m pl*, sue *f pl*
yours (pl formal) *pron* di loro; il / la loro *m f*
young *adj* giovane

Z
zoo *n* lo zoo *m*

ENGLISH–ITALIAN

A

l'abbigliamento *m clothes n* (general attire)

abbinare *v to match* **p20**

abbronzato -a *tanned adj*

abitare *v to live* **p20**

> **Dove abita?** *Where do you live?*
>
> **Abito con il / la mio ragazzo -a.** *I live with my boyfriend / girlfriend.*

accendere *v to start* (a car), *to turn on* **p20**

> **Posso offrirle da accendere?** *May I offer you a light?*

l'accendino *m light, lighter n* (cigarette)

l'accesso ai disabili *m disabled access n*

accettare *v to accept* **p20**

> **Si accettano carte di credito.** *Credit cards are accepted.*

accettato -a *accepted adj*

l'accettazione *f check-in n*

l'acconciatura afro *f afro n*

accontentare *v to please, to be pleasing to* **p20**

l'acne *f acne n*

l'acqua *f water n*

> **l'acqua calda** *hot water*
>
> **l'acqua fredda** *cold water*

acquistare *v to buy* **p20**

addestrare *v to train* **p20**

adesso *now adv*

l'aeroporto *m airport n*

l'affare *m business, deal, bargain n*

> **Fatti gli affari tuoi.** *Mind your own business.*

affittare *v to rent* **p20**

> **Desidero affittare ____.** *I'd like to rent ____.*

affollato -a *crowded, busy adj* (restaurant)

l'afroamericano -a *African American adj*

l'agenzia *f agency n*

aggiornare *v to update* **p20**

l'aglio *m garlic n*

agnostico -a *m f agnostic n*

agosto *m August n*

Ahi! *Ouch! interj*

l'aiuto *m help n*

> **Aiuto!** *m Help! n*

aiutare *v to help* **p20**

l'alba *f dawn n*

> **all'alba** *at dawn*

albergo *m hotel n*

l'alcol *m alcohol n*

allattare *v to nurse* (breast-feed) **p20**

l'allergia *f allergy n*

allergico -a *allergic adj*

l'alluminio *m aluminum n*

l'altitudine *f altitude n*

alto -a *tall, high adj, loudly adv*

> **più alto -a** *higher, taller*
>
> **il / la più alto -a** *the highest, tallest*

altro -a *(an)other adj*

alzare *v to lift, raise, turn up* (sound) **p20**

amare *v to love* **p20**
l'ambasciata *f embassy n*
l'ambiente *m environment n*
l'ambulanza *f ambulance n*
l'americano -a *American adj n*
l'amico -a *m f friend n*
ammaccare *v to dent* **p20**
l'ammaccatura *f dent n*
l'amore *m love n*
l'anatra *f duck n*
anche *too, also adv*
andare *v to go* **p27**

andare fuori al club *to go clubbing*
andare bene *to fit*

l'angolo *m corner n*
all'angolo *on the corner*
l'animale *m animal n*
annebbiato -a *blurry adj*
anni *m pl years n* (age)

Quanti anni hai? *What's your age?*

l'antibiotico *m antibiotic n*
l'anticipo *m advance n*
in anticipo *in advance*
anticoncezionale *birth control adj*

Non ho più pillole anticoncezionali. *I'm out of birth control pills.*

l'antistaminico *m antihistamine n*
l'ape *f bee n*
aperto -a *open adj*
l'appartamento in un albergo *m suite n*

l'appartenenza ad un'associazione *f membership n*
approvare *v approve* **p20**

La sua carta di credito non è stata approvata. *Your credit card has been declined.*

l'appuntamento *m appointment n*
aprile *m April n*
l'arancia *m orange n* (fruit)
arancione *orange adj* (color)
l'area di campeggio *f campsite n*
l'argento *m silver n*
argento *silver adj* (color)
l'aria *f air n*
l'aria condizionata *f air conditioning n*
l'arma *f weapon n*
l'armadietto *m locker n*

l'armadietto della palestra *gym locker*
l'armadietto di deposito *storage locker*

arrivare *v to arrive* **p20**
Arrivederci. *See you later. interj*
l'arrivo *m*, gli arrivi *m pl arrival n, arrivals n pl*
l'arte *f art n*

le belle arti *fine arts*
il museo d'arte *art museum*
la mostra d'arte *art exhibit*

articoli da toelette *m pl toiletries n*
l'artista *m f artist n*
l'ascensore *m elevator, lift n*

l'asciugacapelli m hair dryer n

l'asciugamano m towel n

asciugare v to dry p20

asciutto -a dry, dried adj

l'asiatico -a Asian adj n

l'asilo infantile m nursery n

l'asino m donkey n

l'asma f asthma n

aspettare v to wait, hold p20

l'aspirina f aspirin n

assaggiare v to try (food), to taste p20

l'asse f board n

l'assegno m check n

l'assicurazione f insurance n

l'assicurazione sugli scontri collision insurance

assicurazione sulla responsabilità liability insurance

l'assistenza f assistance n

l'assistenza telefonica f directory assistance n (phone)

assistere v to attend, to assist p20

l'ateo -a atheist adj n

attendere v to wait p20

Attenda, per favore. Please wait.

atterrare v to land p20

l'attesa f wait n

l'attico m penthouse n

attraverso across prep

l'audio m audio adj n

Per favore alza l'audio. Please turn up the audio.

Auguri! Best wishes! interj

l'auricolare m headphones n

l'australiano -a Australian adj n

l'autista m driver n

l'auto f car n

l'autonoleggio car rental agency

l'autobus m bus n

la fermata degli autobus bus stop

l'autobus navetta shuttle bus

l'autobus per gite turistiche sightseeing bus n

l'automobile f car n

l'autunno m autumn n

l'autostrada f highway n

avanzato -a forward adj

avere v to have p27

avere rapporti sessuali to have sex

avere fretta to hurry

l'avvocato -essa m f lawyer n

azzurro -a light blue adj

B

il / la baby-sitter m f babysitter n

il bacio m kiss n

il bagaglio m, **i bagagli** m pl luggage, baggage n

i bagagli smarriti lost baggage

il recupero bagagli baggage claim

il bagno m bath, bathroom, restroom n

i bagni donne *women's restrooms*

i bagni uomini *men's restrooms*

il balcone *m balcony n*

ballare *v to dance* p20

il ballo *m dance n*

il ballo da sala *m ballroom dancing n*

i bambini *pl children n pl*

cibo per bambini *baby food*

passeggini per bambini *baby strollers*

il / la bambino -a *m f baby, child n*

la banca *f bank n*

bancario -a *bank adj*

il conto bancario *bank account*

la tessera bancaria *bank card*

il banco *m counter n* (bar)

il bancomat *m ATM / cash machine n*

la banconota *f bill n* (currency)

la banda larga *f broadband n*

il bar *m bar, café n*

il barattolo *m tin can n*

il barbiere *m barber n*

la barca *f boat n*

basso -a *short, low adj*

più basso -a *lower*

il / la più basso -a *lowest*

il basso *m bass n* (instrument)

i bassifondi *m pl slum n*

bello -a *beautiful, handsome adj*

bene *fine, well adv*

Sto bene. *I'm fine.*

Benvenuto. *Welcome. interj*

Benvenuti in Italia. *Welcome to Italy.*

la benzina *f gasoline, petrol n*

indicatore di benzina *gas gauge*

La benzina è finita. *It's out of gas.*

Dov'è il distributore di benzina più vicino? *Where is the nearest gas station?*

bere *v to drink* p29

la berlina *f sedan n*

la bevanda *f drink n*

bevanda offerta dalla casa *complimentary drink*

Desidero una bevanda. *I'd like a drink.*

la bevanda alcolica *f alcoholic drink n*

la biancheria intima *f underwear n*

bianco -a *white adj*

bianco sporco *off-white adj*

il biberon *m feeding bottle n*

la bibita analcolica *f soda, soft drink n*

la bibita dietetica *f diet soda*

la biblioteca *f library n*

il bicchiere *m glass n*

Lo servite a bicchiere? *Do you have it by the glass?*

Vorrei un bicchiere per favore. *I'd like a glass please.*

un **bicchierino** *m shot n*
(liquor)
bighellonare *v to lounge* **p20**
la **biglietteria** *f ticket
counter, box office n*
il **biglietto** *m ticket n*
un biglietto di sola andata
one-way ticket
**un biglietto di andata e
ritorno** *round-trip ticket*
il biglietto da visita *business
card*
bilanciare *v to balance* **p20**
bilanciato -a *balanced adj*
il **bilancio** *m budget n*
il **biliardo** *m pool n* (game)
bilingue *bilingual adj*
il / la **biondo -a** *blond(e) adj n*
la **birra** *f beer n*
birra alla spina *draft beer*
birazziale *biracial adj*
il **biscotto** *m cookie, biscuit n*
bisognare *v to need* **p20**
Ho bisogno di ____. *I need
(to) ____.*
bloccare *v to block* **p20**
il **blocco** *m block n*
la **bocca** *f mouth n*
la **bomba** *f bomb n*
la **bomba d'ossigeno** *f oxygen tank n*
il **bordo della strada** *m curb n*
a bordo *on board*
la **borsa** *f bag n*
la **borsa portadocumenti** *f
briefcase n*

la **borsetta** *f purse, handbag
n*
il **botteghino** *m box office n*
la **bottiglia** *f bottle n*
il **box** *m garage n*
il **braccio** *m arm n*
il **Braille** *m Braille n*
brillante *bright adj*
il **brillante** *m diamond n*
bronzo *bronze adj*
bruciacchiato -a *charred
(food) adj*
bruciare *v to burn* **p20**
bruno -a *brown adj*
la bruna *f brunette n*
brutto -a *m f ugly*
il **bucato** *m laundry n*
il / la **buddista** *Buddhist adj n*
il **buffet** *m buffet n*
buio -a *dark adj*
il buio *m dark n*
buono -a *good, fine adj*
buon giorno *good morning*
buon pomeriggio *good
afternoon*
buona sera *good evening*
buona notte *good night*
il buono *m voucher n*
il buono per i pasti *meal
voucher*
il buono per la camera
room voucher
il **burro** *m butter n*
la **busta** *f envelope n*

C

la cabina privata *f private berth, cabin n*

cadere *v to fall* **p20**

il caffè *m café, coffee n*

il caffè freddo *iced coffee*

caldo -a *warm, hot adj*

il calzino *m sock n*

i calzoncini corti *m pl shorts n*

i calzoncini da bagno *m swim trunks n*

cambiare *v to change* **p20**

cambiarsi *v to change clothes* **p35**

il cambio *m change n*

il cambio della valuta *m exchange rate n*

il cambio di moneta *m money exchange n*

il cambio di velocità *f transmission n*

il cambio di velocità automatico *automatic transmission*

il cambio di velocità manuale *standard transmission*

il cambiavalute *m currency exchange n*

la camera d'albergo *f hotel room n*

il cameriere *m waiter n*

la cameriera *f waitress, maid n*

il camerino *m changing room n*

la camicetta *f blouse n*

la camicia *f shirt n*

camminare *v to walk* **p20**

il cammino *m walk, path n*

campeggiare *v to camp, to go camping* **p20**

il camper *m camper n*

il campo *m field n (sport)*

canadese *Canadian adj n*

cancellare *v to cancel* **p20**

la candeggina *f bleach n*

il cane *m dog n*

il cane guida *service dog*

la canna da pesca *f fishing pole n*

il canovaccio *m dish towel n*

cantare *v to sing* **p20**

la canzone *f song n*

i capelli *m pl hair n*

dai capelli rossi *redhead adj*

capire *v to understand* **p32**

Non capisco. *I don't understand.*

Capite? *Do you understand?*

il capo *m boss n*

il cappello *m hat n*

il cappotto *m coat n*

la capra *f goat n*

il carabiniere *m policeman n*

caricare *v to charge (a battery), to load* **p20**

a carico del destinatario *collect adj*

la carie *f tooth cavity n*

la carne *f meat n*

caro -a *dear, expensive adj*

la carta *f paper, card n*

la carta igienica *f toilet paper*

il piatto di carta *paper plate*

il **tovagliolo di carta** *paper napkin*

Avete un mazzo di carte? *Do you have a deck of cards?*

la **carta di credito** *credit card*

Si accettano carte di credito. *Credit cards accepted.*

la **carta d'imbarco** *f boarding pass*

la **cartina geografica** *f map n*

la **carta geografica di bordo** *onboard map*

la **cartolina** *f postcard n*

la **casa** *f home, house n*

a **casa mia** *at / in my home*

la **casa editrice** *publishing house*

la **casalinga** *f homemaker n*

il **casinò** *m casino n*

la **cassaforte** *f safe n* (container)

il / la **cattolico -a** *Catholic adj n*

il **cavallo** *m horse n*

celebrare *v to celebrate* **p20**

la **cena** *f dinner, supper n*

il **centimetro** *m centimeter n*

cento *m hundred n*

il **centralinista** *m f operator n* (phone)

il **centro** *m center n*

in **centro** *m downtown*

il **centro benessere** *fitness center*

il **centro commerciale** *mall*

il **centro affari** *m business center*

cercare *v to look for, to attempt* **p20**

la **ceretta** *f waxing n*

che *what interj*

Che tipo di ____? *What sort of ____?*

chi *who pron*

di **chi** *whose*

chiamare *v to call, to shout* **p20**

chiamare all'altoparlante *v to page* (someone) **p20**

la **chiamata sveglia** *f waiting call n*

la **chiamata a carico del destinatario** *collect phone call*

chiarire *v to clear* **p21**

chiaro -a *clear adj*

la **chiave** *f key n*

chiedere *v to order* (request), *to ask for* **p20**

chiedere scusa *v to make up* (apologize) **p20**

la **chiesa** *f church n*

il **chilo** *m kilo n*

il **chilometro** *m kilometer n*

il / la **chiropratico** *m f chiropractor n*

la **chitarra** *f guitar n*

chiudere *v to close* **p20**

chiudere a chiave *v to lock* **p20**

chiuso -a *closed adj*

il **cibo** *m food n*

il **cibo in scatola** *m canned goods n*

cieco -a *blind adj*

le **ciglia** *f eyelashes n*

il **cigno** *m swan n*

il **cinema** *m cinema n*

il / la **cinese** *Chinese adj n*

cinquanta *fifty adj*

cinque *five adj*

la **cinta** *f belt n*

la **cioccolata calda** *f hot chocolate n*

la **città** *f city n*

in città *downtown*

il **ciuccio** *m pacifier n*

il **clarinetto** *m clarinet n*

la **classe** *f class n*

la **classe business** *business class*

la **classe economica** *economy class*

la **prima classe** *first class*

il **climatizzatore** *m air conditioning n*

la **colazione** *f breakfast n*

la **prima colazione** *f breakfast n*

il **collegamento elettrico** *m electrical hookup n*

colorare *v to color* **p20**

il **colore** *m color n*

il **Colosseo** *m Coliseum n*

il **colpo di sole ai capelli** *m highlights n* (hair)

come *how adv*

cominciare *v to begin* **p20**

commerciale *business adj*

il / la **commesso -a** *m f salesperson n*

il / la **compagno -a** *m f partner n*

comportarsi *v to behave* **p35**

comprare *v to buy* **p20**

compreso -a *included adj*

comune *common adj*

con *with prep*

il **concerto** *m concert n*

il **condimento** *m salad dressing n*

la **condizione** *f condition n*

in buone / cattive condizioni *in good / bad condition*

la **conferma** *f confirmation n*

confermare *v to confirm* **p20**

confuso -a *confused adj*

il **congestionamento** *m congestion n* (sinus)

congestionato -a *congested adj*

il **coniglio** *m rabbit n*

conoscere *v to know* (someone) **p20**

il **contachilometri** *m odometer n*

i **contanti** *m pl cash n*

l'**acconto in contanti** *cash advance*

solo contanti *cash only*

il **contatto d'emergenza** *m emergency contact n*

contentissimo -a *delighted adj*

continuare *v to continue* **p20**

il **conto** m account n

il **contraccettivo** m contraceptive n

la **contraccezione** f birth control n

la **coperta** f blanket n

il **coperto** m service charge, cover charge n

coprire v to cover p21

il **corno** m horn n

la **corona dentale** f dental crown n

correggere v to correct p20

la **corrente** f water current n

correre v to run, to jog p20

corretto -a correct adj

il **corridoio** m hallway n

la **corsia** f aisle n (in store)

cortese courteous adj

  per cortesia please

cosa what n

  Cosa c'è? What's up?

costare v to cost p20

costoso -a expensive adj

il **costume** m costume n

  il **costume da bagno** swimsuit

il **cotone** m cotton n

la **crema** f cream n

  la **crema solare protettiva** sunscreen

crescere v to grow, to get larger p32

  Dove sei cresciuto -a? Where did you grow up?

il **crostaceo** m shellfish n

la **cuccetta** f berth n

la **cucina** f kitchen n

cucinare v to cook p20

  cotto -a cooked adj

  non abbastanza cotto -a undercooked adj

il **cucinino** m kitchenette n

cucire v to sew p21

il / la **cugino** -a m f cousin n

la **culla** f crib n

il **cuoio** m leather n

il **cuore** m heart n

il **cuscino** m pillow n

  il **cuscino di piume** down pillow

D

danneggiato -a damaged adj

Dannazione! Damn! expletive

danno m damage n

dare v to give p28

  Dia le carte anche a me. Deal me in.

il **datore di lavoro** m employer n

davanti front adj

  la **porta d'ingresso** front door

davvero really adv

il **dazio** m duty, toll n

  esente da dazio duty-free

decimo -a tenth adj

del m / **della** f / **dei** m pl / **delle** f pl any adj

il **delfino** m dolphin n

la **democrazia** f democracy n

il **denaro** m money n

  il **denaro liquido** cash

il dente *m* tooth *n*
la dentiera *f* denture *n*
la piastra dentale *denture plate*
il / la dentista *m f* dentist *n*
desiderare *v* to wish **p20**
la destinazione *f* destination *n*
la destra *f* right-hand side *n*
È sulla destra. *It's on the right.*
All'angolo, girare a destra. *Turn right at the corner.*
diabetico -a *diabetic adj*
la diarrea *f* diarrhea *n*
Al diavolo! *Damn! expletive*
dicembre *m* December *n*
dichiarare *v* to declare **p20**
diciannove *nineteen adj*
diciassette *seventeen adj*
diciotto *eighteen adj*
dieci *ten adj*
dietro -a *behind prep adv*
difficile *difficult adj*
il / la dipendente *m f* employee *n*
dipingere *v* to paint **p20**
dire *v* to say **p32**
i diritti *m pl* rights *n*
i diritti civili *civil rights*
diritto -a *straight adj adv*
proprio diritto *straight ahead*
Andare diritto. *Go straight.* (giving directions)
il / la disabile *m f* disabled *n*
il / la disegnatore -trice *m f* designer *n*
il disegno *m* drawing *n* (art)

disponibile *available adj*
la disponibilità *f* vacancy *n*
distante *distant adj*
più distante *farther*
il / la più distante *farthest*
il distributore automatico *m* vending machine *n*
il divieto *m* prohibition *n*
Divieto di balneazione *No swimming*
divorziato -a *divorced adj*
la doccia *f* shower *n*
il documento di riconoscimento *n* identification *n*
dodici *twelve adj*
la Dogana *f* Customs *n*
il dolce *m* dessert *n*
la lista dei dolci *dessert menu*
il dollaro *m* dollar *n*
la domanda *f* question *n*
fare una domanda *to ask a question* **p28**
domandare *v* to ask (a question) **p20**
il domani *m* tomorrow *n*
la domenica *f* Sunday *n*
la donna *f* woman *n*
dopo *f* after, later adv, prep
dopodomani *the day after tomorrow adv*
doppio -a *double adj*
il / la dottore -essa *m f* doctor *n*
dove *where adv*
Dov'è? / Dove si trova? *Where is it?*
dovunque *anywhere adv*
la dozzina *f* dozen *n*

il **dramma** m drama n
due two adj
durare v to last p20
duro -a hard adj
il **DVD** m DVD n

E

è v is v. See essere **p24, 26**
ebreo -a Jewish, Hebrew adj
  n
Eccellente! Great! adj
l'**economia** f economy n
economico -a inexpensive adj
l'**educatore** m / l'**educatrice** f
  educator n
elaborare v to process (documents) **p20**
l'**elefante** m elephant n
l'**elezione** f election n
l'**emergenza** f emergency n
entrare v to enter **p20**
  Proibito entrare. Do not
    enter.
l'**entrata** f entrance n
entusiastico -a enthusiastic adj
l'**erbetta** f herb n
l'**errore** m mistake n
esaurito -a sold out adj
  Tutto esaurito No vacancy
l'**esca** f bait n
l'**esercizio fisico** m workout n
espresso -a express adj
essere v to be (permanent
  quality) **p24, 26**
  C'è / Ci sono ____? Is / Are
    there ____?
l'**estate** f summer n

l'**esterno** m outside n
l'**età** f age n
l'**ettaro** m hectare n
l'**etto** m a hundred grams n
extra / in più extra (additional) adj

F

il **facchino** / il **portiere** m
  porter / concierge n
la **famiglia** f family n
fare v to make, to do **p28**
  fare un'escursione a piedi
    to hike
  **Faccio un'escursione a
    piedi.** I'm going on a hike.
  fare il bagno to bathe
  fare il numero to dial
    (phone)
  fare il numero diretto dial
    direct
  fare il surf to surf
  fare le carte to deal (cards)
  fare la doccia to shower
  fare le spese to shop
  fare l'immersione subacquea to snorkel
  fare bene to do good
  fare male to hurt
  Ahi! Questo fa male! Ouch!
    That hurts!
il **farmaco** m medication n
il **faro della macchina** m
  headlight n
fatto -a di made of adj
febbraio m February n
felice m f happy adj

femminile *f female adj*

la ferita *f wound, cut n*

fermare *v to stop* p20

Per favore si fermi. *Please stop.*

Ferma, ladro! *Stop, thief!*

la fermata *f stop n*

la fermata del bus *bus stop*

la festa *f feast, holiday n*

il fiammifero *m match n* (stick)

il / la fidanzato -a *m f boyfriend / girlfriend n fiancé / fiancée n*

il figlio *m son n* 114

la figlia *f daughter n*

il filo *m thread, wire n*

la finestra *f window n*

il finestrino di consegna *pickup window*

fino -a *fine adj*

il fiore *m flower n*

firmare *v to sign* p20

Firmi qui. *Sign here.*

il fiume *m river n*

il flauto *m flute n*

il formaggio *m cheese n*

il formato *m format n*

la formula *f formula n*

fotocopiare *v to photocopy* p20

fragile *fragile adj*

il / la francese *French adj n*

il francobollo *m stamp n* (postage)

il fratello *m brother n*

la freccia *f turn signal n* (car)

il freddo *m cold n*

frenare *v to brake* p20

il freno *m brake n*

fresco -a *fresh adj*

la fronte *f forehead n*

il frullato *m milk shake n*

la frutta *f fruit n* (collective)

i frutti di mare *m pl seafood n*

il frutto *m fruit n*

fumare *v to smoke* p20

funzionare *v to function, to work* p20

le funzioni religiose *f pl religious services n*

il fuoco *m fire n*

Al fuoco! *m Fire! interj*

il furgoncino *m van n*

G

il gabbiano *m gull n*

il gabinetto *m toilet n*

la gamba *f leg n*

il gambero *m shrimp n*

il / la gatto -a *m f cat n*

il / la genitore *m f parent n*

gennaio *m January n*

il ghiaccio *m ice n*

la macchina per il ghiaccio *ice machine*

la giacca *f jacket n*

giallo -a *yellow adj*

il giallo *m mystery novel n*

il / la giapponese *Japanese adj n*

ITALIAN—ENGLISH

il giardino di ricreazione *m*
  playground n
il / la ginecologo -a *m f gyne-*
  cologist n
giocare *v to play* (a game)
  p20
  giocare a golf *to go golfing*
il giocattolo *m toy* n
  il negozio di giocattoli *toy*
  store
il gioco *m play* n
il giornalaio *m newsstand* n
il giornale *m newspaper* n
il giorno *m day* n
  questi ultimi giorni *these*
  last few days
giovane *young adj*
il giovedì *m Thursday* n
girare *v to turn* **p20**
  girare a sinistra / destra *to*
  turn left / right
il girello *m walker* n (ambula-
  tory device)
il giro turistico *m sightseeing* n
la gita *f tour* n
  la gita guidata *guided tour*
giù *down, downward adv*
giugno *m June* n
giusto -a *correct adj*
il golf *m golf* n
  il campo da golf *golf course*
la gomma *f rubber* n (material), *eraser, tire* n (wheel)
  Ho una gomma a terra. *I*
  have a flat tire.

graffiare *v to scratch* **p20**
graffiato -a *scratched adj*
il graffio *m scratch* n
il grammo *m gram* n
grande *big adj*
  più grande *bigger*
  il / la più grande *biggest*
il grasso *m*, grasso -a *fat adj n*
Grazie. *Thank you. interj*
il / la greco -a *Greek adj* n
gridare *v to shout* **p20**
grigio -a *gray adj*
la gruccia *f clothes hanger* n
il gruppo *m band* n (musical
  ensemble), *group* n
il guanto *m glove* n
guardare *v to look, watch*
  p20
  Guarda qui! *Look here!*
la guardia *f guard* n
  la guardia di sicurezza *secu-*
  rity guard
la guerra *f war* n
la guida *f guide* (publication), *tour guide* n
guidare *v to drive, guide* **p20**
il gusto *m taste* n (discernment)

H
la hostess *f flight attendant* n

I
ieri *m yesterday* n *adv*
  ieri l'altro *the day before*
  yesterday

imbarazzato -a *embarrassed adj*

l'imbarcazione *f boat n*

immergersi con l'apparecchiatura subacquea *v to scuba dive* **p35**

importante *important adj*

Non è importante. *It's no big deal.*

l'imposta *f tax n*

l'imposta sui valori aggiunti (IVA) *value-added tax (VAT)*

incassare *v to cash, to collect (money)* **p20**

incassare la vincita *to cash out (gambling)*

incendiare *v to burn* **p20**

l'incidente *m accident n*

incinta *pregnant adj*

incominciare *v to start, to begin* **p20**

l'incrinatura *f crack n (glass)*

indicare *v to point* **p20**

l'indigestione *m indigestion n*

l'indirizzo *m address n*

Qual'è l'indirizzo? *What's the address?*

indossare *v to wear* **p20**

l'indù *Hindu adj n*

l'infarto *m heart attack n*

l'infermiere -a *m f nurse n*

l'informazione *f information n*

il chiosco delle informazioni *information booth*

l'ingegnere *m engineer n*

inghiottire *v to swallow* **p21**

l'inglese *m f English adj n*

l'Inghilterra *f England n*

l'ingorgo stradale *m congestion n (traffic)*

l'insalata *f salad n*

inserire la spina *v to plug in* **p21**

l'insetto *m bug, insect n*

insultare *v to insult* **p20**

intasato -a *backed up (toilet) adj*

interno -a *inside adj*

l'interprete *m f interpreter n*

l'intervallo *m intermission n*

intollerante al lattosio *lactose-intolerant adj*

l'invalidità *f disability n*

l'inverno *m winter n*

io *I pron*

l'ipovedente *m f visually-impaired n*

l'irlandese *m f Irish adj n*

l'italiano -a *m f Italian adj n*

J

il jogging *m jogging n*

K

kasher *kosher adj*

L

là *there adv (demonstrative)*

di là *over there*

la lampada *f light n (lamp)*

largo -a *wide adj*

il lato *m side n*

dall'altro lato di *across prep*
dall'altro lato della strada *across the street*
il **latte** *m milk n*
il **latte in polvere** *formula*
il **lavabo** *m sink n*
il **lavaggio a secco** *m dry cleaning n*
lavanda *f lavender n*
la **lavanderia a secco** *f dry cleaner n*
lavorare *v to work* **p20**
Io **lavoro per** _____. *I work for* _____.
la **legge** *f law n*
leggere *v to read* **p20**
leggero -a *light adj*
lei *f she, her pron*
lentamente *slowly adv*
le **lenti a contatto** *f contact lens n*
la **lentiggine** *f freckle n*
lento -a *slow adj*
le **lenzuola** *f sheets n* (linens)
il **letto** *m bed n*
il **lettore di DVD** *m DVD player n*
levare *v to take off* **p20**
la **lezione** *f lesson n*
libero -a *free adj*
la **libreria** *f bookstore n*
il **libro** *m book n*
il **limite di velocità** *m speed limit n*
la **limousine** *f limo n*
la **lingua** *f language n*

il **liquore** *m liqueur n*
liscio -a *smooth adj, straight adj* (drinks)
il **litro** *m liter n*
locale *local adj*
lontano -a *far adj*
più lontano -a *farther*
il / la **più lontano -a** *farthest*
loro *they, them pron*
la **luce** *f light n*
luglio *m July n*
lui *m he, him pron*
luminoso -a *bright adj*
luna *f moon n*
lunedì *m Monday n*
lungo -a *long adj*
più lungo -a *longer*
il / la **più lungo -a** *longest*
di lusso *upscale adj*

M
la **macchina** *f machine, car n*
la **macchina decappottabile** *convertible car*
la **madre** *f mother n*
maggio *m May n* (month)
la **maglia** *f sweater n*
il **maiale** *m pig n*
malato -a *sick adj*
male *badly adv*
il **mal d'auto** *carsickness*
il **mal di denti** *toothache*
il **mal di mare** *seasickness*
il **mal di testa** *headache*
il / la **manager** *m f manager n*

la mancia *f* tip *n* (gratuity)
  Mancia compresa. *Tip included.*
mandare *v* to send **p20**
  mandare la posta elettronica / e-mail to send e-mail
  mandare il conto to bill
maneggiare *v* to handle **p20**
  Maneggiare con cura. *Handle with care.*
mangiare *v* to eat **p20**
  mangiare fuori to eat out
la mano *f sing* / le mani *f pl* hand *n*
mantenere *v* to hold, to keep **p20**
il manuale d'istruzioni *m* manual *n* (book)
il marciapiede *m* sidewalk *n*
il marito *m* husband *n*
marroncino -a tan *adj*
marrone brown *adj*
il martedì *m* Tuesday *n*
marzo *m* March *n* (month)
maschile male *adj*
il maschio *m* male *n*
massaggiare *v* to massage **p20**
il massaggio alla schiena *m* back rub *n*
il mattino *m* morning *n*
  al mattino in the morning
medio -a middle, medium *adj* (size)
meno *adv* less
meno *adv* lesser
il meno *n* least

il menù *m*, la lista *f* menu *n*
  il menù dei bambini children's menu
  il menù per i diabetici diabetic menu
  il menù da asporto takeout menu
il mercato *m* market *n*
  il mercatino delle pulci flea market
  il mercato all'aperto open-air market
il mercoledì *m* Wednesday *n*
il mese *m* month *n*
il mestiere *m* occupation, trade *n*
  Che mestiere fa? What do you do for a living?
la metà *f* half *n*
il metro *m* meter *n*
il metrò *m*, la metropolitana *f* the subway, tube *n*
  la linea della metropolitana subway line
  la stazione della metropolitana subway station
  Che linea di metropolitana devo prendere per____?
  Which subway do I take for ____?
mettere *v* to place, to put **p20**
  mettere in borsa to bag
la mezzanotte *f* midnight
il mezzogiorno *m* noon *n*
migliore better, best *adj*
il militare *m* military *n*

mille *thousand adj n*

il millilitro *m milliliter n*

il millimetro *m millimeter n*

la minestra *f soup n*

il minimo *m least n*

il minuto *m minute n*

in un attimo *in a minute*

la misura *f size n* (clothing)

in modo sospetto *suspiciously adv*

la moglie *f wife n*

molti -e *many adj*

molto -a *much, very adj adv*

la moneta *f coin n*

la montagna *f mountain n*

scalare la montagna *mountain climbing*

morbido -a *soft adj*

la moschea *f mosque n*

la mostra *f exhibit n*

mostrare *v to show* **p20**

Può mostrarmelo? *Would you show it to me?*

la moto *f motorcycle n*

il motore *m engine n*

il motorino *m scooter n*

la mucca *f cow n*

la multa *f fine n* (penalty)

il museo *m museum n*

la musica *f music n*

il / la musicista *m f musician n*

il / la musulmano -a *Muslim adj n*

N

il naso *m nose n*

il nastro trasportatore *m conveyor belt n*

il naufragio *m shipwreck n*

la nausea *f nausea n*

la nave *f ship n*

la navetta *f shuttle n* (transportation)

navigare a vela *v to sail* **p20**

la nazionalità *f nationality n*

il negozio *m store, shop n*

il negozio duty-free *duty-free shop*

il neo *m mole n* (facial feature)

il / la neonato -a *f baby, infant n*

nero -a *black adj*

nessuno -a *m f nobody n*

il niente *m nothing n*

il night *m nightclub n*

il / la nipote *m f nephew, niece, grandchild n*

no *no adv*

la nocciolina americana *f peanut n*

la noce *f nut n*

noi *us pron*

noleggiare *v to charter* (transportation), *to rent* **p20**

a noleggio *chartered, rented*

il nome *m name n*

nome e cognome *first and last name*

non-fumatori *nonsmoking adj*

la zona non-fumatori *nonsmoking area*

la carrozza non-fumatori *nonsmoking car*

la sala non-fumatori *non-smoking room*

la nonna *f grandmother n*

il nonno *m grandfather n, grandparent n*

nono -a *ninth adj 9*

la notte *f night n*

  a notte *per night*

novanta *ninety adj*

nove *nine adj n*

novembre *m November n*

nubile *f maiden adj n*

  lo conservato il mio nome da nubile. *I kept my maiden name.*

il numero *m number, size n* (shoes)

nuotare *v to swim* **p20**

la Nuova Zelanda *f New Zealand n*

il / la neozelandese *New Zealander adj n*

nuovo -a *new adj*

nuvoloso -a *cloudy adj*

O

l'oca *f goose n*

gli occhiali *m pl glasses n pl* (spectacles)

  gli occhiali da sole *sunglasses*

l'occhio *m eye n*

occupato -a *busy adj* (phone line), *taken adj* (seat)

  Questo posto è occupato? *Is this seat taken?*

offrire *v to offer* **p21**

l'oggi *m today n*

l'olio *m oil n*

l'oliva *f olive n*

l'ombrello *m umbrella n*

l'onorario *m fee n*

l'opera *f opera, work n*

il / la operatore -trice *m f phone operator n*

l'optometrista *m f optometrist n*

l'ora *f hour, time n*

  A che ora? *At what time?*

  Che ora è? *What time is it?*

l'orario *m hours* (at museum), *schedule, timetable n* (train)

  È in orario? *Is it on time?*

ordinare *v to order* **p20**

ordinato -a *neat adj* (tidy)

organico -a *organic adj*

l'organo *m organ n*

l'oro *m gold adj n*

l'orso *m bear n*

l'ospite *m guest n*

l'ostello *m hostel n*

l'otorino *m ear / nose / throat specialist n*

ottanta *eighty adj*

l'ottavo -a *eighth adj*

  tre ottavi *three eighths n*

otto -a *eight adj*

ottobre *October n*

P

il pacco *m package n*

il padre *m father n*

il paesaggio *m landscape n* (painting)

pagare *v to pay* **p20**

  pagare il conto dell'albergo *check out* (of hotel)

la palestra *f gym n*

la palla *f ball n*

  il pallone *ball, soccer* (sport)

pallido -a *pale adj*

il pane *m bread n*

il pannolino *m diaper n*

  il pannolino di stoffa *cloth diaper*

il parabrezza *m windshield n*

la parata *f parade n*

parcheggiare *v to park* **p20**

il parcheggio *m parking n*

il parco *m park n*

il parente *m relative n*

parlare *v to talk, to speak* **p20**

  Si parla inglese. *English spoken here.*

la parola di accesso *f password n*

il parrucchiere *m hairdresser n*

la partenza *f departure n*

la partita *f match m* (sport)

il partito politico *m political party n*

il passaggio pedonale *m walkway n*

passare *v to pass* **p20**

il passaporto *m passport n*

il passeggero *m passenger n*

il passeggino *m stroller n*

la passerella *f walkway, cat-walk n*

  la passerella mobile *moving walkway*

il passero *m sparrow n*

il pasto *m meal n*

  il pasto per diabetici *diabetic meal*

  il pasto kasher *kosher meal*

  il pasto vegetariano *vegetarian meal*

la patente *f driver's license n*

il pavimento *m floor n* (ground)

pazzo -a *m crazy n*

il pedaggio *m toll n*

il pediatra *m pediatrician n*

pedonale *pedestrian adj*

  la zona pedonale *pedestrian area*

il pedone *m pedestrian n*

la pelle *f skin, leather n*

pentito -a *sorry adj*

perdere *v to lose, to miss* (a flight) **p20**

  Mi sono perso. *I'm lost.*

per favore *please* (polite entreaty) *interj*

il pericolo *m danger n*

la permanente *f permanent* (hair) *n*

il permesso *m license, permit n 50*

  Permesso. *Excuse me, pardon me.*

permettere *v to permit* **p20**

il personale *m staff n*

pesare *v to weigh* **p20**

  Pesa ____. *It weighs ____.*

i pesi *m pl* weights *n*

il pettine *m* comb *n*

il pettirosso *m* robin *n*

il pezzo *m* / il pezzetto *m* bit (small amount) *n*

piacere *v* to like (take pleasure in) p33

Mi piacerebbe _____. I would like ____.

il piacere *m* pleasure *n*

per piacere please (polite entreaty)

È un piacere. It's a pleasure.

il piano *m* floor *n*

il piano terra ground floor

il secondo piano first floor

il piano rateale *m* rate plan *n* (for purchases)

il piatto *m* dish *n*

il piatto del giorno special (featured meal)

il piccione *m* pigeon *n*

piccolo -a little, small *adj*

più piccolo -a littler, smaller

il più piccolo, la più piccola littlest, smallest

il piede *m* foot (body part) *n*

pieno -a full *adj*

il pieno full tank (fuel)

la pila *f* battery (electric) *n*

la pillola *f* pill *n*

la pillola contro il mal di mare seasickness pill

piovere *v* to rain p20

piovoso -a rainy *adj*

la piscina *f* swimming pool *n*

la pista *f* runway *n*

più tardi later *adv*

A più tardi. See you later.

piuttosto rather *adv*

la pizza *f* pizza *n*

la plastica *f* plastic *n*

lo pneumatico *m* tire *n* (wheel)

Ho lo pneumatico sgonfio. I have a flat tire.

poco -a (a) little *adj* (quantity)

poco costoso -a cheap *adj*

meno costoso -a cheaper

il / la meno costoso -a cheapest

poco profondo -a shallow *adj*

poi then, later *adv*

la polizia *f* police *n*

il poliziotto *m* officer *n*

il pollame *m* poultry *n*

il pollice *m* thumb *n*

il pollo *m* chicken *n*

la polpetta *f* meatball *n*

le poltroncine nella sezione orchestra *f pl* orchestra seats *n pl*

il pomeriggio *m* afternoon *n*

nel pomeriggio / di pomeriggio in the afternoon

la pompa *f* pump *n*

il ponte *m* bridge (across a river, dental prosthesis) *n*

popolare popular *adj*

la porta *f* door *n*

il portabagagli *m* trunk *n* (car)

il portafogli *m* wallet *n*

portare *v* to take, to bring p20

portare indietro *v to return (something to a store)* **p20**

il portiere *m goalie (sport), concierge n*

il porto *m port (beverage, ship mooring) n*

la porzione *f portion n*

la posta *f mail n*

 la posta aerea *air mail*

 la posta raccomandata *certified mail*

 la posta celere *express mail*

 la posta prioritaria *first class mail*

 spedire per assicurata *to send by registered mail*

posta elettronica *f e-mail n*

 messaggio di posta elettronica, messaggio e-mail *e-mail message*

 Posso avere il suo indirizzo di posta elettronica / e-mail per favore? *May I have your e-mail address?*

il posto *m seat, place n*

 il posto sul corridoio *aisle seat*

 Sei a posto? *Are you okay?*

potere *v can (be able to), may v aux* **p30**

 Posso ____? *May I ____?*

la pozza *f pool n*

il pozzo *m pit, well n*

il pranzo *m lunch, dinner, meal n*

preferire *v to prefer* **p32**

prelevare *v to withdraw* **p20**

il prelievo *m withdrawal n*

la prenotazione *m reservation n*

preoccupato -a *anxious adj*

preparato -a *prepared adj*

presentare *v to introduce* **p20**

 Ho il piacere di presentarti ____. *I'd like to introduce you to ____.*

il preservativo *m condom n*

 Hai un preservativo? *Do you have a condom?*

 non senza un preservativo *not without a condom*

preventivare *v to budget* **p20**

le previsioni del tempo *f weather forecast n*

il prezzo *m price n*

 il prezzo del biglietto *fare / ticket price*

 il prezzo d'ingresso *admission fee*

 a prezzo modico *moderately priced*

presto -a *early, quick adj*

 È presto. *It's early.*

 Fai presto! *Be quick!.*

la primavera *f spring (season) n*

primo -a *first adj*

il problema *m problem n*

il prodotto *m product n*

professionale *professional adj*

profondo -a *deep adj*

il programma *m program n*

prossimo -a *next adj*

 la prossima stazione *the next station*

il / la **protestante** *Protestant adj n*

provare *v to try, to try on* (clothing) **p20**

provare gioia *to enjoy* **p20**

pulire *v to clean* **p21**

la **pulizia** *f cleanliness n*

puntare *v to bet, to put* (gambling) **p20**

Punti sul rosso / nero! *Put it on red / black!*

il **punteggio** *m score n*

in **punto** *o'clock adv*

puzzare *v to smell* **p20**

Q

a **quadretti** *checked* (pattern) *adj*

il **quadro** *m painting n*

qualche *some adj*

qualcosa *f something n*

qualcuno -a *someone adj n*

quale *which adv*

qualsiasi cosa *f anything n*

quando *when adv*

la **quantità** *f amount n*

quanto *sing* / **quanti** *pl how much adj pron*

Quanti? *How many?*

Quanto? *How much?*

quaranta *forty adj*

quarto -a *fourth adj*

il **quarto** *m quarter n*

quasi al sangue *medium rare* (steak) *adj*

quattordici *m fourteen adj*

quattro *m four adj*

quello -a *that adj*

quelli -e *those adj*

questo -a *this adj*

questi -e *these adj*

qui *here n*

quindici *m fifteen adj*

quinto -a *fifth adj*

R

raccomandare *v to recommend* **p20**

Ti raccomando! *I beg you!*

la **radio** *f radio n*

la **radio satellitare** *satellite radio*

il **raffreddore** *m cold n* (sickness)

il **ragazzo** *m boy, boyfriend n*

la **ragazza** *f girl, girlfriend n*

i **ragazzi** *m f pl kids n*

rallentare *v to slow down* **p20**

Rallenta! *Slow down!*

il **rame** *m copper n*

la **rampa** *f ramp n*

il **rapporto sessuale** *m sexual intercourse n*

il **recapito domiciliare** *m home address n*

il **reclamo** *m complaint n*

il / la **redattore** -trice *m f editor n*

il **regalo** *m gift n*

reggere *v to hold* **p20**

il **repellente insetticida** *m insect repellent n*

restare *v to stay* **p20**

resto *m change n* (money)

la rete *f network n*
riappacificarsi *v to make up, to make peace* **p35**
riccio -a *curly adj*
il ricciolo *m curl n*
la ricerca *f search n*
la ricetta medica *f prescription n*
ricevere *v to receive* **p20**
la ricevuta *f receipt n*
richiesta *f order, request n*
riempire *v to fill* **p21**
rifiutare *v to refuse, to decline* **p20**
il rifornimento *m stock n*
rilassarsi *v to relax, to hang out* **p35**
ripetere *v to repeat* **p20**
   Può ripetere per favore? *Would you please repeat that?*
riscuotere *v to collect* (pay) **p20**
rispondere *v to answer, to reply* **p20**
   Per cortesia, rispondimi. *Answer me, please.*
risposta *f answer n*
   Ho bisogno di una risposta. *I need an answer.*
il ristorante *m restaurant n*
il ritardo *m delay n*
   Per favore non fare ritardo. *Please don't be late.*
   in ritardo *late adv*
ritirare *v to withdraw* **p20**

ritornare *v to return* (go back to) **p20**
il ritratto *m portrait n*
il ritrovo *m hangout* (hot spot) *n*
il rivelatore di metalli *m metal detector n*
la rivista *f magazine n* (periodical)
la roccia *f rock n*
   scalare le roccie *rock climbing*
romantico -a *romantic adj*
il romanzo *m novel n*
rompere *v to break* **p20**
rosa *pink adj*
   la rosa *f rose n*
rosso -a *red adj*
a rotelle *wheeled adj* (luggage)
la rottura *f break n*
rovesciare *v to spill* **p20**
rubare *v to steal, to rob* **p20**
   Qualcuno ha rubato il mio portafogli. *Someone stole my wallet.*
rubato -a *stolen adj*
il rubinetto *m faucet n*
rumoroso -a *loud, noisy adj*
la ruota di scorta *f spare tire n*

S
il sabato *m Saturday n*
il sacchetto *m bag n*
   il sacchetto per il mal d'aria *airsickness bag*
la sala d'aspetto *f lounge n*

la sala **non-fumatori** f non-smoking room n

il **saldo** m balance (bank account) n

il **sale** m salt n

Con poco sale low-salt

salire v to climb p21

salire le scale to climb the stairs

salire a bordo di to board

Lei salirà a bordo della nave. She will board the ship.

salpare v to set sail, to sail away p20

Quando salpiamo? When do we sail?

il **saluto** m greeting n

Il **salvagente** m life preserver n

al **sangue** rare (meat) adj

sapere v to know (something) p20

il **sapone** m soap n

il **sapore** m taste (flavor) n

il **sapore di cioccolato** chocolate flavor

il **sarto** m tailor n

il **satellite** m satellite n

la **radio satellitare** satellite radio

il **tracking satellitare** satellite tracking

sazio -a full adj (after a meal)

sbagliare v to make a mistake p20

lo **sbaglio** m mistake n

la **scala** m staircase, straight (gambling) n

la **scala mobile** f escalator n

scalare v to climb p20

scalare una montagna to climb a mountain

scalare delle rocce rock climbing

la **scalata** f climbing n

l'**attrezzatura per scalate** climbing gear

le **scale** f pl stairs n

scalfito -a scratched adj

la **scalinata** f steps n

scaricare v to download, to unload p20

lo **scarico** m drain n

la **scarpa** f shoe n

la **scheda** f phone card n

la **schiena** f back n

sciolto -a loose adj

la **scogliera** f reef n

la **scommessa** f bet n

Eguaglio la tua scommessa I'll see your bet.

scommettere v to bet p20

scomparire v to disappear p21

lo **sconto** m discount n

lo **sconto per i bambini** children's discount

lo **sconto per gli anziani** senior discount

lo **sconto per gli studenti** student discount

lo **scontrino** m receipt n

la **scottatura solare** f *sunburn* n

il / la **scozzese** *Scottish* adj

lo / la **scrittore -trice** m f
  writer n

scrivere v *to write* **p20**

  Come si scrive? *How do you
  spell that?*

  **Per favore potreste scriver-
  melo?** *Would you write
  that down for me?*

la **scultura** f *sculpture* n

la **scuola** f *school* n

  la **scuola media** *junior high
  / middle school*

  la **scuola superiore** *high
  school*

  la **facoltà di giurisprudenza**
  law school

  la **facoltà di medicina** *medical school*

  la **scuola elementare** *pri-
  mary school*

scusare v *to excuse* (pardon)
  p20

  Mi scusi. *Excuse me.*

secco -a *dry* adj

secondo -a *second* adj

sedersi v *to sit* **p35**

la **sedia a rotelle** f *wheelchair*
  n

  l'accesso alle sedie a rotelle
  wheelchair access

  la **rampa delle sedie a
  rotelle** *wheelchair ramp*

  la **sedia a rotelle motorizzata** *power wheelchair*

sedici *sixteen* adj

il **sedile** m *seat* n

il **sedile di sicurezza** m *car
  seat, child's safety seat* n

il **segnale di strada bloccata** m
  road-closed sign n

il **segnale di precedenza** m
  yield sign n

sei *six* adj

self-serve *self-serve* adj

sembrare v *to look, to
  appear* **p20**

sempre *always* adv

senso unico *one way* (traffic
  sign) adj

il **sentiero** m *trail* n

sentire v *to hear, to feel* **p21**

senza *without* prep

separato -a *separated* (marital status) adj

la **sera** f *evening* n

  di sera *at night*

la **serratura** f *lock* n

servire v *to serve* **p21**

servizio m *service* n

  Fuori servizio *Out of service*

sessanta *sixty* adj

il **sesso** m *sex* (gender, activ-
  ity) n

la **seta** f *silk* n

settanta *seventy* adj

sette *seven* adj

settembre m *September* n

la **settimana** f *week* n

  questa settimana *this week*

  la **settimana scorsa** *last week*

tra una settimana / la settimana prossima *a week from now / next week*

il settimo -a *seventh adj*

sgocciolare *v to drip* **p20**

si *yes adv*

la sicurezza *f security, safety n*

il sedile di sicurezza *child's safety seat*

il punto di controllo di sicurezza *security checkpoint*

la guardia di sicurezza *security guard*

sicuro -a *safe (secure) adj*

il sigaro *m cigar n*

la sigaretta *f cigarette n*

un pacchetto di sigarette *a pack of cigarettes*

silenzioso -a *quiet adj*

simpatico -a *nice adj*

la sinfonia *f symphony n*

single *single (unmarried) adj*

E' single? *Are you single?*

singolo -a *single (one) adj*

sinistro -a *left adj*

a sinistra *on the left*

smarrirsi *v to get lost, to go astray* **p35**

Ho smarrito il mio passaporto. *I lost my passport.*

smarrito -a *missing adj*

il socialismo *m socialism n*

il socio *m member n*

la soda *f seltzer n*

soffrire *v to suffer* **p21**

che soffre il mal di mare *seasick*

il sole *m sun n*

soleggiato -a *sunny adj*

solo -a *alone adj adv*

solo scotch *straight scotch*

sopra *above prep adv*

il sopracciglio *m eyebrow n*

sordo -a *deaf adj*

la sorella *f sister n*

la sostituzione *f substitution n*

sottile *thin adj*

sotto *below prep, adv*

il sottotitolo *m subtitle n*

spaccare *v to break* **p20**

la Spagna *f Spain n*

il / la spagnolo -a *Spanish adj n*

lo spago *m twine n*

le spalle *f back n*

la spazzola *f brush n*

le spazzole del tergicristallo *f wiper blades n*

specificare *v to specify* **p20**

spedire *v to send, to ship* **p21**

le spesa *f groceries n*

lo spettacolo *m show n (performance)*

la spezia *f spice n*

la spia *f spy, lamp n (dashboard)*

la spia dell'olio *oil light*

la spiaggia *f beach n*

gli spiccioli *m change (money) n*

spiegare *v to explain* **p20**

la spina *f plug n*

spingere *v to push* **p20**

lo spinotto adattore *m adapter plug n*

sporco -a *dirty adj*

gli sport *m sports n*

sposarsi *v to marry* **p35**

sposato -a *married adj*

spuntare *v to trim* (hair) **p20**

lo spuntino *m snack n*

la squadra *f team n*

staccato -a *disconnected, detached adj*

lo stadio *m stadium n*

stampare *v to print* **p20**

stanco -a *tired, exhausted adj*

stare *v to be v* (temporary state, condition, mood) **p24**

stare in piedi *to stand*

lo stato *m state n*

gli Stati Uniti *the United States*

la stazione *f station n*

la stazione di polizia *police station*

la stazione termale *spa*

la stella di Natale *f poinsettia n*

stitico -a *constipated adj*

lo STOP *m STOP* (traffic sign)

stordito -a *dizzy adj*

la storia *f history n*

storico -a *historical adj*

la strada *f road, street n*

dall'altra parte della strada *across the street*

giù per la strada *down the street*

stressato -a *stressed adj*

stretto -a *tight, narrow adj*

a striscie *striped adj*

lo studio del medico *m doctor's office n*

su *up adv prep*

subire un furto *v to get mugged, to get robbed* **p21**

Ho subito un furto. *I've been robbed.*

il succo *m juice n*

il succo d'arancia *orange juice*

il succo di frutta *fruit juice*

il sugo *m sauce n*

suo -a *his adj*

suonare *v to play* (an instrument) **p20**

surriscaldare *v to overheat* **p20**

la sveglia *f alarm clock n*

svenire *v to faint* **p21**

T

il tachimetro *m speedometer n*

il tacchino *m turkey n*

la taglia *f size n* (clothes)

tagliare *v to cut* **p20**

il taglio *m cut n*

il tamburo *m drum n*

la targa *f license plate n*

la tariffa *f fare, rate n* (car rental, hotel)

la tassa *f tax, fee n*

il tasso d'interesse *m interest rate n*

la tavola di surf *f surfboard n*

il tavolo *m table n*

il taxi *m* taxi *n*

la stazione dei taxi *taxi stand*

il tè *m* tea *n*

il tè con latte e zucchero *tea with milk and sugar*

il tè con il limone *tea with lemon*

la tisana *herbal tea*

il teatro *m* theater *n*

il teatro dell'opera *m* opera house *n*

la tecno-musica *f* techno *n*

il / la tedesco -a *m f* German *adj n*

telefonare a *v* to call (phone) **p20**

la telefonata *f* phone call *n*

una telefonata internazionale *an international phone call*

una telefonata interurbana *a long-distance phone call*

telefonico -a telephone *adj*

elenco telefonico *phone directory*

il telefonino *m* cell / mobile phone *n*

Vendete i telefonini prepagati? *Do you sell prepaid phones?*

il telefono *m* phone *n*

Può darmi il suo numero di telefono? *May I have your phone number?*

la televisione *f* television *n*

la televisione via cavo *cable television*

la televisione satellitare *satellite television*

il televisore *m* television set *n*

il tempio *m* temple *n*

il tempo *m* time *n*

Per quanto tempo? *For how long?*

la tenda *f* curtain, tent *n*

tenere *v* to keep, to hold **p20**

tenersi per mano *to hold hands*

il tennis *m* tennis *n*

il campo da tennis *tennis court*

il tergicristallo *m* windshield wiper, wiper *n*

il terminale *m* terminal *n* (airport)

terzo -a third *adj*

la tessera *f* permit *n*

Abbiamo bisogno di una tessera? *Do we need a permit?*

il tessuto *m* fabric *n*

il tettuccio apribile *m* sunroof *n*

il tipo *m* kind *n* (type)

Che tipo è? *What kind is it?*

tirare *v* to pull **p20**

Tira vento. *It's windy out.*

tirare a riva *to beach*

tirare l'acqua del gabinetto *to flush*

togliere *v* to remove **p20**

la tonnellata *f* ton *n*

il topo *m* mouse *n*

il torto *m* fault *n*

Ho torto. *I'm at fault.*
Lui ha torto. *He's at fault.*
la tosse *f cough n*
tossire *v to cough* **p21**
il totale *m total n*
   Qual'è il totale? *What is the total?*
il tovagliolo *m napkin n*
traboccante *overflowing adj*
il traffico *m traffic n*
   Com'è il traffico? *How's the traffic?*
   Il traffico è orribile. *The traffic is terrible.*
   il regolamento del traffico *traffic rules*
la transazione *f transaction n*
il trasferimento *m transfer n*
   trasferimento di valuta / di fondi *money transfer*
   Ho bisogno di fare un trasferimento dei fondi. *I need to transfer funds.*
trasferire dei dati *v to upload* **p21**
traslocare *v to move* **p20**
trasmettere *v to transfer* **p20**
tre *three adj*
la treccia *f braid n*
tredici *thirteen adj*
il treno *m train n*
trenta *thirty adj*
   Sono le due e trenta. *It's two-thirty.*
il tribunale *m court* (legal) *n*
triplo -a *triple adj*
triste *sad adj*

troppo *too* (excessively) *adv*
   troppo caldo -a *too hot*
   troppo cotto -a *overcooked*
trovare *v to find* **p20**
truccarsi *v to make up* (apply cosmetics) **p35**
il trucco *m makeup n*
tu *you pron* (singular, informal)
tuffarsi *v to dive* **p35**
tuo *m sing* / **tua** *f sing* / **tuoi** *m pl* / **tue** *f pl your adj*
il tuo *m* / **la tua** *f* / **i tuoi** *m pl* / **le tue** *f pl yours n*
tutto- a *all adj*
   È tutto, grazie. *That's all, thank you.*
   tutto esaurito -a *sold out adj*

U

l'uccello *m bird n*
udire *v to hear* **p21**
l'ufficio postale *m post office n*
   Dov'è l'ufficio postale? *Where is the post office?*
ultimo -a *last adj*
umido -a *humid adj*
undici *eleven adj*
l'università *f university, college n*
uno -a *one adj*
l'uomo *m man n*
usare *v to use* **p20**
uscire *v to exit* **p32**

l'**uscita** f gate (at airport), exit n

senza sbocco not an exit
l'**uscita d'emergenza** emergency exit n

l'**uscita USB** f USB port n

l'**uva** f grapes n

V

la **vacanza** f vacation, holiday n

il **vagone letto** m sleeping car n

la **valigia** f suitcase n

la **valvola fusibile** f fuse n

la **vasca da bagno** f bathtub n

vecchio -a old adj

vedere v to see p22

Posso vederlo? May I see it?

il / la **vedovo -a** m f widower, widow n

il **vegetale** m vegetable n

vegetariano -a vegetarian adj

la **vela** f sail n

veloce fast adj

la **velocità di connessione** f connection speed n

vendere v to sell p20

il **venditore all'aperto** m street vendor n

venerdì m Friday n

il **ventaglio** m fan n

venti twenty adj

verde green adj

la **verdura** m vegetables n (food)

verificare v to check p20

la **verruca** f wart n

la **versione** f version n

il **vestito** m dress (garment) n

vestirsi v to dress p35

viaggiare v to travel, to ride p20

il **viaggio** m trip, tour n

vicino -a close, near adj, nearby adj, adv

più vicino -a closer, nearer
il / la più vicino -a closest, nearest
il / la vicino -a neighbor

il **video (registratore)** m VCR, video n

Vietato Fumare No Smoking (sign)

Vietato l'ingresso Do not enter (sign)

il **vigneto** m vineyard n

il **vinile** m vinyl n

il **vino** m wine n

il vino bianco white wine
il vino rosso red wine
il vino frizzante sparkling wine
il vino dolce sweet wine

viola purple adj

la **viola del pensiero** f pansy n

il **violino** m violin n

la **visione** f vision n

visitare v to visit p20

il **viso** m face n

la **vista** f view n

la vista della spiaggia beach view

la vista della città *city view*
il visto *m visa n*
la vita *f life n*
il vivere *m living n*
il vocabolario *m dictionary n*
voi *you* (pl informal) *pron*
volere *v to want* **p31**
il volo *m flight n*
la volpe *f fox n*
votare *v to vote* **p20**
il voto *m grade, mark n*
  (school)

W
il water (*VAH-tehr*) *m toilet
  bowl n*

X

Y

Z
la zia *f aunt n*
lo zio *m uncle n*
zitto -a *quiet adj*
la zona periferica *f suburb n*
la zona non-fumatori *f nonsmoking area n*
lo zoo (*ZOH-oh*) *m zoo n*